Joint Insolvency Examinations Board

Liquidations

Study Manual

For the November 2010 examination

JIEB Liquidations Study Manual

ISBN: 9780 7517 8264 6 (previous edition 9780 7517 6563 2)
Third edition November 2009
First edition 2008

British Library Cataloguing-in-Publication Data
A catalogue record for this book has been applied for from
the British Library

We are grateful to the Joint Insolvency Examinations Board
for permission to reproduce the syllabus and past examination
questions and answers.

Printed in the United Kingdom

Your learning materials, published by BPP Learning Media,
are printed on paper sourced from sustainable, managed
forests.

A note about copyright

Dear Customer

What does the little © mean and why does it matter?

Your market-leading BPP books, course materials and
elearning materials do not write and update
themselves. People write them: on their own behalf
or as employees of an organisation that invests in this
activity. Copyright law protects their livelihoods. It
does so by creating rights over the use of the
content.

Breach of copyright is a form of theft – as well being
a criminal offence in some jurisdictions, it is
potentially a serious breach of professional ethics.

With current technology, things might seem a bit
hazy but, basically, without the express permission of
BPP Learning Media:

• Photocopying our materials is a breach of
  copyright

• Scanning, ripcasting or conversion of our digital
  materials into different file formats, uploading
  them to facebook or emailing them to your
  friends is a breach of copyright

You can, of course, sell your books, in the form in
which you have bought them – once you have
finished with them. (Is this fair to your fellow
students? We update for a reason.) But the ilearns
are sold on a single user license basis: we do not
supply 'unlock' codes to people who have bought
them second hand.

And what about outside the UK? BPP Learning Media
strives to make our materials available at prices
students can afford by local printing arrangements,
pricing policies and partnerships which are clearly
listed on our website. A tiny minority ignore this and
indulge in criminal activity by illegally photocopying
our material or supporting organisations that do. If
they act illegally and unethically in one area, can you
really trust them?

Contents

		Page

Liquidations

iv

Introduction

This is the third edition of BPP Learning Media's ground-breaking new study manual for the Liquidations paper of the Joint Insolvency Examinations Board. It has been published specifically for the November 2010 JIEB exam.

Features include:

▶ Full syllabus coverage

▶ Fully up-to-date at 31 July 2009

▶ A user friendly style for easy navigation

▶ Chapter introductions to put the topic into context and explain its significance in the exam

▶ Section overviews and chapter summaries

▶ Self test questions and answers

▶ Suggested practice on past exam questions.

Other JIEB papers and products

BPP Learning Media publishes a range of learning materials for the three JIEB examinations, including Question Banks, Passcards, Audio CDs and Home Study programmes.

For further information, or to order, call 0845 0751 100 (within the UK) or +44 (0)20 8740 2211 (from overseas) or order online at www.bpp.com/learningmedia

Feedback

We at BPP Learning Media always appreciate feedback about our products. If you have any comments about this book or any other products in the BPP Learning Media JIEB range, please contact Pippa Riley, Publishing Projects Director by e-mail at pippariley@bpp.com.

v

JIEB Liquidations syllabus

Candidates must be able to demonstrate a thorough working knowledge of Insolvency Practice, including relevant law and guidance as described in this syllabus, sufficient to enable them to carry out the functions of an authorised insolvency practitioner. Insolvency Practice includes both non-formal and formal practice. Non-formal practice is defined as the provision of analysis and advice to stakeholders concerning an entity in financial difficulties. Formal practice is defined as acting as office holder, from appointment through all the stages of the relevant insolvency procedures to release from the office. The jurisdictions for the purposes of this syllabus are England and Wales; and Scotland. The offices and procedures described in this syllabus relate to both jurisdictions except to the extent that legislation applies differently between them. The relevant offices for the purposes of this syllabus are as follows: those described in the Insolvency Act 1986 and the Bankruptcy (Scotland) Act 1985; receiverships under the Law of Property Act 1925, the Agricultural Credits Act 1928, the Agricultural Credits (Scotland) Act 1929: court appointments; and offices held by virtue of EU Insolvency Regulation 1346/2000.

Relevant law and guidance comprises the legislation referred to above, the Company Directors' Disqualification Act 1986, the Insolvency Rules 1986, the Insolvency (Scotland) Rules 1986, all as from time to time amended, and any other primary legislation, secondary legislation, case law or other guidance that is directly relevant to the performance of an office holder's duties. Examination questions will be based on the relevant law and guidance in force on 30th April for the year of the examination. Questions will not require more recent case law, but demonstrating knowledge of any that is relevant may attract additional marks.

Candidates will also need to demonstrate knowledge of cross-border insolvency issues (including foreign entities located in the respective jurisdictions) but not of the insolvency legislation in foreign regimes. Candidates will need to be aware of industry licensing, environmental and other regulatory requirements, agency and other issues, and the civil and criminal risks arising from them, but will not need in-depth knowledge of industry-specific legislation.

Candidates will be assessed by means of three separate papers, all of which may include questions relating both to non-formal practice and to formal practice although the emphasis will be on the latter. The three papers are distinguished by the different types of entity and the different formal insolvency procedures to which they relate.

The Personal Insolvency paper may include questions relating to any of the following types of entity: individuals, partnerships (except Limited Liability Partnerships) and the estates of deceased individuals. Questions on formal practice will focus on the following procedures: Bankruptcy and Individual Voluntary Arrangements; Voluntary Trust Deeds and Sequestrations. However, questions may also test knowledge of Administrations, Liquidations and Receiverships as they relate to individuals (e.g., individuals in partnerships or individuals subject to Receivership).

The Liquidations paper may include questions relating to any of the following types of entity: all forms of registered and unregistered companies (whether or not in a group structure), including Limited Liability Partnerships (but excluding other partnerships). Questions on formal practice will be limited to the following procedures: Members' Voluntary Liquidations (including Section 110 schemes); Creditors' Voluntary Liquidations; Compulsory Liquidations; and the appointment of Provisional Liquidators or Special Managers. Candidates will be expected to recognise that the following types of entity require special treatment, but they will not be required to deal with these entities in detail: Industrial Societies, Provident Societies, Friendly Societies, Commonhold Associations and Community Interest Companies.

The Administrations, Company Voluntary Arrangements and Receiverships paper may include questions on any of the same types of entity as for the Liquidations paper. Questions on formal practice will be limited to the following procedures: Company Voluntary Arrangements; Partnership Voluntary Arrangements; Administrations, Administrative Receiverships, Receiverships (Scotland), Court Appointed Receiverships and Receiverships under the Law of Property Act 1925.

Non-formal Insolvency Practice

This section of the syllabus refers to engagements for the provision of analysis and advice about matters relating to entities that might already be, or that are at risk of becoming, insolvent. The potential clients for this advice include the entities, their representatives, their creditors, and any other stakeholders.

Engagement

The following learning outcomes refer to the process of engagement for non-formal Insolvency Practice. They do not refer to the process of appointment to an office in a formal insolvency procedure, which is addressed later in the syllabus.

1   Candidates should be able to identify legal, regulatory and ethical considerations affecting the engagement, and also practical considerations (eg staffing levels, relevant experience, and qualifications) to determine whether the engagement can be accepted.

2   Candidates should be able to set out and confirm the adviser's and the client's duties, responsibilities and obligations in connection with the engagement.

Analysis and Advice

The following learning outcomes refer to analyses of the entity's financial affairs, and to the provision of advice with regard to those affairs.

The analyses will be necessary to provide the basis for the advice, which is why the learning outcomes dealing with analyses are in this part of the syllabus. Similar analyses will be required for formal Insolvency Practice, which is addressed in the next section of the syllabus.

3   Candidates should be able to assess an entity's overall financial state and solvency by:

- ▶   ascertaining the value of assets and the amount of liabilities, including contingent and prospective liabilities

- ▶   considering the achievability of profit and loss, and cash flow forecasts.

4   Candidates should be able to establish whether an entity that appears to be insolvent should be made subject to a formal insolvency procedure or whether a non-formal insolvency procedure such as a turnaround or a debt management scheme might be appropriate. However, candidates are not required to be able to advise on the detailed techniques that may be used in any such non-formal insolvency procedures.

5   Candidates should be able to identify the most appropriate formal insolvency procedure and estimate the financial outcome of an entity's insolvency by:

- ▶   ascertaining the values of assets and the amounts of liabilities that would arise in the formal insolvency

- ▶   comparing and contrasting the estimated outcomes from the available procedures, and from alternative strategies within the available procedures.

6   Candidates should be able to provide advice to the entity or its representatives with regard to:

- ▶   their duties, responsibilities and potential liabilities
- ▶   any need to seek additional legal or other guidance
- ▶   how best to proceed.

7   Candidates should be able to provide advice to others who are affected by the financial state of the entity with regard to protecting their interests.

8   Candidates should be able to adapt their advice to take account of new information and changing circumstances.

Formal Insolvency Practice

This section of the syllabus refers to appointments as office holder.

The different subsections refer in turn to case management, case strategy, and the operational requirements to make realisations, to deal with any misconduct, and to agree and pay claims.

Questions on formal Insolvency Practice may also include requirements to carry out the same sorts of analyses as are described above in the previous section of the syllabus on non-formal Insolvency Practice.

Case Management

The following learning outcomes refer to any appointment as an office holder under relevant legislation.

9   Candidates should be able to identify legal, regulatory and ethical considerations affecting the appointment as office holder, and also practical considerations (eg staffing levels, relevant experience, and qualifications) to determine whether the appointment can be accepted.

10   Candidates should be able to manage the statutory, regulatory and contractual procedures required to institute, progress and close the relevant insolvency procedure, including:

- ▶ establishing and maintaining files, including Insolvency Practitioner Records
- ▶ appointment to the office
- ▶ obtaining bonding and insurance
- ▶ calling and holding statutory meetings of relevant participants as required, including initial, general and final meetings
- ▶ banking, managing and disbursing funds
- ▶ obtaining sanction for specific actions, as required from creditors (or the relevant committee/s), the court, or the Official Receiver
- ▶ ceasing to act and release from office.

11   Candidates should be able to prepare and file the relevant notices, reports and returns required by the office, including to:

- ▶ the insolvent entity
- ▶ creditors
- ▶ members
- ▶ HM Revenue and Customs
- ▶ the Secretary of State for The Department of Business Enterprise and Regulatory Reform
- ▶ Companies House
- ▶ the London Gazette
- ▶ the relevant court
- ▶ the Serious Organised Crime Agency
- ▶ the office holder's authorising body
- ▶ the Pension Protection Fund, the Pensions Regulator, and the trustees or managers of the pension scheme.

Case Strategy

The following learning outcomes refer to the overall strategies, which will guide the office holder's actions to optimise the result.

12   Candidates should be able to identify whether the optimum result is more likely to be achieved by

- ▶ a formal procedure that involves disposals of assets; and/or
- ▶ a formal procedure not involving disposals but which may include, for example, voluntary contributions, debt rescheduling and/or debt restructuring.

13   Where appropriate, candidates should be able to identify the overall strategy that is likely to optimise realisations by means of disposals, which strategy may include

▶   continued trading; and/or
▶   the sale of assets (either as a whole or piecemeal).

14   When determining the most appropriate strategy, candidates should be able to take into account:

▶   the taxation implications of the different possible strategies
▶   the possible effects of interactions between concurrent and/or consecutive procedures.

15   Candidates should be able to identify steps that might properly be taken to mitigate liabilities (including any liabilities arising from the strategy itself).

16   Candidates should be able to adapt their strategies to take account of new information and changing circumstances.

Realisations

The following learning outcomes provide a general list of the activities which candidates should be able to carry out to achieve realisations by disposals of the entity's assets and by other means as appropriate.

17   Candidates should be able to identify, seek out, establish ownership, take control of and protect the entity's assets and records, including by means of:

▶   investigation
▶   physical and practical controls
▶   legal proceedings
▶   insurance
▶   banking arrangements and investment of funds.

18   Candidates should be able to manage the continuation and/or cessation of an entity's business having proper regard to the rights of all affected parties, including dealing with:

▶   finances, using cash flow forecasts and trading budgets

▶   employees, taking account of their rights (including Transfer of Undertakings and pension rights) and of the office holder's duties

▶   management of operations

▶   tax including VAT compliance

▶   compliance with industry licensing, environmental and other regulatory requirements, including for personnel and premises

▶   business assets, including:

–   freehold and leasehold premises
–   fixtures and fittings
–   plant and equipment
–   motor vehicles
–   stock and work in progress
–   contracts
–   intellectual property, including goodwill.

19   Candidates should be able to realise value from the entity by executing:

▶   sales of the business as a going concern, either as a whole or in part/s, making use of hive-down companies if appropriate; and/or

> ▶ sales of assets, either as a whole or piecemeal, including, where relevant and appropriate, dealing with assets that are subject to:
>
> - security
> - execution, attachment or distress
> - lien
> - reservation of title
> - special legal requirements
> - onerous provisions.

20 Candidates should also be able to achieve realisations from sources other than asset disposals, including from:

> ▶ actions that may only be available to the office holder, including those in respect of misconduct, or voidable transactions
>
> ▶ amounts that may be recoverable by the entity in its own name
>
> ▶ contributions from net income
>
> ▶ contributions from third parties.

21 Candidates should be able to identify circumstances that give rise to potential recovery actions, the creditors who might benefit from pursuing them, how such actions might be funded, and whether they should be pursued.

Dealing with Misconduct

The following learning outcomes refer to the duties of the office holder to assess and report on conduct.

22 Candidates should be able to identify and, where appropriate, investigate misconduct relating to the insolvency, including such matters as are identified in the Insolvency Act 1986 and in the Company Directors' Disqualification Act 1986.

23 Candidates should be able to prepare and submit reports as required in cases of misconduct, including to the:

> ▶ Official Receiver
> ▶ Secretary of State for The Department of Business Enterprise and Regulatory Reform
> ▶ Serious Organised Crime Agency.

Agreeing and Paying Claims

The following learning outcomes provide a general list of the activities by which candidates should be able to agree and pay claims in an insolvency procedure. Not all of them will apply in every case.

24 Candidates should be able to determine the validity of charges and the charge holders' rights, and to compute the amounts payable.

25 Candidates should be able to determine the validity and quantum of preferential claims and compute the amounts payable.

26 Candidates should be able to evaluate and resolve claims in special categories, including:

> ▶ retention of title
> ▶ lien
> ▶ hire purchase and leasing
> ▶ execution and distress.

27 Candidates should be able to determine the validity and quantum of unsecured claims and compute the amounts payable.

28 Candidates should be able to rank all of the valid claims, and duly pay them in the statutory order having taken into account, as appropriate, interest, set off, the Prescribed Part, subrogation and marshalling.

29 Where there is a surplus after the payment of relevant creditors, candidates should be able to determine the amounts and entitlements to the surplus and the procedures for passing it across.

The JIEB exam

The exam paper

(a) The JIEB exam consists of three papers, each of three hours, with an additional 30 minutes' reading and planning time per session. (In 2010 the examination will be held on 2, 3 and 4 November.)? to check1!!!

(b) Exam questions are set on the basis of European and UK legislation on insolvency and statements of insolvency practice in force on the 30th day of April for the year of examination. Knowledge of case law after 30 April will not be specifically examined, however demonstration of knowledge of recent case law may attract additional marks.

(c) The subject of the three papers is:

▶ Liquidations
▶ Administrations, Company Voluntary Arrangements and Receiverships
▶ Personal Insolvency

(d) Each paper consists of four compulsory questions, with two questions attracting 20% of the marks and two questions attracting 30% of the marks.

(e) The examination is essentially practical and relevant experience, while not essential, is an advantage. The examination aims to assess whether candidates have sufficient knowledge of insolvency law and practice to enable them to carry out the functions of an authorised insolvency practitioner. Candidates are expected to have a basic knowledge of taxation, accountancy and business law, directly relevant to the performance of an office holder's duties in the practice of insolvency.

(f) Marks are awarded in the exam for the ability to communicate effectively.

(g) The exam is open book and candidates are provided, in the exam hall, with the latest edition of the Butterworths Insolvency Law Handbook.

How to use this Study Manual

This is the third edition of the BPP Learning Media study manual for the Liquidations paper of the Joint Insolvency Examinations Board. It has been written to cover the JIEB syllabus.

To pass the examination you need a thorough understanding in all areas covered by the syllabus.

Recommended approach

(a) To pass you need to be able to answer questions on **everything** specified by the syllabus. Read the text very carefully and do not skip any of it.

(b) Learning is an **active** process. Do **all** the activities as you work through the manual so you can be sure you really understand what you have read.

(c) After you have covered the material in the Study Manual, work through the questions suggested in the Exam Practice section.

(d) Before you take the exam, check that you still remember the material using the following quick revision plan.

　(i) Read through the chapter learning objectives. Are there any gaps in your knowledge? If so, study the section again.

　(ii) Read and learn the defined terms.

　(iii) Read and learn the diagrammatic summary of each chapter.

　(iv) Do the self test questions again. If you know what you're doing, they shouldn't take long.

This approach is only a suggestion. You or your college may well adapt it to suit your needs.

Remember this is a **practical** course. Try to relate the material to your experience in the workplace or any other work experience you may have had.

Enrolment

To enrol for the JIEB exam you must be registered with one of the recognised professional bodies.

It is your responsibility to enrol with your respective Professional Body for the JIEB exam and to pay the exam fee – this is not included in the BPP course fees.

Application information is also available from the JIEB examinations office, telephone 01908 248 040.

Chapter summary

Chapter 1 – Legislation

This Chapter introduces the main legislation governing insolvency law and the Insolvency Code of Ethics and provides important background information. The principles of the Insolvency Code of Ethics are a very examinable topic in the JIEB exam.

Chapter 2 – Statements of Insolvency Practice (SIPs)

This Chapter introduces Statements of Insolvency Practice (SIPs) and Technical Releases, what they are and who produces them, and lists what SIPs are currently in use. A good knowledge of the SIPs is essential. SIPs cover all aspects of insolvency work so this material has been repeated in the Personal Insolvency and Administrations manuals for the JIEB course.

Chapter 3 – Introduction to liquidation

Essential background information is provided in this chapter which introduces the different types of liquidation and details the powers of the liquidator. The Insolvency Code of Ethics is also covered which is a very examinable topic.

Chapter 4 – Members' Voluntary Liquidation

Members' voluntary liquidation (MVL) is introduced in this chapter which covers the procedure to place a company into MVL, the statutory requirements with regard to the Directors' Declaration of Solvency and the duties of the liquidator if the company turns out not to be solvent. This is a very important chapter with the topics covered being regularly tested in the JIEB exam.

Chapter 5 – Creditors' Voluntary Liquidation

Creditors' voluntary liquidation (CVL) is introduced in this chapter: the procedure to place a company into CVL, statutory provisions re convening meetings of creditors and members and the preparation of the Statement of Affairs and Deficiency account. The liquidation committee is also discussed, including its role, powers and duties. The content of SIP 8 and SIP 15 are also detailed in this chapter. All of this chapter is important and should be learnt in detail.

Chapter 6 – Compulsory liquidation

This chapter covers all aspects of compulsory liquidation: the grounds for compulsory liquidation, the petition, the procedure to follow to place a company into compulsory liquidation, the first meeting of creditors, the provisional liquidator and special manager. Whilst compulsory liquidations are regularly tested in the JIEB exam, the grounds for compulsory liquidation are not as important a topic as the procedure to follow to place a company into compulsory liquidation, or the provisional liquidator and special manager.

Chapter 7 – Liquidators' investigations

This chapter discusses why a liquidator has to carry out investigations, the form such investigations will take per SIP 2, director's disqualification and the content of SIP 4. The completion of director's returns and liquidator's investigations are both topics which are regularly tested in the JIEB exam.

Chapter 8 – Antecedent transactions

These are examined in nearly every exam paper. You should focus on being able to identify an antecedent transaction and understanding the main features of the rules, including relevant time periods for action to be taken. This chapter covers transactions at an undervalue, preferences, extortionate credit transactions, avoidance of floating charges, transactions defrauding creditors, fraudulent trading, wrongful trading, misfeasance and re-use of company names.

Chapter 9 – The Asset Protection Regime

This is an important topic which is often tested in the JIEB exam. It is important to understand the rules outlined in this chapter and how matters are dealt with differently in a compulsory and voluntary liquidation. This chapter covers actions or proceedings against the company, execution, distress and post commencement dispositions.

Chapter 10 – Proof of debts

This chapter details what debts may be proved for and how a creditor proves for his debt, the difference between proving for voting and dividend purposes, how certain claims are dealt with and the procedure to follow when making a dividend payment to creditors. This material is very similar to the chapter in the Personal Insolvency manual. The agreement of creditors' claims and the payment of dividends are popular topics in the JIEB exam.

Chapter 11 – Remuneration

This is a very practical topic which is very likely to be examined in the JIEB exam. It could be examined in any of the three papers, so the material has been repeated in the Personal Insolvency and Administration and Receiverships Study Manual for the course. This chapter details the statutory provisions relating to the calculation of liquidator's remuneration, the provision of information to those responsible for the approval of fees, the drawing of disbursements and the Schedule 6 scale.

Chapter 12 – Practical issues

This is a very practical chapter dealing with matters which the liquidator will have to deal with during the course of the liquidation, including sale of assets to directors, continuing to trade, employee claims, ROT, hiving down, banking, receipts and payments accounts, bonding and IP case records.

Chapter 13 – Vacation of office

This chapter details how a liquidator may vacate office, his duties on doing so and provides a closure checklist. This is not a very examinable topic in respect of the liquidation paper, but the closure checklist is also relevant to other insolvency appointments so should be reviewed.

Legislation

> > > > > > > > > > > > > > > >

Introduction

Learning objectives

▶ Understand the main legislation governing insolvency law ☐

▶ Identify the fundamental principles and apply the Insolvency Code of Ethics in practice in relation to appointments as supervisor of a voluntary arrangement, administrator or administrative or other receiver ☐

▶ Understand implications of money laundering regulations for an office holder ☐

▶ Understand the implications of the EC Regulations for office holders ☐

Working context

All aspects of insolvency work are governed by legislation, it is therefore important to understand the requirements of the legislation in your daily working lives.

Stop and think

Why should the area of insolvency require regulating? Why shouldn't an administrator act as an auditor of a company? What are the fundamental principles? Why are they important?

Examination context

Ethics is a very examinable topic appearing regularly in any of the three JIEB exam papers. It is important to learn not just the fundamental principles but also to be able to apply the requirements of the Code of Ethics in practice.

The EC Regulations are unlikely to be tested in their own right, however an understanding of the Regulations is required.

Money Laundering Regulations came into force in 2003 and therefore in terms of the exam this is relatively new material for the examiner. It appeared in the 2005 exam (Sec A Question 1(a)) and you should therefore be aware of the issues for office holders in respect of money laundering.

Past exam questions to look at include:

2008	Question	1(a)
2002	Question	2(a)
2000	Question	1
1996	Question	4(b)

1 The Insolvency Act 1986

Section overview

▶ The Insolvency Act 1986 ("the Act") consolidated the Insolvency Act 1985 (never brought fully into force) and those provisions of the Companies Act 1985 relating to receiverships and corporate insolvencies.

▶ The Act came into force on the 29 December 1986 (effect of s443 of the Act, s236(2) of the Insolvency Act 1985 and the Insolvency Act 1985 (commencement No 5) Order 1986).

1.1 The Act and corporate recovery procedures

The Act introduced two new procedures which it was hoped would aid in the rescuing of financially troubled but viable businesses.

▶ The Company Voluntary Arrangement (Part I, ss.1-7 of the Act) and

▶ The Administration Order (Part II, ss.8-27 of the Act)

In addition the Act introduced the concept of the 'administrative receiver' a statutory modification of existing and familiar 'receiver and manager' appointments.

The Insolvency Act 1994 amended the provisions of the Act in relation to the liability of administrative receivers on adopted employment contracts.

1.2 Impact of the Insolvency Act 2000 and Enterprise Act 2002 on the Insolvency Act 1986

The Insolvency Act 2000 received Royal Assent on 20 December 2000. The provisions relating to administrations and disqualifications were brought into force on 2 April 2001 (Insolvency Act 2000 (Commencement No. 1 and Transitional Provisions) Order 2001) and provisions relating to CVAs and IVAs were not brought into force until 1 January 2003 (Insolvency Act 2000 (Commencement No.3 and Transitional Provisions) Order 2002).

The Enterprise Act received the Royal Assent on 7 November 2002. Much of the Act relates to competition law and is not directly related to insolvency. The main insolvency reforms introduced by the Enterprise Act 2002 are contained in Part X (ss248 – 272). The corporate provisions were brought into force on 15 September 2003 and the personal insolvency provisions on 1 April 2004 (Enterprise Act 2002 (Commencement No.4 and Transitional Provisions and Savings) Order 2003).

Neither the Insolvency Act 2000 nor the Enterprise Act 2002 constitute "stand alone" items of insolvency legislation. In both cases their function is to amend or make additions to the Insolvency Act 1986.

It follows that it is not necessary either in the Joint Insolvency Exam nor generally in practice to refer to the 2000 and 2002 Acts.

In these notes 'the Act' refers, therefore, to the 1986 Act and all references unless otherwise stated are to that Act.

1.3 The Insolvency (Amendment) (No.2) Rules 2002

These rules came into force on 1 January 2003 and made amendments to the Insolvency Rules 1986 consequential on the changes made by the Insolvency Act 2000. It follows that the main changes were to parts 1 (CVAs) and 5 (IVAs) of those rules.

In particular a new chapter 9 in Part 1 of the 1986 Rules (R1.35 – 1.54) applies where Directors have filed for a 'small company' moratorium.

In some cases the old rules (i.e. without the 2002 amendment rules changes) will continue to apply. These are where

▶ Written notice of a proposal for an IVA or CVA was endorsed before 1 January 2003

▶ Or where in the case of a CVA a liquidator or administrator summonsed a meeting of creditors before that date.

1.4 The Insolvency (Amendment) Rules 2009

These rules came into force on 6 April 2009 and made amendments to the Insolvency Rules 1986.

The new rules:

▶ Introduced Debt Relief Orders

▶ Made changes to the rules on publication or advertisement of notices

▶ Throughout the rules 'forthwith' was changed to 'as soon as reasonably practicable'.

2 The Companies Act 2006

Section overview

The Companies Act 2006 (CA 06) was given Royal Assent in November 2006. Its aim was to modernise existing company law to provide a simple, efficient and cost effective framework for British businesses in the 21st century.

2.1 Implementation

The CA 85 was changed in order to meet four key objectives:

(i) To enhance shareholder engagement and a long term investment culture.
(ii) To ensure better regulation and a 'Think Small First' approach.
(iii) To make it easier to set up and run a company.
(iv) To provide flexibility for the future.

The overall arrangement of the CA 06 is as follows:

PART	SUMMARY
1 to 7	The fundamentals of what a company is, how it can be formed and what it can be called.
8 to 12	The members (shareholders) and officers (management) of a company.
13 and 14	How companies may take decisions.
15 and 16	The safeguards for ensuring that the officers of a company are accountable to its members.
17 to 25	Raising share capital, capital maintenance, annual returns and company charges.
26 to 28	Company reconstruction, mergers and takeovers.
29 to 39	The regulatory framework, application to companies not formed under the CA and other company law provisions.
40 to 42	Overseas disqualification of directors, business names and statutory auditors.
43	Transparency obligations.
44 to 47	Miscellaneous and general.

The company law provisions of the 2006 Act (Parts 1 to 39) restate almost all of the provisions of the 1985 CA, together with the company law provisions of the CA 1989 and the Companies (Audit, Investigations and Community Enterprise) Act 2004.

The 2006 CA was not fully implemented until October 2009. The provisions of the Act were implemented in stages in April 2007, April 2008 and October 2008 with the final implementation in October 2009.

3 The Insolvency Code of Ethics

Section overview

The Code of Ethics governs the conduct of practitioners. All practitioners should be guided by the fundamental principles contained in the Code of Ethics. It sets out to assist the Insolvency Practitioner (IP) in the application of legislation and also in matters not covered by legislation. Failure to observe the code may not, of itself, constitute professional misconduct, but will be taken into account in assessing the conduct of an IP. An IP should not engage in any business, occupation or activity that impairs or might impair integrity, objectivity or the good reputation of the profession and as a result would be incompatible with the fundamental principles.

3.1 Fundamental principles

The Code identifies five fundamental principles with which the IP is required to comply:

1 Integrity – an IP should be straightforward and honest in all professional and business relationships.

2 Objectivity – an IP should not allow bias, conflict of interest or undue influence of others to override professional or business judgements.

3 Professional competence and due care – an IP has a continuing duty to maintain professional knowledge and skill at the level required to ensure that a client or employer receives competent professional service based on current developments in practice, legislation and techniques. An IP should act diligently and in accordance with applicable technical and professional standards when providing professional services.

4 Confidentiality – an IP should respect the confidentiality of information acquired as a result of professional and business relationships and should not disclose any such information to third parties without proper and specific authority unless there is a legal or professional right or duty to disclose. Confidential information acquired as a result of professional and business relationships should not be used for the personal advantage of the IP or third parties.

5 Professional behaviour – an IP should comply with relevant laws and regulations and should avoid any action that discredits the profession. IPs should conduct themselves with courtesy and consideration towards all with whom they come into contact when performing their work.

3.2 Threats

The Code requires the IP to identify, evaluate and address threats to the fundamental principles. Many threats fall into five categories:

1 Self interest threats – these may occur as a result of the financial or other interests of a practice or an IP or of an immediate or close family member of an individual within the practice.

2 Self review threats – these may occur when a previous judgement made by an individual within the practice needs to be re-evaluated by the IP.

3 Advocacy threats – these may occur when an individual within the practice promotes a position or opinion to the point that subsequent objectivity may be compromised.

4 Familiarity threats – may occur when, because of a close relationship, an individual within the practice becomes too sympathetic or antagonistic to the interests of others.

5 Intimidation threats – these may occur when an IP may be deterred from acting objectively by threats, actual or perceived.

3.3   Safeguards

IPs should ensure that safeguards are in place to reduce the level of any threat. These may include:

▶ Leadership that stresses the importance of compliance with the fundamental principles.

▶ Policies and procedures to implement and monitor quality control of engagements.

▶ Documented policies regarding the identification of threats to compliance with the fundamental principles, the evaluation of the significance of these threats and the identification and the application of safeguards to eliminate or reduce the threats, other than those that are trivial, to an acceptable level.

▶ Documented internal policies and procedures requiring compliance with the fundamental principles.

▶ Policies and procedures to consider the fundamental principles of the Code before the acceptance of an insolvency appointment.

▶ Policies and procedures regarding the identification of interests or relationships between individuals within the practice and third parties.

▶ Policies and procedures to prohibit individuals who are not members of the insolvency team from inappropriately influencing the outcome of an insolvency appointment.

▶ Timely communication of a practice's policies and procedures, including any changes to them, to all individuals within the practice, and appropriate training and education on such policies and procedures.

▶ Designating a member of senior management to be responsible for overseeing the adequate functioning of the safeguarding system.

▶ A disciplinary mechanism to promote compliance with policies and procedures.

▶ Published policies and procedures to encourage and empower individuals within the practice to communicate to senior levels within the practice and/or the IP any issue relating to compliance with the fundamental principles that concerns them.

Safeguards specific to an appointment may include:

▶ Involving and/or consulting another IP from within the practice to review the work done.

▶ Consulting an independent third party, such as a committee of creditors, a licensing or professional body or another IP.

▶ Involving another IP to perform part of the work, which may include another IP taking a joint appointment where conflict arises during the course of the appointment.

▶ Seeking directions from the court.

▶ Obtaining knowledge and understanding of the entity, its owners, managers and those responsible for its governance and business activities.

▶ Acquiring an appropriate understanding of the nature of the entity's business, the complexity of its operations, the specific requirements of the engagement and the purpose, nature and scope of the work to be performed.

▶ Acquiring knowledge of relevant industries or subject matters.

▶ Possessing or obtaining experience with relevant regulatory or reporting requirements.

▶ Assigning staff with the necessary competencies.

▶ Using experts where necessary.

▶ Complying with quality control policies and procedures designed to provide reasonable assurance that specific engagements are accepted only when they can be performed competently.

Where a threat cannot be eliminated the IP should evaluate the significance of such a threat and apply necessary safeguards to reduce them to an acceptable level.

In situations where no safeguards can mitigate a threat, the IP should conclude that it would not be appropriate to accept the insolvency appointment.

The nature of the safeguards to be applied will vary depending on the circumstances. In exercising judgement, an IP should consider what a reasonable and informed third party, having knowledge of all relevant information, including the significance of the threat and safeguards applied, would conclude to be unacceptable.

The IP should always be aware of how his actions will be perceived by others. Sometimes the mere perception of risk or conflict will undermine confidence in the practitioner's objectivity. In such circumstances, acceptance of an insolvency appointment would be unwise.

IPs should document their consideration of the fundamental principles and the reasons behind their agreement or otherwise to accept an insolvency appointment.

3.4 Fees and other types of remuneration

The special nature of insolvency appointments makes the payment or offer of any commission for, or the furnishing of any valuable consideration towards, the introduction of insolvency appointments inappropriate. This does not, however, preclude an arrangement between an IP and a *bona fide* employee whereby the employee's remuneration is based in whole or in part on introductions obtained for the practitioner through the efforts of the employee.

3.5 Significant professional and personal relationships

The environment in which IPs work can lead to threats to the principles of objectivity and integrity. The most common threats arise from ongoing and previous relationships.

▶ 'Self review threats' – where the practitioner has had a significant professional relationship with the company or individual in relation to which or whom an appointment is taken, and

▶ 'Self interest threats' – threats which refer to personal relationships which may affect the reasoning the practitioner applies.

The IP should identify and analyse the significance of any professional or personal relationship which may affect compliance with the fundamental principles. The IP should consider whether any individual within the practice, or the practice itself, has or had a professional or personal relationship with a principle or employee of an entity for which an insolvency appointment is being considered, or any business controlled by or under the same control as the entity or part of it.

A professional relationship includes where an individual within the practice is carrying out or has carried out audit work or any other professional work. A professional relationship may also arise from an individual within the practice having an interest in an entity.

An IP should not accept an insolvency appointment in relation to an entity where any personal, professional or business connection with a principle is such as to impair or reasonably appear to impair the IP's objectivity.

In assessing whether a relationship is significant the IP should consider:

▶ How the relationship will be viewed by others.

▶ How recently any work was carried out.

▶ Whether the fee received for the work by the practice is or was significant to the practice itself or is or was substantial.

▶ The impact of the work conducted by the practice on the financial state and/or the financial stability of the entity.

▶ The nature of the previous duties undertaken by a practice or an individual within the practice during an earlier relationship with the entity.

▶ The extent of the insolvency team's familiarity with the individuals connected with the insolvency appointment.

If there is a significant relationship, the IP should consider whether that relationship gives rise to any particular threat. In situations where no threat arises, an IP will be able to undertake or continue the insolvency appointment.

Where a threat arises from a significant relationship, and the threat cannot be overcome by safeguards, the professional work cannot be undertaken or continued.

3.6 Audit work previously undertaken for a company or individual to which an appointment is being sought

Where the IP or a practice has previously carried out audit work within the previous three years for a company or individual to which the appointment is being considered, the IP should not accept an appointment.

Where the audit work was conducted over three years ago, the IP should still consider whether any self review threats may arise and impose any necessary safeguards before the appointment is accepted.

3.7 Professional work undertaken by an individual within the practice for an entity or any principle of an entity to which an insolvency appointment is being considered

Where an individual within the practice is undertaking professional work (eg. tax work) for an entity or any principle of an entity to whom an insolvency appointment is being considered, this will give rise to a threat to independence. The nature of the professional work will have to be considered. For example, basic tax work for the director of an entity may not be regarded as so significant as tax planning work undertaken for the entity.

3.8 Appointment as Nominee and/or Supervisor of a Company Voluntary Arrangement, Administrator or Administrative Receiver or other receiver

Where there has been a significant professional relationship with a company or a personal relationship with a director, former director or shadow director of a company, no individual within the practice should accept appointment as nominee or supervisor of a voluntary arrangement, administrator or administrative or other receiver in relation to that company.

3.9 Appointment as Investigating Accountant at the instigation of a creditor

A significant professional relationship would not normally arise following the appointment of the practice by a creditor of a company to investigate its affairs provided that:

(a)   There has not been a direct involvement by an individual within the practice in the management of the company, and

(b)   The practice continues to have its principal client relationship with the creditor, rather than the company and the company is aware of this.

Where an IP or the practice has undertaken an investigation into the financial affairs of the company at the request of a secured creditor of the company, and is asked, as a consequence, by that creditor to accept appointment as administrator or administrative receiver, the IP should be satisfied that the company (acting by its board of directors) does not object to the acceptance of the appointment.

IPs may be called upon to justify the propriety of acceptance where the circumstances of the initial appointment are such as to prevent open discussion of the financial affairs of the company with the directors.

3.10 Administration following appointment as supervisor of a voluntary arrangement

Appointment as administrator may be accepted where an individual in the practice has acted as the supervisor of a voluntary arrangement, provided the appointment is made by the holder of a floating charge and consideration has been given to the principles set out in the Code.

3.11 Administrator, nominee and/or supervisor of a voluntary arrangement following appointment as administrative receiver or LPA or other receiver

Appointment should not be accepted where an individual within the practice is, or in the previous three years has been an administrative or other receiver of a company or a LPA receiver unless the previous appointment was made by the court.

3.12 Audit following appointment as supervisor of a voluntary arrangement, administrator or administrative or other receiver

Appointment as auditor of a company should not be accepted for any accounting period during which an individual within the practice has acted as supervisor of a voluntary arrangement, administrator or administrative or other receiver of a company.

3.13 Liquidation following appointment as supervisor of CVA or administrator

Appointment as liquidator can be accepted where administration is followed by compulsory winding up, however the administrator should not accept appointment as liquidator unless he has the agreement of the creditors' committee or of a meeting of creditors. Appointment as liquidator following a voluntary arrangement is acceptable.

Where an individual within the practice is, or in the previous three years has been, administrative receiver of a company, or a receiver under LPA 1925 or otherwise, of any of its assets, no individual within that practice should accept appointment as liquidator of the company in an insolvent liquidation. This does not apply however where the previous appointment was made by the court.

3.14 Pre-agreed business sales

Where the assets and business of an insolvent company are sold by an IP shortly after appointment on pre agreed terms, this could lead to an actual or perceived threat to independence. To reduce the threat the IP should obtain an independent valuation of the assets and seek to identify other potential purchasers.

3.15 Relationships between insolvent individuals and insolvent companies

An IP, or an individual within the practice, who acts as an IP in relation to an individual may be asked to accept an insolvency appointment in relation to a company of which the debtor is a major shareholder or creditor or where the company is a creditor of the debtor. Acceptance should not be taken unless the IP is satisfied that steps can be taken to minimise problems of conflict and the IP's overall integrity and objectivity are, and are seen to be, maintained.

3.16 Joint appointments

Where an IP is specifically precluded by the guidance given in the Code from accepting an appointment as an individual, a joint appointment will not render the appointment acceptable.

3.17 Relationship with a debenture holder

An IP should, in general, decline to accept an insolvency appointment in relation to a company if an individual within a practice has such a personal or close and distinct business connection with the debenture holder as might impair or appear to impair the IP's objectivity. It is not considered likely that a close and distinct business connection would normally exist between an IP and a clearing bank or other major financial institution.

3.18 'Independent trustees' of Pension schemes

The Pensions Act 1995 (brought into force on 6 April 1997) requires the IP or OR to ensure that the trustee is independent. Where there is no independent trustee, one should be appointed as soon as reasonably practicable.

In corporate insolvency, members should not appoint a principal or employee of their firm (or connected parties) as independent trustee of a pension scheme of a company in respect of which they are the responsible IP.

The guide warns of the threat to objectivity posed by reciprocal arrangements in respect of these appointments with other firms.

Interactive question: Biome Limited

One of the partners in the accountancy firm you work for has been approached to act as administrator to Biome Limited. You will be the manager with day-to-day responsibility for the assignment.

Requirement

List the practical steps to be taken regarding conflicts of interest and qualification to act as administrator, before your partner accepts the appointment.

See **Answer** at the end of this chapter.

4 Money Laundering

Section overview

▶ There are a number of Acts that contain law relating to money laundering. The main ones are:

- Money Laundering Regulations 2007

- Part 7 Proceeds of Crime Act 2002 (Money Laundering) (POCA 2002)

- s18 and s21A Terrorism Act 2000 (TA 2000)

▶ Compliance with the 2007 Money Laundering Regulations is a legal requirement. The regulations came into force on 15 December 2007 and apply to all appointments held by an IP at that date.

Definition

Money Laundering: a number of offences involving the proceeds of crime (including tax evasion and fraud) or terrorist funds. It is the process by which the identity of dirty money (ie. The proceeds of crime and the ownership of those proceeds) is changed so that the proceeds appear to originate from legitimate sources. It includes possessing, dealing with or concealing the proceeds of any crime or similar activities in relation to terrorist funds, which includes funds from legitimate sources which are likely to be used for terrorism, as well as the proceeds of terrorism.

4.1 Money laundering process

Money laundering is conventionally described as being a three stage process:

▶ Placement – where cash (literally money in the form of coins and banknotes) is deposited into the banking system. Serious and organised criminals need access to the international banking system due to the practical difficulties in using cash to settle large transactions.

▶ Layering – a series of transactions designed to disguise the audit trail.

▶ Integration – whereby the now apparently cleaned funds are invested in the legitimate economy.

An Insolvency Practitioner can be targeted at any of the three stages, for instance:

▶ Placement – A potential purchaser of a business who wishes to pay for assets in cash.

▶ Layering – A criminal sends a cheque made payable to a liquidator of a company purporting to be in payment of a debt owed to the company which is being wound-up. The liquidator pays the cheque into an account maintained in the name of his firm in compliance with SIP 11. The debtor ledger is then checked and when it becomes apparent that the debt in question does not exist a cheque in the name of the firm is sent to the criminal. The funds appear legitimate.

▶ Integration – A criminal acquires a business through an office holder using funds which have already passed through a money laundering process and now appear to be legitimate.

4.2 Offences

There are a wide range of offences under POCA 2002, TA 2000 and 2007 Regulations. The main ones relate to where a person:

▶ Conceals, disguises, converts or transfers criminal property from the UK.

▶ Enters into or becomes concerned in an arrangement which he knows or suspects facilitates the acquisition, retention, use or control of criminal property by or on behalf of another person.

▶ Acquires, uses and/or possesses criminal property.

A second tier of offences relate to the regulated sector and relate to where a person:

▶ Fails to disclose knowledge or suspicion of money laundering to the nominated officer or Serious Organised Crime Agency (SOCA).

▶ Tips off any person that such a disclosure has been made.

4.3 IPs' obligations re money laundering

IPs are required to:

▶ Establish procedures to identify customers and verify their identities.

▶ Carry out ongoing monitoring of business relationships.

▶ Appoint a nominated officer called a 'Money Laundering Reporting Officer' (MLRO) to whom principals and employees must make money laundering reports. This does not apply to sole practitioners who do not employ any staff or act in association with any other parties.

▶ Establish internal systems, procedures, policies and controls to forestall and prevent money laundering.

▶ Provide relevant individuals with training on money laundering.

▶ Maintain records of client identification and of business relationships for at least five years.

▶ Report suspicions of money laundering to SOCA.

4.4   Identification procedures

Reg 5 Money Laundering Regulations 2007 details identification procedures which IPs must have in place for identifying the customer and verifying their identity on the basis of documents, data or information obtained from a reliable and independent source.

Identification procedures are required when:

▸ Entering a business relationship
▸ Carrying out an occasional transaction
▸ Where there is suspicion of money laundering or terrorist financing
▸ Where there are doubts concerning the validity of previous identification evidence.

Definition

Occasional transaction: a transaction amounting to 15,000 euros or more. (This would include the sale of assets of an insolvent involving the paying of 15,000 euros or more to the IP.)

Identification procedures for an individual would include the IP seeing and taking copies of evidence establishing the applicant's full name and address ie. Passport, photo driving licence, recent utility bill, HMRC Tax notification, Benefits Agency benefits book.

Identification procedures for a company may also involve identifying the controllers of the company. Suitable evidence for a company includes:

▸ Certificate of incorporation
▸ Evidence of company's registered address
▸ Copy of company's annual return.

4.5   Reporting suspicions of money laundering

Internal reports of money laundering should be made to the MLRO who is required to decide whether to report the matter on to the SOCA. If in doubt, the MRLO should seek legal advice. Reports should be made as soon as possible, irrespective of the amounts involved.

There are two types of form for reporting to the SOCA:

▸ Standard Disclosure Form
▸ Limited Intelligence Value Report Form.

Care must be taken that a money launderer is not tipped off (this constitutes an offence under POCA 2002 and TA 2000).

Having made the report, no action that would assist the launderer or otherwise constitute money laundering by the IP may take place for seven working days, unless SOCA gives consent for it to go ahead. This may impact on a potential sale in which case reports to SOCA may be marked urgent.

4.6   High Value Dealers

High value dealers are required to register with the Commissioners of HM Revenue & Customs.

Definition

High value dealer: the activity of dealing in goods whenever a transaction involves accepting a total cash payment of 15,000 euros or more in one operation or several if they are linked.

---

5 The EC Regulation on Insolvency Proceedings 2000

Section overview

▶ The EC Regulation on Insolvency Proceedings 2000 (The "EC Regulation") was adopted by the Council of Ministers of the European Union on 29 May 2000 and came into force on 31 May 2002.

▶ The EC Regulation applies throughout the European Union with the exception of Denmark which exercised its right of opt-out.

▶ Note that although the European Community has become the European Union it is still usual to refer to EC legislation. This is because the Legislation is intended to promote the single market rather than other EU aims such as a common foreign and security policy.

5.1 Significance of 'Regulation' status

A Regulation is an item of European secondary legislation (as opposed to primary legislation such as the Treaty of Rome). A Regulation is said to be "directly applicable" i.e. on coming into force it is automatically part of the law of each member state without the need for (in the UK) an implementing statute or piece of delegated legislation.

This should be contrasted with Directives which are not directly applicable. For example, the 1977 European Acquired Rights Directive designed to protect an employee's rights on transfers of undertakings was enacted in UK law by the Transfer of Undertakings (Protection of Employment) Regulations 1981 (TUPER).

European law is normally broadly drafted and a purposive rather than literal approach to interpretation will be taken by the courts. For instance in *Litster v Forth Dry Dock and Engineering Co. Ltd 1989* where staff had been dismissed one hour before the transfer in an attempt to evade the effect of TUPER, mentioned above, the House of Lords interpreted the words "immediately before the transfer" as meaning "or would have been so employed if not unfairly dismissed before the transfer".

Under the European Community Act 1972 European Law has supremacy over UK made law and it follows that courts will not be bound to follow UK law which is inconsistent with the EC Regulation.

5.2 The UK under the EC Regulation

The UK is treated as one jurisdiction i.e. Scotland and Northern Ireland where insolvency law differs from that in England and Wales are not considered separate territories.

Gibraltar is included within the UK.

5.3 Application of the EC Regulation

The EC Regulation will apply to a debtor company or individual where its Centre of Main Interests ("COMI") is within the European Union (para 14 of the Recitals: "This Regulation applies only to proceedings where the centre of the debtor's main interests is located in the community").

Definition

Centre of main interests: this is the place of command or control, the place where the debtor conducts the administration of its business on a regular basis. This could be where the registered office is, but may not always be so.

If the COMI is outside the EU the EC Regulation will not apply. Where a company has its COMI in the US for instance and that company has assets in the UK, domestic UK law and not the EC Regulation will apply to those UK assets.

Paragraph 1 of Article 3 of the EC Regulation provides that in the case of a company the registered office shall be presumed to be the COMI in the absence of proof to the contrary. However

▶ Paragraph 13 of the Recitals provides that the COMI "should correspond to the place where the debtor conducts the administration of his interests on a regular basis and is therefore ascertainable by third parties".

▶ In *Re Brac Rent-a-car Ltd* concerning a company registered in *Delaware* the High Court held that the EC Regulation applied as the company's operations were conducted almost entirely in the UK and the COMI was therefore also situated in the UK.

▶ The Eurofoods decision of the European Courts of Justice (02.05.06) emphasised that:

– The EC Regulation is to be applied separately to each company in a group.

– The registered office presumption can only be rebutted by objective evidence ascertainable by creditors. A parent-subsidiary relationship or evidence that a parent determined the economic choices of a subsidiary was insufficient on its own to rebut the presumption.

– Where a party disagreed with the decision of a national court in relation to the opening of main proceedings the appropriate remedy was to appeal through the national courts not to appeal to the ECJ.

▶ In *Geveran Trading v Skjevesland* the court held that the EC Regulation did not apply as the debtor's COMI was in Switzerland, and commented that a company's head office was more likely to correspond to its COMI than the registered office which in the UK might simply be the address of a firm of accountants.

5.4   Types of insolvency procedure governed by the EC Regulation

Article 1 of the EC Regulation provides that it applies to "collective insolvency proceedings which entail the partial or total divestment of a debtor and the appointment of a liquidator".

"Collective insolvency proceedings" consist in the UK of (see Article 2(a) and Annex A):

▶ Winding up by the court

▶ Creditors' voluntary winding-up. However here, as a CVL is not a court procedure, "confirmation by the court" is required

▶ Administration – and the EC Reg will also apply to subsequent insolvency proceedings such as a CVL under para 83 of Schedule B1 of the Insolvency Act 1986

▶ IVAs and CVAs

▶ Bankruptcy.

Those who qualify as "liquidators" are listed in Annex C and include liquidators, administrators, supervisors, the OR and a trustee in bankruptcy, i.e. the term "liquidator" in the EC Regulation is used loosely to mean the office holder in an Annex A insolvency proceeding.

There are some notable omissions from the Annex A list:

▶ Members' voluntary liquidations (EU cross-border issues here are covered by the Brussels Convention).

▶ Administrative receivership or receivership under a fixed charge. The EC Regulation is concerned with processes designed to deal with creditors generally. Receiverships concern the enforcement of private contractual rights by a secured creditor. Administrators will therefore have advantages over administrative receivers where there are assets outside the UK in more readily being able to "export" their powers to other EU jurisdictions.

▶ S.895 CA 2006 Schemes of arrangement.

Article 1 (2) excludes insurance undertakings, credit institutions, investment undertakings holding funds or securities for third parties and collective investment undertakings (eg. unit trusts). These financial services sector businesses have their own separate European regulatory framework.

5.5 Main proceedings

(i) Concept of 'main proceedings'

Article 3(1) "The courts of the Member State within the territory of which the centre of a debtor's main interests is situated shall have jurisdiction to open insolvency proceedings." These proceedings will be "main proceedings" (see next section for significance of the expression).

Remember that the COMI will not necessarily be the same as the jurisdiction of incorporation or the domicile of the registered office of the company. In the *Daisytek* case for instance, both the UK High Court and the French Court of Appeal held that the COMI of a French subsidiary of a UK holding company was in the UK, the courts being presented with evidence that the French company was managed from the UK (following *Eurofoods* this would need to be ascertainable by creditors). The UK High Court was able to make separate, UK administration orders in relation to both the holding and subsidiary companies.

(ii) Significance of 'main proceedings'

All other Member State courts must recognise the judgement of the court opening main proceedings (this is the court in the territory of the COMI of the relevant debtor. (Article 16(1))

Courts in other Member States may not open main proceedings in relation to the same debtor i.e. there can only be one set of main proceedings in relation to a company or individual.

The rights of courts in other Member States to open any other form of insolvency proceeding are restricted. By Article 3(2) these (non-main) proceedings:

▸ Can only be opened in another Member State if the debtor possesses an 'establishment' within that territory,

▸ An 'establishment' is defined as 'any place of operations where the debtor carries out a non-transitory economic activity with human means and goods',

▸ And, the effect of those proceedings is restricted to the assets of the debtor situated in the territory in which the non-main proceedings are opened,

Where main proceedings have been opened any proceedings opened subsequently in another member state are termed 'secondary' proceedings. Secondary proceedings must be 'winding-up' proceedings, defined in Annex B as a winding-up by the court, CVL or bankruptcy.

Proceedings which were opened prior to the opening of main proceedings in another Member State are called 'territorial' proceedings in the Regulation. Territorial proceedings can only be opened if:

▸ Opening of main proceedings in the jurisdiction of the debtor's COMI is not possible under that jurisdiction's law or

▸ The territorial proceedings are opened at the request of a creditor who is domiciled, habitually resident or has its registered office in that jurisdiction or whose claim arises from the operation of that establishment (Article 3(4)).

By Article 18 'The liquidator appointed by a court which has jurisdiction' to open main proceedings may exercise all the powers conferred on him by the law of the state of the opening of proceedings.

▸ If a UK court opens main administration proceedings therefore the administrator's powers are 'exportable' to other EU states where the debtor company has assets or interests.

▸ These powers would include the power to challenge voidable transactions and the power to enforce co-operation under Ss. 234-237 of the Act.

5.6 Cross border insolvency within UK and outside EU

Insolvency law differs widely between nations. This can lead to difficulties in dealing effectively with insolvencies of entities whose interests straddle international borders. Procedures governing cross border insolvencies are mainly dependant on regulations in force in the particular country and whether the country is signed up to EC regulations, the UNCITRAL Model Law or has its own regulations.

The United Nations Commission on International Trade Law (UNICTRAL) developed a Model Law on Cross Border Insolvency, the purpose of which was to ensure a fair distribution of an insolvent entity's assets where those assets are in more than one country.

Unlike EC regs (which are automatic throughout the EU), the Model Law provides for countries to modify or opt out of provisions if they wish.

The Model Law was adopted by the UK in The Cross Border Insolvency Regulations 2006.

The Regulations apply where:

▶ Assistance is sought in the UK by a foreign court in connection with a 'foreign proceeding'.

▶ Assistance is sought in one state in connection with a proceeding under British Insolvency Law.

▶ A foreign proceeding in one state and a proceeding under British Insolvency Law in respect of the same debtor are taking place concurrently.

▶ Creditors in a different state have an interest in commencing or participating in a proceeding under British Insolvency Law.

The Regulations entitle a foreign representative to apply directly to the UK courts to commence British Insolvency proceedings and to participate in such proceedings once commenced. They set out a procedure for a foreign representative to seek recognition and relief for insolvency proceedings and they enable British Insolvency office holders (excluding administrative receivers) to act in other states in respect of a proceeding under British Law.

In any conflict between the Model Law and the EC Regulations, the EC Regulations will take precedence.

Summary and self-test

Summary

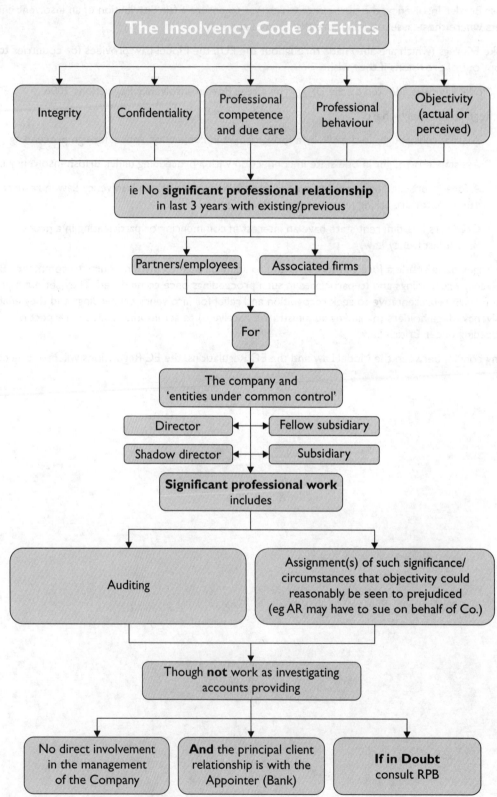

The Insolvency Code of Ethics

- Integrity
- Confidentiality
- Professional competence and due care
- Professional behaviour
- Objectivity (actual or perceived)

ie No **significant professional relationship** in last 3 years with existing/previous

- Partners/employees
- Associated firms

For

The company and 'entities under common control'

| Director | ↔ | Fellow subsidiary |
| Shadow director | ↔ | Subsidiary |

Significant professional work includes

- Auditing
- Assignment(s) of such significance/ circumstances that objectivity could reasonably be seen to prejudiced (eg AR may have to sue on behalf of Co.)

Though **not** work as investigating accounts providing

- No direct involvement in the management of the Company
- **And** the principal client relationship is with the Appointer (Bank)
- **If in Doubt** consult RPB

Self-test

Answer the following questions.

1   What are the five fundamental principles?

2   If you were asked to act as administrator of a company, what practical steps would you take to establish whether there were any ethical reasons why you should not accept the appointment?

3   What is a 'centre of main interests (COMI)'?

4   What is an 'establishment'?

5   To what insolvency procedures do the EC Regulations not apply?

6   You have just been appointed administrator of Parry Stationers Ltd. How can you ensure that you comply with the money laundering regulations?

7   What is the role of a MLRO?

Now, go back to the Learning Objectives in the Introduction. If you are satisfied that you have achieved these objectives, please tick them off.

Answers to Self-test

1 – Integrity

– Objectivity

– Professional competence and due care

– Confidentiality

– Professional behaviour

2 Obtain company search (including for any associated or connected companies) to identify the directors of the company.

Prepare group structure chart and identify directors and shareholders to check if conflicts exist.

Ask the directors if they are aware of any involvement of my firm with them or the company.

Do I have a personal connection with any of the directors of the company?

Circulate partners, managers etc in my firm and ask them if they are aware of any previous professional involvement with the company or directors.

Ensure that my firm has not acted as auditors of the company within the last three years.

Check own practice management system / client lists for details of any involvement.

Ensure my firm has not acted as administrative receivers or LPA receivers of the company within the last three years.

Consider the nature and impact of any advice given to the directors pre insolvency by my firm.

Consult my professional body for advice.

Ensure that I am duly qualified to act as administrator.

Ensure that I hold the required general penalty bond.

3 **Centre of main interests**: this is the place of command or control, the place where the debtor conducts the administration of its business on a regular basis. This could be where the registered office is, but may not always be so.

4 **Establishment**: Any place of operations where the debtor carries out a non-transitory economic activity with human means and grounds.

5 Members' voluntary liquidation.

Administrative receivership.

Fixed charge receivership.

S895 CA 06 scheme of arrangement.

6 (i) ▸ Obtain satisfactory evidence of the identity of the business and of any individual business who expresses an interest in purchasing the assets of the company in administration ie. Passport, photo driving licence, credit card bill, bank statement, utility bill;

▸ Evidence of major shareholders and directors, company search, latest accounts.

(ii) Ensure office:

▸ Has appointed a MLRO (money laundering reporting officer)
▸ Has procedures in place for reporting suspicious transactions
▸ Carries out staff training re money laundering issues
▸ Keeps records of checks made

(iii)   If become suspicious re any transaction, must report suspicions to the MLRO who will then make a suspicious activity report to SOCA. The transaction will be halted until permission is received from the SOCA (should receive within seven working days or if no response after seven days transaction may continue).

7   He is a nominated officer to whom principals and employees report suspicions of money laundering. He decides whether matters need reporting on to the SOCA.

Answer to interactive question

Interactive question: Biome Limited

The following practical steps should be taken relating to conflicts of interest:

▶   Circulate partners, managers etc in own firm to ask if any previous professional or personal involvement with the company or the directors (asking for nil returns as well).

▶   Check own practice management system / client lists etc for details on any such involvement.

▶   Check company search to see if your firm is auditor of the company (or has been during previous three years).

▶   Ask the directors if they are aware of any involvement of your firm with them or the company.

▶   Consider the nature and impact of any advice that your firm has given to the directors pre-insolvency.

▶   Make a file note evidencing that you have considered all the above factors and concluding that it is in order for you to accept the appointment.

In relation to qualifications:

▶   Ensure that you have current authorisation to accept insolvency appointments
▶   Ensure that you have a self-certification borderau limit sufficient to bond the case
▶   If the limit is too low, contact the bond provider before accepting the appointment.

2

Statements of Insolvency Practice

> > > > > > > > > > > > > > > > >

Contents

Introduction

Examination context

Topic List

Self-test

Answers to Self-test

Introduction

Learning objectives

▶ Understand what a Statement of Insolvency Practice (SIP) is, who produces them and why they are important

▶ Learn relevant SIP numbers and names

▶ Understand what a Technical Release is

▶ Understand what an Insolvency Guidance Paper (IGPs) is, who produces them and why they are important

Working context

Due to the differing nature of insolvency appointments there is a need to co-ordinate and promote best practice amongst insolvency professionals. Statements of Insolvency Practice outline best practice and basic principles which must be followed by insolvency professionals. A good knowledge of the SIPs is therefore fundamental to ensure that all areas of your work are carried out with the appropriate levels of competence and skill.

Stop and think

Why do office holders need a uniform approach to practical issues relating to insolvency appointments? Why are there only 16 SIPs?

Examination context

It is unlikely in the exam that a question will appear testing your knowledge of a particular statement in its own right. However a good, detailed knowledge of the SIPs are required in order to pass the exam, for example, a question regarding CVAs would require a detailed knowledge of the content of SIP 3 and a question can director's disqualification will require a detailed knowledge of SIP 4.

Past exam questions to look at include:

2007   Question   2(i)

1 Statements of Insolvency Practice and Technical Releases

Section overview

▶ Statements of Insolvency Practice (SIPs) set out basic principles and essential procedures with which office holders are required to comply.

1.1 Statements of Insolvency Practice (SIPs)

Statements of Insolvency Practice (SIPs) are issued under procedures agreed between the insolvency regulatory authorities acting through the Joint Insolvency Committee. SIPs should be used as guidance only and should not be relied upon as definitive statements. The introduction to each SIP details who it is issued by and sets out the context in which it is to be used.

1.2 Technical Releases

SIP 5 and SIP 6 were withdrawn by the Society of Practitioners of Insolvency in August 1999 and replaced by Technical Releases. These apply in exactly the same way as the original SIPs.

2 List of Statements of Insolvency Practice

Section overview

▶ The following is a list of SIPs in force at July 2009. Where a detailed knowledge of the content of the SIP is required reference is made to the relevant chapter in this Study Manual.

2.1 Summary of SIPs

SIP	Name	Chapter
1	An administrative receiver's responsibility for the company's records	8
2	A liquidator's investigation into the affairs of an insolvent company	
3	Voluntary arrangements	13
4	Disqualification of directors	11
5	Non preferential claims by employees dismissed without proper notice by insolvent employers (replaced by Technical Release 5)	10
6	Treatment of director's claims as employees in insolvency administrations (replaced by Technical Release 6)	10
7	Preparation of insolvency office holder's receipts and payments	12
8	Summoning and holding meetings of creditors convened pursuant to s98	
9	Remuneration of insolvency office holders	
10	Proxy forms	
11	The handling of funds in formal insolvency appointments	
12	Records of meetings in formal insolvency proceedings	13

LEARNING MEDIA

SIP	Name	Chapter
13	Acquisition of assets of insolvent companies by directors	10
14	A receiver's responsibility to preferential creditors	8
✱ 15	Reporting and providing information on their functions to committees in formal insolvencies - *covers all syllabus!*	11
16	Pre-packaged sales in administrations	

3 Insolvency Guidance Papers

Section overview

▶ Insolvency Guidance Papers (IGPs) are developed and approved by the Joint Insolvency Committee and are issued to insolvency practitioners to provide guidance on matters that may require consideration in the conduct of insolvency work or in an insolvency practitioner practice.

▶ Unlike SIPs, which set out required practice, IGPs are purely guidance and practitioners may develop different approaches to the areas covered by the IGPs.

3.1 List of IGPs

The following IGPs have been issued to date:

▶ Control of cases
▶ Succession planning
▶ Bankruptcy – family homes

Appendix I

Insolvency Guidance Paper – Control of cases

Introduction

Insolvency appointments are personal to an individual practitioner, who has an obligation to ensure that cases are properly controlled and administered at all times. However, issues can arise when an insolvency practitioner delegates work to others, or takes appointments jointly with other practitioners. In such circumstances, a practitioner's planning and administrative arrangements will need to consider how best to ensure that cases are properly controlled at all times and that proper regard is paid to the interests of creditors and other affected parties.

Delegation

Given the wide variation in the size of firms dealing with insolvency work, each practitioner will have different case loads and resources and thus a different requirement to delegate work. Delegation can take on a number of forms, including:

▶ Delegation of work to staff in the practitioner's own office or to sub-contractors.

▶ Delegation of work to staff within a firm but in another location.

▶ Taking a reduced role on an appointment taken jointly with an insolvency practitioner in the practitioner's office.

▶ Taking a reduced role on an appointment taken jointly with an insolvency practitioner within the same firm but in another location.

▶ Allowing a specialist insolvency practitioner within a firm to take responsibility for all work of a specific type.

▶ Allowing a specialist within a firm to handle work of a specific type (eg tax).

▶ Sharing work on an agreed basis on an appointment taken jointly with a practitioner from another firm.

▶ Employing another firm to give specialist advice (eg tax) or to undertake specific work (eg an investigation) and

▶ Allowing a practitioner in a former firm (following either the practitioner's move to another firm or retirement) to take responsibility for appointments for a short time pending the transfer of cases.

For each of the above examples (and in other cases where delegation takes place) the practitioner must be satisfied at all times that work is being carried out in a proper and efficient manner, appropriate to the case.

Control

In determining the procedures to be put in place to ensure that an appropriate level of control can be established in relation to delegated work, it is recommended that a practitioner have regard to the following matters:

▶ The structure within a firm, and the qualifications and experience of staff.

▶ The need for the practitioner to be involved in setting case strategy at the outset, depending on the nature, size and complexity of the case.

▶ The procedures within a firm to ensure consultation by joint appointees, other practitioners and staff.

▶ The extent to which levels of responsibility are defined, and the circumstances in which a reference to, or approval by, the practitioner is required.

▶   Whether there are clear guidelines within a firm to deal with the administration of cases at locations remote from the practitioner.

▶   The ways in which compliance and case progress are monitored, and then reported to the practitioner.

▶   The frequency of case reviews, and who carries them out.

▶   The systems for dealing with correspondence received and, in particular, complaints.

▶   The process by which work is allocated on a joint appointment with a practitioner from another firm, the rationale for that split, and the controls to be put in place, subject always to statutory requirements and

▶   The way in which specialist advisers (including agents and solicitors) and sub-contractors are chosen and engaged, and how their work is monitored.

Insolvency practitioners are aware that they may be required to justify their decisions and demonstrate that appropriate levels of control have been established. It is recommended that for firm wide procedures guidance is set out in writing, and that on a case by case basis contemporaneous working papers or file notes are prepared.

Appendix 2

Insolvency Guidance Paper – Succession planning

Introduction

Insolvency appointments are personal to an insolvency practitioner, who has an obligation to ensure that cases are properly managed at all times, and to have appropriate contingency arrangements in place to cover a change in the insolvency practitioner's circumstances. The over-riding principle is that the interests of creditors and other stakeholders should not be prejudiced.

Continuity

It is important for insolvency practitioners to consider on a regular basis the arrangements in place to ensure continuity in the event of death, incapacity to act, retirement from practice, or the practitioner otherwise retiring from a firm.

Sole practitioners

A sole practitioner should consider the steps necessary to put a workable continuity agreement in place, although there may well be considerations as to whether a sole practitioner's cases would be accepted by another insolvency practitioner. The full consequences, both practical and financial, of the relationship with another insolvency practitioner have to be recognised by both the office holder and the nominated successor, so that continuity can be achieved and the interests of creditors and other stakeholders safeguarded. In particular, the nominated successor would have to consider whether the obligations arising from a successor arrangement can be discharged properly and expeditiously, having regard to the number and nature of cases to be taken over.

A retiring office holder should normally make arrangements for the transfer of cases (including, where appropriate, an application to Court) in sufficient time to ensure that the cases are transferred before the retirement takes place.

The nominated successor may need to make an application to Court for the transfer of cases as soon as possible after the other office holder's death, incapacity or, if no other arrangements have been made, retirement.

The arrangements with the nominated successor will need to be reviewed as circumstances dictate, but preferably at least annually.

The principal matters that might routinely be dealt with in a continuity agreement are set out in the Appendix to this paper.

Firms

Every insolvency practitioner in a firm (whether a principal or employee) should consider the comments made above regarding sole practitioners, and should discuss with the firm the arrangements for succession planning, to cover death, incapacity to act, retirement, or leaving the firm. It is recommended that this is reflected in the partnership agreement or in a separate insolvency practice agreement.

In a firm with other insolvency practitioners, it is likely that the arrangements would include, at the least, an understanding that another insolvency practitioner will take over open cases, and make an application to court for the transfer of those cases, if the office holder is unable to do so. It will be the professional responsibility of the remaining partners (as insolvency practitioners) to take prompt action to safeguard the interests of creditors and other stakeholders.

When an office holder retires from a firm, it may be acceptable for the office holder to remain in office for a short period, with an insolvency practitioner in the firm dealing with the administration of cases. However, there the office holder needs to receive appropriate information on the progress of cases, and be consulted when decisions are to be made; the office holder is likely to require unrestricted access to case files. Such an arrangement, however, is unlikely to be appropriate other than for cases that are clearly in their closing stages. In normal circumstances, the retiring office holder should be replaced within a reasonable period, likely to be within 12 months of retirement.

Where there are no other insolvency practitioners in a firm, and in the absence of any contractual arrangements to deal with death, incapacity to act, or retirement, the remaining partners (presumably themselves members of professional bodies) should consider their own professional obligations to ensure the proper management of their practice, including making arrangements for another insolvency practitioner to step in as office holder. The firm may have to procure an application to court for the transfer of cases as soon as possible after the office holder's death, incapacity or retirement.

The principal matters that might routinely be dealt with in an insolvency practice agreement (or a partnership agreement) are set out in the Appendix to this paper.

Disputes

There can be disputes between firms and partners (and employees who are office holders) who leave the firm, principally arising from the personal nature of insolvency appointments. However, commercial disputes should not be allowed to obscure the over-riding principle set out at the beginning of this paper - that the interest of creditors and other stakeholders should not be prejudiced.

It is important therefore, that the contractual arrangements referred to above should provide for the (essentially) mechanistic and financial consequences of an office holder leaving the firm (or upon incapacity to act). There will be similar considerations when an office holder (either partner or employee) is suspended by a firm, or is otherwise excluded from the firm's offices.

Where there are no contractual arrangements, or where a dispute arises, both parties should consider their professional obligations, and the standard of conduct required by their professional bodies. Further, an office holder must have regard to the statutory obligations of the offices held.

If there is a dispute, it is for the office holder to decide how best to ensure that the obligations of office can be discharged; an application to court may be the only means of finding a solution. It is always open to an office holder to consult with his or her authorising body.

As noted above, there may be professional obligations on remaining partners to arrange for the proper management of their practice, and so ensure that they do not bring their own professional bodies into disrepute.

Appendix

Principal matters that might be dealt with in a continuity agreement:

1   A clear statement of the circumstances upon which the agreement would become operative, and also the circumstances in which the nominated successor can decline to act.

2   The extent and frequency of disclosure to the nominated successor of case details and financial information.

3   Detailed provisions to provide for:

▸   The steps to be taken by the nominated successor when the agreement becomes operative
▸   Ownership of, or access to, case working papers
▸   Access to practice records
▸   Financial agreements.

Principal matters that might be dealt with in an insolvency practice agreement (or in a partnership agreement):

1   Clear statements of what happens in the event of an insolvency practitioner (whether partner or employee)

▸ .   Dying, or being otherwise incapable of acting as an insolvency practitioner
▸   Retiring from practice
▸   Being suspended or otherwise excluded from the firm's offices or
▸   Leaving the firm.

2 Where the agreement provides for another insolvency practitioner (whether in the firm or in another firm) to take over appointments

▶ The time within which transfers of cases will take place and the arrangements for the interim period, including provisions for access to information and files

▶ The obligations placed on the practitioner, the firm and the successor practitioner, both in the interim period and thereafter

▶ Professional indemnity insurance arrangements and

▶ Financial arrangements.

3 Where the insolvency practitioner is to remain as office holder following retirement or leaving the firm

▶ Ownership of, or access to, case working papers
▶ Access to practice records
▶ Professional indemnity insurance arrangements and
▶ Financial arrangements.

Self-test

Answer the following questions.

1   You have just been appointed administrative receiver of Whole Foods Limited. To which SIP would you look to for guidance regarding your responsibility for the company's records?

2   What matters are dealt with by SIP 7?

3   What matters are dealt with by SIP 13?

4   As an administrator of a company, to which SIP would you look to for guidance on drawing your remuneration?

5   Which SIP deals with a receiver's responsibility to preferential creditors?

6   As an administrator, to which SIP would you look for guidance when reporting to a creditors' committee?

7   What matters are dealt with by SIP 10?

8   What matters are dealt with by SIP 11?

9   What matters are dealt with by SIP 12?

Now, go back to the Learning Objectives in the Introduction. If you are satisfied that you have achieved these objectives, please tick them off.

Answers to self-test

1	SIP 1
2	Preparation of insolvency office holders' receipts and payments accounts
3	Acquisition of assets of insolvent companies by directors
4	SIP 9
5	SIP 14
6	SIP 15
7	Proxy forms
8	The handling of funds in formal insolvencies
9	Records of meetings in formal insolvencies

3

Introduction
to liquidations

> > > > > > > > > > > > > > >

Contents

Introduction

Learning objectives

▶ Identify different types of liquidation

▶ Qualification of an individual required to act as liquidator

▶ State the powers of the liquidator, including those which require sanction and those which don't

▶ Understand when a company may be dissolved without first being wound up

Working context

In a working context you may be asked to assist on both compulsory and voluntary liquidations, it is important therefore to understand the main differences between each type of liquidation.

Stop and think

Why are there different types of liquidation? Why might an Insolvency Practitioner (IP) sometimes be prevented from accepting an appointment as liquidator? What powers does a liquidator have and why does the exercise of certain powers require sanction?

Examination context

Dissolution has been examined only once as a five marker question in the 2000 JIEB exam. While it is not a very examinable topic for Paper 1 Liquidations, it is still worth being familiar with the principles of dissolution, particularly as an alternative to Members' Voluntary Liquidation.

An understanding of the powers of the liquidator is required, including being able to identify when the exercise of certain powers requires sanction.

Exam requirements

Past exam questions to look at include:

2002	Question 4(b)
2001	Question 3(a)
2000	Question 5(a)
1995	Question 3(b)
1994	Question 2(c)

1 Introduction to liquidations

Section overview

▶ There are two types of liquidation, voluntary liquidation and compulsory liquidation. Voluntary liquidations commence with the passing of a resolution by the members of the company and compulsory liquidations commence with the making of a winding-up order by the court.

▶ The legislation governing liquidations is found in Part IV IA 1986 (s73 – s251) and Part 4 of the Rules (r4.1 – 4.231).

1.1 Types of voluntary winding-up

There are two types of voluntary liquidations:

▶ Members' voluntary liquidation (MVL) – solvent liquidation where directors swear a Declaration of Solvency.

▶ Creditors' voluntary liquidation (CVL) – insolvent liquidation, creditors have an opportunity to appoint a liquidator of their choice.

Members' voluntary liquidation is dealt with in more detail in Chapter 4.

Creditors' voluntary liquidation is dealt with in more detail in Chapter 5.

Compulsory liquidation is dealt with in Chapter 6.

1.2 Commencement of winding-up

A compulsory liquidation is deemed to commence on the date of the presentation of the petition on which a winding-up order is made.

A voluntary liquidation is deemed to commence on the date of the members' resolution to wind up the company.

Interactive question: Liquidations

Briefly outline the main features of:

(i)   Members' voluntary liquidation
(ii)   Creditors' voluntary liquidation
(iii)   Compulsory liquidation.

See **Answer** at the end of this chapter.

1.3 Qualification as liquidator

In order to act as a liquidator a person must be:

▶ An individual (a firm cannot act as liquidator)
▶ A qualified IP

A person is not qualified unless:

▶ He is authorised by membership of a professional body
▶ He is authorised by a competent body under s392
▶ He has lodged security in accordance with the regulations

2 Powers of the liquidator

Section overview

▶ The powers of the liquidator are detailed in Schedule 4. The exercise of some of the powers by the liquidator require sanction. By s165(1), in a voluntary liquidation sanction is obtained:

    – in a MVL, by the passing of an special resolution by the company in general meeting

    – in a CVL, either from the liquidation committee (or if there is none, a creditors' meeting) or the court

▶ In practice, the Secretary of State will give sanction to liquidators in situations where there is no liquidation committee.

▶ In a compulsory liquidation sanction is obtained from the liquidation committee, or if there is none, the OR (s167).

▶ If the OR is himself liquidator, sanction can be obtained from the Secretary of State or from the court.

2.1 Powers exercisable with sanction (Part I)

The following powers require sanction in any type of liquidation:

▶ To pay any class of creditor in full
▶ To make compromises or arrangements with creditors or claimants against the company
▶ To compromise claims by the company against debtors, potential debtors and contributories
▶ To bring legal proceedings under s 213, 214, 238, 239, 242, 243 or s423

2.2 Powers exercisable without sanction in a voluntary winding-up (Part II)

The following powers are exercisable without sanction in a voluntary winding-up, however they would require sanction in a compulsory winding-up:

▶ To bring or defend any action or other legal proceedings in the name and on behalf of the company
▶ To carry on the business of the company so far as may be necessary for its beneficial winding-up.

2.3 Powers exercisable without sanction in any type of liquidation (Part III)

▶ To sell company property.
▶ To execute all documents.
▶ To claim in the insolvency of debtor individuals and companies.
▶ To draw/make etc bills of exchange and promissory notes.
▶ To raise money on the security of company assets.
▶ To take out letters of administration in the name of deceased contributories.
▶ To appoint an agent.
▶ To do all such other things as may be necessary for winding-up the company's affairs.

2.4 Powers which require notice to be given to the liquidation committee

In a voluntary liquidation if the liquidator disposes of any company property to a party connected with the company, he must give notice of it to the liquidation committee.

In a compulsory liquidation notice must be given of the appointment of a solicitor or the sale of assets to an associate of the company.

2.5 Other powers

The liquidator can apply to the Court for Directions (Compulsory winding-up s168(3), Voluntary winding-up s112). The official receiver can apply for directions under r10.3

Under s147 the liquidator or the official receiver or creditors or contributories can apply to have the winding-up stayed.

The liquidator may summon meetings of creditors and contributories to ascertain their wishes (s168).

The liquidator can, with special court leave or sanction of the liquidation committee, make calls on any or all of the contributories of the company to the extent necessary to satisfy the company's debts, liabilities and expenses of the winding-up (ss150, 160).

The liquidator has the power to make payments to employees:

▶ Any resolution under s247 CA 06 to pay employees on cessation or transfer of business is valid providing:

– It was passed pre commencement of winding-up
– It is made out of distributable profits.

▶ The company can, post commencement of winding-up, resolve to pay employees but this can only be out of assets, which would otherwise be available to members.

Power to transfer assets (s110).

Power to challenge directors for fraudulent/wrongful trading (s213, s214).

Power to apply for private examination (s236).

Power to insist on continuation of supplies (s233). The liquidator can be required to personally guarantee payments for future supplies however suppliers can't insist on payment for past supplies.

Power to get in the company's property (s234).

Power to require co-operation (s235).

Power to set aside transactions under (s238, s239, s244, s245).

Power to apply to vest property in the liquidator (s145).

Power to disclaim onerous property (s178).

2.6 Centrebind procedure   *presumably n/a to MVL?*

Usually the General Meeting (GM) and the s98 creditors' meeting will be held on the same day. However, if the members agree to calling the GM at short notice a liquidator may be appointed and the company placed into liquidation. The s98 meeting of creditors may be held at any time within the following 14 days. This is called a 'centrebind' procedure.

In the period between the GM and the s98 creditors' meeting the members' liquidator's powers are limited.

S166 limits the exercise of the liquidator's powers to:

▶ Take into custody or control all of the company's property
▶ Dispose of perishable/wasting goods
▶ Do all things necessary for the protection of the company's assets.

The exercise of any other powers requires the sanction of the court.

The members' liquidator must attend the s98 creditors' meeting and report to it on the exercise of his powers.

The introduction of s166 was to limit the acts of less than scrupulous Insolvency Practitioners who previously would arrange the sale of company assets at a marked down price to connected companies prior to the meeting of creditors.

3 Dissolution without winding up

Section overview

The Companies Acts provide for two situations where a company may be dissolved without it being wound up first.

▶ Under s895 CA 2006 the court may order the dissolution of a company on the application to the court for the sanctioning of a compromise or arrangement. The court will order the dissolution in appropriate circumstances where the compromise or arrangement involves a reconstruction or amalgamation and the transfer of whole or any part of the undertaking of property of one company to another.

▶ A private company which is not trading may be dissolved by striking it from the register at Companies House under s1000 CA 06.

Definition

Dissolution: where a company is struck off the register and ceases to exist.

3.1 S1000 CA 06

The company itself may apply to be struck off (where the business has achieved the objectives for which it was set up or the owners wish to retire) or the Registrar of Companies may strike a company's name off the register where he has reasonable cause to believe that a company is not carrying on business or is not in operation (ie. documents required have not been received or mail is returned unopened).

A company struck off under s1000 CA 06 may still be wound up by the court, but it should be restored to the register first. If the court makes an order restoring a company to the register, the company shall be deemed to have continued in existence as if its name had not been struck off.

3.2 Dissolution as an alternative to MVL

Where there is a trading company which is no longer required there is a choice whether to put the company into members' voluntary liquidation or apply under s1003 CA 06 for the company to be struck off.

If the liquidation route is chosen the liquidator will distribute the assets as a capital distribution to the shareholders. Once the liquidation is complete a final return will be sent to Companies House and the company will be dissolved three months after this is filed. (See Chapter Four for more details.)

If the s1003 CA 06 route is chosen the directors complete an application form and file it with the Registrar Of Companies with the £10 fee. (The company must not have traded or otherwise carried on business for three months or more.)

The directors must, within seven days of the application, notify interested parties (shareholders, creditors, employees, trustees of employee's pension fund, any directors who did not sign the application).

The Registrar advertises the proposed dissolution in the Gazette, but will not strike the company off for three months, pending any obligations.

The company will be dissolved when the Registrar publishes a notice to that effect in the Gazette.

Advantages of striking off:

▶ Cheaper option than MVL, no liquidator's costs.

▶ Quicker option than MVL, minimum three-month period.

▶ Avoids requirement to indemnify the liquidator.

▶ HMRC will treat the distribution of funds to shareholders as a capital distribution for tax purposes (under C16 statutory concession).

Disadvantages to striking off:

▸ Application may be made by an 'aggrieved person' for the company to be restored to the register within 20 years of the dissolution being published in the Gazette.

▸ Despite the tax treatment of distributions made under extra statutory concession C16 the *of profits* distribution of capital is still unlawful. Where the company has been dissolved the Crown has the right to recover funds from members. (However, the Treasury Solicitor has stated that where the amount distributed to shareholders under the concession does not exceed £4,000 the Treasury Solicitor will waive the right to recover the money.) If funds are greater than £4,000 members' voluntary liquidation would be a more beneficial route.

▸ An application under s1003 CA 06 cannot be made if the company is subject to formal insolvency process or a scheme under s895 CA 06.

▸ There is a risk that a creditor may be missed or declined to qualify for a claim. The liquidator in a MVL has the power to advertise for and agree creditor claims.

▸ Any breach by the directors in making the application or furnishing false or misleading information renders them liable to prosecution.

▸ Any property of the company on dissolution will be *bona vacantia*.

3.3 Restoration to the register

The Registrar cannot restore a company to the register without a court order. When the Registrar receives an office copy of the court order for restoration, the company is regarded as having continued in existence as if it had not been struck off and dissolved.

For companies struck off following a s1003 CA 06 application, any of the parties who must be notified of the application can apply to the court within six years of the dissolution for the name of the dissolved company to be restored to the Register.

If a members' voluntary liquidation had been used and the company has been dissolved, the period for such applications is limited to two years.

(**Note:** S1024 CA 06 introduces a six-year time limit for all applications to restore a company whether dissolved under a MVL or under s1003 CA 06.)

Summary and self-test

Summary

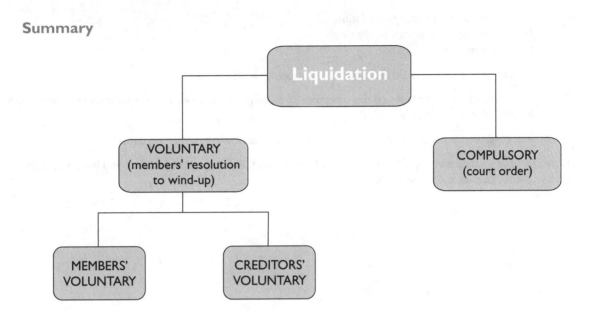

Self-test

Answer the following questions.

1.   When do the following liquidations commence?

    (a)   Members' voluntary liquidation
    (b)   Creditors' voluntary liquidation
    (c)   Compulsory liquidation

2.   When might a company be dissolved without being wound up first?

3.   What are the disadvantages to the directors of dissolving a dormant company rather than entering a Members' Voluntary Liquidation?

4.   In a creditors' voluntary winding-up who sanctions the powers of the liquidator?

Now, go back to the Learning Objectives in the Introduction. If you are satisfied that you have achieved these objectives, please tick them off.

Answers to self-test

1   (a)   Date members pass special resolution to wind up.
    (b)   Date members pass special resolution to wind up.
    (c)   Date of petition on which a winding-up order is made.

2   (a)   Under s895 CA 06 – on application to the court for the sanctioning of a compromise or arrangement.
    (b)   Under s1000 CA 06 – where company is not carrying on business or is not in operation.

3   Disadvantages of dissolution to the directors:

    ▶   An application cannot be made if the company is subject to a formal insolvency process or a scheme under s895 CA 2006

    ▶   An aggrieved person could apply to have the company restored within twenty years of dissolution

    ▶   Risk that a creditor may be missed

    ▶   Any breach by the directors in making the application, or furnishing false or misleading information renders them liable to prosecution

    ▶   The company can distribute profits to shareholders but not assets.

4   In a creditors' voluntary liquidation, sanction is obtained from the liquidation committee (or if there is none a meeting of creditors) or the court.

Answer to interactive question

Interactive question: Liquidations

(i)   Members' voluntary liquidation:

- Solvent liquidation
- Directors swear Declaration of Solvency
- Commences on date members pass resolution to wind up
- Members control liquidation (no creditors' meeting)

(ii)   Creditors' voluntary liquidation:

- Insolvent liquidation
- Statement of Affairs
- Creditors' meeting, creditors choose liquidator and have control of the liquidation
- Commences date members pass resolution to wind up

(iii) Compulsory liquidation:

- OR becomes liquidator initially
- Court process
- Commences with presentation of a petition to wind up the company

4

Members'
Voluntary Liquidation

> > > > > > > > > > > > > > > > > >

Contents

Introduction

Learning objectives

▶ Procedure to place a company into members' voluntary liquidation ☐

▶ Statutory regulations re Declaration of Solvency ☐

▶ Duties of liquidator in Members' Voluntary Liquidation ☐

▶ Consequences of company becoming insolvent post resolution to wind up ☐

▶ S110 arrangements ☐

Working context

This is a very practical subject. You may be asked to assist with a members' voluntary liquidation in a work environment advising directors on the procedure to follow to place a company into members' voluntary liquidation and the content of the director's Declaration of Solvency.

Stop and think

How does a members' voluntary liquidation differ to other forms of liquidation? When is it appropriate to use members' voluntary liquidation? What happens if the company turns out to be insolvent? What is a distribution in specie?

Examination context

Members' voluntary liquidation is a very important topic in the JIEB exam. It is important to learn all of the topics covered in this chapter.

Exam requirements

Past exam questions to look at include:

2008	Question 1(a)
2007	Question 1(a)
2006	Question 4
2004	Question 2(b)
2002	Question 2
2000	Question 5
1998	Question 2
1994	Question 3

1 Procedure for Members' Voluntary Liquidation (MVL)

Section overview

A MVL is a solvent liquidation. The directors swear a Declaration of Solvency (if no declaration is sworn the liquidation must proceed as a Creditors' Voluntary Liquidation). The members control the winding-up, because the creditors will be paid in full they have no interest in how it is conducted.

1.1 Procedure for MVL

The directors hold a Board Meeting where the following resolutions are passed:

▶ Ask the members to resolve to wind up the company as a MVL
▶ To convene an General Meeting (GM)
▶ Appoint a director to chair the GM
▶ To allow a distribution in specie
▶ Make out and swear a Declaration of Solvency

Hold GM:

▶ 14 days' notice must be given to the members (s307 CA 2006), this can be waived by 90% in nominal value of those having the right to attend and vote. (95% for a general meeting held by a public company.)

▶ The notice must set out the special resolution in full.

▶ The company must give notice of the resolution to any qualifying floating charge holders. The resolution cannot be passed until either the charge holder consents or five business days have expired (s84 (2A)).

▶ Quorum is two persons present (unless a one member company (s318(1) CA 2006))

The following resolutions will be placed before the members:

▶ Special resolution to wind up the company as a members' voluntary liquidation. This requires at least 75% of those attending and voting to vote in favour.

▶ Ordinary resolution to appoint a liquidator. This requires a simple majority of members voting in favour.

▶ Ordinary resolution to agree the liquidator's remuneration.

▶ A special resolution for the members to agree to a distribution in specie. (This is where assets are distributed as a dividend to shareholders as well as cash.) A minimum majority of 75% of members entitled to vote must vote in favour of it.

Proxies may be appointed. Voting is initially on a show of hands, however a poll vote may be demanded (this means voting by equity – share ownership).

If the company can't agree on a liquidator, but has resolved to wind up, the court can appoint a liquidator under s108.

The liquidator must provide the chair of the members' meeting with a statement that he:

▶ Is an IP, duly qualified to act as liquidator
▶ Accepts the appointment (r4.139(2)).

The chair fills in Form 4.27 (certificate of appointment) and gives it to the liquidator who must retain it as part of the records of the winding-up.

The liquidator must give notice of his appointment to all creditors of whom he is aware within 28 days of his appointment (r4.139(4)).

A copy of the special resolution to wind up the company must be sent to the Registrar of Companies within 15 days. Failure to do so will render the responsible officers liable to a fine.

The company must give notice of the passing of the resolution by advertisement in the London Gazette within 14 days.

Minutes of the meeting must be signed by the Chairman.

The winding-up is deemed to commence from the passing of the special resolution to wind up the company (s86).

1.2 Effect of MVL on the directors

All powers of the directors cease, except so far as the company in General Meeting, or the liquidator, sanctions their continuance.

2 Declaration of solvency

Section overview

In order for the liquidation to proceed as a MVL the directors must swear a declaration of solvency.

2.1 Who swears the declaration?

The declaration must be sworn by the directors. If the company has one director, that director will swear. If the company has two directors, both directors must swear. If the company has more than two directors, a majority of the directors must swear.

The declaration must be sworn at a directors' meeting before a solicitor/ notary public/ JP/ commissioner for oaths.

2.2 Content of the declaration

The declaration states that the directors have made a full enquiry into the company's affairs and are of the opinion that the company will be able to pay its debts in full, together with interest at the official rate, within such period, not exceeding 12 months, from the commencement of the winding-up as may be specified in the declaration (s89 (1)).

It must be made before the members' resolution is passed, but not more than five weeks before the resolution is passed.

It must contain a statement of the company's assets and liabilities as at the latest practicable date before the making of the declaration (s89(2)(b)).

It must be filed with the Registrar of Companies within 15 days of the resolution (s89(3)).

2.3 Penalties

A director who makes a declaration without reasonable grounds is liable to a fine and/or imprisonment. It is presumed that the director did not have reasonable grounds if it turns out that all creditors cannot be paid (s89(5)).

Interactive question: Brown and Co Ltd

You have been approached by the ageing directors of Brown and Co Limited for advice regarding placing the company into members' voluntary liquidation.

Requirement

Write a letter to the directors dealing with:

(i)   The procedure to follow to place the company into MVL.

(ii)   Advice to the directors regarding their dealings with the company's assets and liabilities both pre and post winding up.

See **Answer** at the end of this chapter.

3 Duties of the liquidator in MVL

Section overview

The liquidator has a number of statutory duties with which he must comply:

▶   Must convene a general meeting 12 months after commencement of the winding-up (s93) and on succeeding anniversaries of the winding-up (or at least no more than 15 months from the last one).

▶   Must lay before those meetings an account of his acts and dealings and of the conduct of the winding-up during the preceding year.

▶   On the company's affairs being fully wound up:

    –   Convene general meeting

    –   Advertise it in London Gazette at least one month before holding it

    –   Prepare an account of the winding-up

    –   Lay the account before the General meeting and explain it to the shareholders

    –   Within seven days of the meeting send to the Registrar a copy of the accounts and a return as to the holding of the meeting and its date.

4 Company becomes insolvent post resolution to wind up

Section overview

If the company is in members' voluntary liquidation and the liquidator becomes aware that it will not, after all, be able to pay its debts (including interest and expenses) within 12 months from the date of commencement of the winding-up, action must be taken under s95.

4.1 Duties of liquidator on becoming aware company insolvent

Within 28 days of the day after the discovery was made that the company was in fact insolvent, the liquidator must convene a meeting of the company's creditors.

At least seven days' notice must be given.

The meeting must be advertised in the London Gazette and may be advertised in such other manner as the liquidator thinks fit.

Prior to the meeting the liquidator must furnish the creditors, free of charge, with such information concerning the affairs of the company as they may reasonably require. This duty applies during the period before the day on which the creditors' meeting is to be held. The duty must be stated on the notices of the creditors' meeting.

The meeting is deemed to be the creditors' meeting in a CVL.

The liquidator must also:

▶   Make a statement in the prescribed form as to the affairs of the company
▶   Lay that statement before the creditors' meeting
▶   Attend and preside at the meeting.

The Statement of Affairs must include the following information:

▶   Particulars of the company's assets, debts and liabilities
▶   The name and addresses of the company's creditors
▶   The securities held by them respectively
▶   The dates when the securities were respectively given
▶   Such further or other information as may be prescribed.

S96 provides that as from the day on which the creditors' meeting is held under s95, this Act has effect as if:

▶   The directors' declaration under s89 had not been made, and

▶   The creditors' meeting and the company meeting at which it was resolved that the company be wound up voluntarily were the meetings mentioned in s98 (see next chapter),

And accordingly the winding-up becomes a creditors' voluntary winding-up.

4.2 Ethical considerations

In these circumstances the liquidator will be under a duty to consider resigning from office. If there is any prospect of a conflict of interest or if objectivity or independence are in any way compromised, the office holder must consider resigning (for example, if the office holder has had a significant professional relationship with the company he may act as a liquidator in a members' voluntary liquidation but not in a creditors' voluntary liquidation). (See Chapter 1 para 5.9 for more details on the liquidator's ethical considerations.)

5   S110A arrangements

Section overview

The liquidator is allowed (with the requisite sanction) to accept shares in a company as consideration for the distribution of assets of the company being wound up. Where the whole or part of the company's business is being transferred or sold to a transferee company, the liquidator can accept shares, policies or 'other like interests' in that company for distribution amongst the creditors. The procedure is only available in a voluntary liquidation.

Sanction is obtained by (s110(3)): In a MVL, by the passing of a special resolution at a general meeting which can be passed at the same time as the resolution to wind up or appoint a liquidator (s110(3)).

In a CVL, by the court or the liquidation committee.

The liquidator may enter into an arrangement (with the creditors' sanction) where a right to participate in profits or some other benefit are received instead of cash, shares etc. (s110(4)).

Any member who did not vote in favour of the resolution may express their dissent, in writing, to the liquidator (may be left at the company's registered office), within seven days after the passing of the resolution. The liquidator may be required to abstain from carrying the resolution into effect, or purchase the shareholder's interest at a price to be determined by agreement or arbitration.

If the liquidator elects to purchase the shareholder's interest the purchase money must be raised by the liquidator in such manner as may be determined by special resolution.

6 Distribution in specie

Section overview

▶ Article 117 of Table A allows a liquidator with the sanction of a special resolution to divide among the members in specie the whole or any part of the company and for such purpose to put a fair value on the property.

▶ A distribution in specie would ordinarily be pro rata to shareholding, based on the nominal value of the shares (not paid up value).

▶ Agreement must be reached as to the value of the assets being distributed – the liquidator usually has the power to determine the fair value of property, but it is prudent to obtain the agreement of the members.

▶ A distribution in specie may give rise to a chargeable gain in the company with the disposal being treated as a disposal of the asset at market rate (s17 TCGA 1992).

6.1 Procedure to follow to make a distribution in specie

1 The liquidator must produce a distribution list showing shareholders' names and addresses, class(es) of shares held, rights, nominal value, paid up value.

2 He should establish whether all shares participate equally.

3 If some shares are part paid, he must consider whether a call is appropriate. If no call is made, the liquidator should make an adjustment when making the distribution. Calls on shares can't be set off against cross claims against the company.

4 A distribution note must be sent to each share holder requesting directions regarding payment and the original share certificate.

5 Share certificates must be checked against the member's register and the distribution statement.

6 Details of the distribution should be endorsed on the share certificate.

7 The cheque (or asset title documents) for distribution and the endorsed share certificate should be returned to the shareholder.

8 Members should be advised that each distribution is a part or full disposal of their shares for CGT purposes.

9 Details of the distribution must be recorded on the IP's statutory record.

10 Unclaimed payments should be banked in the unclaimed dividends account at the Bank of England.

Surplus assets must be distributed in accordance with the company's memorandum and articles of association.

Summary and self-test

Summary

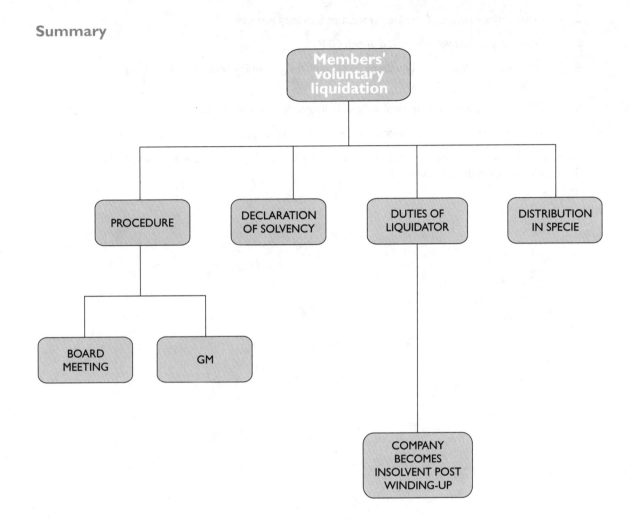

Self-test

Answer the following questions.

1   What are the main features of an MVL?

2   What is the content of the Declaration of Solvency per s89?

3   What resolutions will be passed at the GM?

4   What are the duties of a liquidator in a members' voluntary liquidation if he believes that the company is in fact insolvent?

5   What is the effect of members' voluntary liquidation on the directors?

6   What are the duties of a liquidator on the company's affairs being fully wound up?

Now, go back to the Learning Objectives in the Introduction. If you are satisfied that you have achieved these objectives, please tick them off.

Answers to self-test

1   Solvent liquidation
     Directors swear declaration of solvency
     Creditors have no interest in the winding-up
     Special resolution to wind up the company.

2   The directors of the company have made a full enquiry into the company's affairs, they have formed the opinion that the company will be able to pay its debts, in full, together with interest at the official rate, within such period, not exceeding 12 months, from the commencement of the winding-up, as may be specified in the declaration.

3   Special resolution to wind up the company as a members' voluntary liquidation

     Ordinary resolution to appoint a liquidator

     Ordinary resolution to agree the liquidator's remuneration

     Special resolution for the members to agree a distribution in specie.

4   Within 28 days of the day after the discovery that the company is insolvent, the liquidator must:

     ▶   Summon a creditors' meeting on at least seven days' notice
     ▶   Advertise creditors' meeting in London Gazette and advertised in such other manner as the liquidator thinks fit.
     ▶   Furnish creditors, free of charge, with information re affairs of the company
     ▶   Make out a Statement of Affairs
     ▶   Lay Statement of Affairs before creditors' meeting
     ▶   Attend and preside at the meeting.

5   All powers of the directors cease except so far as the company in general meeting or the liquidator sanctions their continuation.

6   Convene General Meeting.

     Advertise meeting in London Gazette at least one month before.

     Prepare an account of the winding-up.

     Lay the account before General Meeting and explain it to the shareholders.

     Within seven days send to the Registrar of Companies a copy of the accounts and a return as to the holding of the meeting and its date.

Answer to interactive question

Interactive question: Brown and Co Ltd

Letter format

(i)   Procedure to follow to place company into MVL:

1   The directors hold a Board Meeting where the following resolutions are passed:

▶   Ask the members to resolve to wind up the company as a MVL
▶   To convene a General Meeting (GM)
▶   Appoint a director to chair the GM
▶   To allow a distribution in specie
▶   Make out and swear a Declaration of Solvency.

The declaration of solvency states that the directors have made a full enquiry into the company's affairs and are of the opinion that the company will be able to pay its debts in full, together with interest at the official rate, within such period, not exceeding 12 months from the commencement of the winding up as may be specified in the declaration (s89(1)).

2   Hold GM:

▶   14 days' notice must be given to the members (s307 CA 06), this can be waived by 90% in nominal value of those having the right to attend and vote.

▶   The notice must set out the special resolution in full.

▶   The company must give notice of the resolution to any qualifying floating charge holders. The resolution cannot be passed until either the charge holder consents or five business days have expired (s84(2A)).

▶   Quorum is two persons present (unless a one member company (s318(1) CA 06)).

The following resolutions will be placed before the members:

▶   Special resolution to wind up the company as a members' voluntary liquidation. This requires at least 75% of those attending and voting to vote in favour.

▶   Ordinary resolution to appoint a liquidator. This requires a simple majority of members voting in favour.

▶   Ordinary resolution to agree the liquidator's remuneration.

▶   A special resolution for the members to agree to a distribution in specie. (This is where assets are distributed as a dividend to shareholders as well as cash.) A minimum majority of 75% of members entitled to vote must vote in favour of it.

Proxies may be appointed. Voting is initially on a show of hands, however a poll vote may be demanded (this means voting by equity – share ownership).

If the company can't agree on a liquidator, but has resolved to wind up, the court can appoint a liquidator under s108.

The liquidator must provide the chair of the members' meeting with a statement that he:

▶   Is an IP, duly qualified to act as liquidator
▶   Accepts the appointment (r4.139(2)).

The Chair fills in Form 4.27 (certificate of appointment) and gives it to the liquidator who must retain it as part of the records of the winding up.

The liquidator must give notice of his appointment to all creditors of whom he is aware within 28 days of his appointment (r4.139(4)).

A copy of the special resolution to wind up the company must be sent to the Registrar of Companies within 15 days. Failure to do so will render the responsible officers liable to a fine.

The company must give notice of the passing of the resolution by advertisement in the London Gazette within 14 days.

Minutes of the meeting must be signed by the Chair.

The winding up is deemed to commence from the passing of the special resolution to wind up the company (s86).

(ii)   Advice to directors when dealing with assets and liabilities:

The directors should ensure that the assets are secure and insured in the period prior to the passing of a winding up resolution.

Any assets disposed of prior to the winding up should be properly valued and accounted for.

Because the company is solvent, trade creditors should be paid in the normal way. However, since interest will run on all claims under s189 from the passing of the resolution to wind up the company, creditor claims should, wherever possible, be agreed and paid before the resolution is passed.

Dividends declared on shares can be paid but there must be no other distribution to members.

Once the winding up resolution has been passed the directors should have no further powers to deal with the assets or liabilities. It passes to the liquidator to deal with them.

The members may, at the general meeting convened to consider the winding up resolution, pass a resolution sanctioning that the directors' powers continue, if necessary.

5

Creditors' Voluntary Liquidation

› › › › › › › › › › › › › ›

Contents

Introduction

Learning objectives

▶   Identify the main characteristics of a creditors' voluntary liquidation

▶   Understand the procedure for creditors' voluntary liquidation including statutory provisions re convening meetings of members and creditors

▶   Statutory requirements re preparation of the Statement of Affairs and deficiency account

▶   The liquidation committee – its establishment, functions, duties and the duties of the liquidator in relation to the committee

▶   Content of SIP 15

Working context

A large number of companies enter into voluntary liquidation each year. It is likely therefore that you will be involved in working on liquidation cases in an office environment. You may be asked to prepare the relevant notices to convene a s98 meeting of creditors or advise directors on the procedure to follow to place a company into creditors' voluntary liquidation. You may also be asked to attend a s98 meeting on behalf of a client and sit on a creditors' committee on their behalf.

Stop and think

When is a creditors' voluntary liquidation the most appropriate insolvency option for a company? What is a Statement of Affairs? How is a liquidator appointed? What is a liquidation committee? Why is it required? Why is there no committee in a members' voluntary liquidation?

Examination context

The topics covered in this chapter should be learnt in detail, creditors' voluntary liquidations and creditors' committees are very examinable topics in the JIEB exam. You may be asked to simply outline the rules for example, steps to establish a liquidation committee, or you may be presented with a scenario and asked to advise the directors on the most appropriate course of action to take and the procedures to be followed. Dealings by committee members are the main subject of JIEB questions about liquidation committees.

Exam requirements

Past exam questions to look at include:

2008	Question 2(a) and (b)
2006	Question 3
2004	Question 1
2003	Question 2
2001	Question 3
1999	Question 2
1996	Question 3(a)
1995	Question 1
1995	Question 2
1995	Question 4(c)
1994	Question 2
1993	Question 2(a)
1992	Question 1(a)

1 Procedure for Creditors' Voluntary Liquidation

Section overview

A Creditors' Voluntary Liquidation (CVL) is a voluntary liquidation where no declaration of solvency has been made (s90). The company is insolvent, so the creditors have control of the liquidation. The legislation is contained in s97 – s116 and chapters 6 to 12 of the Rules. SIP 8 provides guidance to office holders when summoning and holding meetings of creditors convened pursuant to s98.

1.1 Ethical considerations

Where there has been a significant professional relationship with a company or a personal relationship with a director, former director or shadow director thereof, no individual within the practice should accept appointment as liquidator of the company if the company is insolvent.

The 'Advising Member' should obtain written instructions from the Board of Directors defining matters on which he is to advise.

Where instructions are materially contrary to SIP 8 guidelines:

▶ The member should only accept after careful consideration.

▶ If directors act contrary to the guidelines the member may have to show this was contrary to his advice or without his knowledge.

▶ He should not accept instructions unless he has good grounds for believing that a liquidator will be appointed at the GM.

Continuing professional relationship in previous three years does not preclude acting as advising member (but does preclude accepting appointment as Liquidator). As usual, though, careful consideration should be given.

The member should ensure that he feels competent to provide the required level of advice.

The member should ensure the directors understand it is their responsibility to convene the creditors' meeting and to ensure that arrangements are made for the meeting to be held in accordance with current legislation.

Definition

Advising member: An office holder who has received instructions from the company's directors to advise in relation to the convening of the creditors' meeting.

1.2 Procedure for CVL

▶ The directors should be advised to convene a meeting of the board of directors where the following resolutions will be passed:

– Ask members to resolve to wind up the company as a CVL.
– Convene a General Meeting (GM).
– Convene a creditors' meeting under s98.
– Appoint a director to chair both meetings.
– Make up and swear a Statement of Affairs.

- Convene a GM:

14 days' notice of the GM must be given to the members (21 days' if the meeting is a public company AGM s307 CA 06). The notice period may be waived by 90% of those entitled to attend and vote at the GM (95% if it is a public company).

Notice of the resolution to wind up the company must also be given to any Qualifying Floating Charge Holders. The resolution to wind up cannot be passed until either the charge holder consents or five business days have elapsed.

The special resolution can be passed by written resolution if 75% of the members agree. The written resolution must be passed as a special resolution (s283 CA 06).

The following resolutions will be placed before the members:

- Special resolution to wind up the company as a CVL (this requires at least 75% of those attending and voting to vote in favour).

- Ordinary resolution to appoint a liquidator (this requires a simple majority of members voting in favour).

The special resolution must be filed with the Registrar of Companies within 15 days and advertised in the London Gazette within 14 days.

- Convene s98 meeting of creditors:

SIP 8 gives guidance to office holders when summoning and holding meetings of creditors convened pursuant to s98.

The creditors' meeting has to be held within 14 days of the members' meeting (s98(1)(a)).

The powers of the members' choice of liquidator are strictly limited until the creditors' meeting has been held.

The rules are in s166 which says that the members' choice of liquidator cannot exercise the powers conferred under the Act except to:

- Take control and custody of the company's property
- Dispose of goods of wasting nature
- Do all things necessary to protect the company's assets.

If the members' appointed liquidator wants to do anything else he has to apply to the court.

The members' liquidator will also have to attend the creditors' meeting and report to it on the exercise by him of his powers; the powers under the Act, or those granted by the court (s166(4)).

The company must send notices of this meeting to all creditors. At least seven days' notice is required.

The company must advertise this notice:

- In the London Gazette

- May cause notice of the meeting to be advertised in such other manner as the directors see fit.

Prior to the meeting the office holder must provide information to the creditor's. The notice calling the creditors' meeting must state either:

- Name and address of IP (members' liquidator) who will furnish them with free information pre-meeting.

- Place in relevant locality where on the two business days next before date of meeting the creditors can inspect a list of creditors' names and addresses.

Individual notice can be dispensed with under the court's general power to do so in relation to meetings of creditors and contributories in Rule 4.59. It seems that the need for advertisement cannot be dispensed with.

The notice must contain the following information:

– Creditors' right to information. The liquidator must furnish the creditors, free of charge with such information concerning the affairs of the company as they may reasonably require.

– Date/time/place of meeting.

– Place where, and deadline within which, proxies must be deposited if a creditor is to be able to vote through a proxy.

Deadline must not be later than 12.00 noon on day before meeting (IR 4.51(2)).

SIP 9 now requires notices of s98 meetings to state that resolutions regarding the Liquidator's remuneration and the costs of preparing the Statement of Affairs and calling the meeting may be taken. The notice should be accompanied by a SIP 9 (or equivalent) explanatory guidance note to creditors.

Reasonable and necessary costs will qualify as costs of the liquidation.

By s166(5) if the company defaults in its duties under s98(1) or (2) the liquidator shall apply to the court for directions as to how that default is to be remedied. The application must be made within seven days of the date of nomination of the liquidator or the date the liquidator became aware of the default whichever is the later (s166(6)). In default the liquidator will be liable to a fine (s166(7)). Where there is no need to apply for directions then the liquidator need not apply for them. (*Re Salscombe Hotel Development Ltd*)

In fixing the venue for meeting of creditors and contributories the convenor must have regard to the convenience of persons who are to attend.

The meeting should commence between 10.00 and 16.00 hours on a business day (r4.60).

The advising member should ensure that the proposed accommodation is adequate. He may hold the meeting at his own offices (and charge accordingly) providing r4.60 is complied with.

He should advise the directors as to whether in the circumstances the GM and s98 meeting should be held on the same day.

Before notices are sent out the advising member should advise the company to notify any secured creditors who are entitled to appoint an Administrative Receiver that a s98 meeting is to be convened.

The member should ensure that the directors' list of creditors is complete (includes, eg HP companies, lessors and former lessors and public utilities).

Notice of the meeting should be despatched as early as possible, and no later than the date on which notices are despatched to shareholders.

Advertising of meeting should also be carried out as soon as possible.

Copies of the notice convening the GM should not be circulated to creditors, however, it is useful for notice of the s98 meeting to note convening of GM as creditors will not from the date of that notice be able to retain the benefit of execution or attachment against the liquidator (see ss183(1) and (2)(a)).

Notice of s98 meeting should be sent to solicitors or debt collection agencies known to be acting for creditors.

VAT bad debt relief documentation should not be issued with the notice of s98 meeting (unless company already in liquidation).

Notice of GM should be sent to all High Court Enforcement Officers, etc. known by member to be interested in company.

▶ Information to be given prior to the meeting:

The advising member must provide information to creditors free of charge prior to the creditors' meeting.

Where the directors have arranged for the office holder to provide information under s98(2)(a), he may respond to oral requests for information (but should first take steps to verify that the caller is a creditor or creditor's representative).

Information which is 'reasonable' would include the Statement of Affairs and the list of creditors.

It is legitimate to refuse a request where it is unreasonable to expect information within the time available before the s98 meeting or the information requested is confidential on grounds that its release would be prejudicial to the company or its creditors.

Where the directors decide to make a list of names and addresses available under s98(2)(b) the following information should be given:

– Names of creditors to be in alphabetical order

– No need to provide details of amounts due to each creditor

– List should be available between 10.00 and 16.00 on the two days prior to the meeting, and there should be sufficient copies available for inspection

– Place where list available should be reasonably convenient for creditors.

▶ Proxy forms:

Proxies should be sent out with the notice of the s98 meeting. These should incorporate the name of the company and the date of the meeting.

Proxies will be invalid if:

– They are lodged after the time stated in the notice of the meeting.
– They are incorrectly completed in a material way.
– They are not signed by the principal or a person authorised by him.

Proxies should not be rejected because of a minor error in their completion providing:

– Form of proxy sent with notice or substantially similar form has been used, and

– The following matters are clear:

    – Identity of creditor and proxy holder
    – Nature of proxy holders authority
    – Instructions given to proxy holder.

If the advising member who intends to be appointed liquidator has an interest he should, in appropriate circumstances, advise the chair of meeting to seek independent advice on validity of proxies.

▶ Proofs of debt:

Proofs may be submitted at any time and at the meeting itself.

Admission/rejection is responsibility of the Chair who should check they can identify creditor and amount claimed.

Proofs should be admitted for lower of:

– Amount stated in the proof and
– Amount considered by the company to be due to the creditor.

The advising member can advise the Chair (but again should watch for conflicts).

All proofs and proxies should be made available for inspection by any person entitled to attend and vote.

▶ Attendance at the meeting:

Attendance at the creditors meeting is required of:

– Director to act as Chair.

– Liquidator appointed at GM (both if joint appointment) who must report to the meeting on any exercise of powers.

– Company personnel required to attend by notice (21 days) under r4.58(2) by the convenor of the meeting. Member should advise as to whether any such personnel who should be given notice under this rule are able to provide information relevant to the meeting.

– Others who may attend include:

– Creditors

– Representatives of creditors (persons holding themselves out as such should be allowed admittance and permitted to ask questions, in the absence of contrary evidence)

– Chair has discretion to admit others, eg shareholders and press – but should take into account the views of the creditors present.

▶ Hold s98 meeting of creditors:

The following information should be provided at the meeting:

– Summary or copy of Directors' sworn Statement of Affairs handed to all those attending the meeting and an explanation of the contents of that statement to be given verbally.

– Details of any prior involvement with the company or its directors of the advising member or proposed liquidator.

– Details of the GM:

▶ Venue of the meeting and date notice of GM despatched (explaining how notice period waived if called on short notice)

▶ Resolutions passed

▶ If Liquidator appointed at GM has not yet consented to act – that fact

▶ If GM adjourned without resolving to wind up:

– Date to which adjourned
– Fact that resolutions passed at s98 meeting will now only be conditional.

▶ In relation to s98 meeting:

– Date directors gave instructions for calling of meeting and date on which actually called

– Costs paid by the company in connection with organising the meeting

– Costs in respect of the preparation of the Statement of Affairs.

▶ Brief report on the company's relevant trading history. Apart from formalities, this should include the directors' reasons for the failure of the company, as well as:

– Extracts from any audited, or if none, draft accounts produced for periods covering the previous three years

– A deficiency account reconciling most recent balance sheet with deficiency shown in statement of affairs.

Note: Advising member can rely on information obtained from company personnel and company accounts and records and is not expected to conduct an investigation to ensure this information is accurate.

The Chair will be the director, however the advising member may conduct the meeting on his behalf. This should be explained to the meeting and that the report is the director's responsibility.

Creditors and their representatives should sign an attendance list which should be available for later inspection.

The Chair presents the company's Statement of Affairs to the meeting and creditors are invited to ask questions. Any creditor wishing to ask a question should first formally identify themselves. All questions should be answered unless they are considered prejudicial to the liquidation.

Nominations for the appointment of liquidator should be taken. The Chair should accept all nominations.

The procedure for the appointment of the liquidator should be explained to the meeting. Providing all parties accept the result, initial voting can be on a simple show of hands. Otherwise, a formal vote may be taken. Voting papers should be issued stating the name of all persons nominated for the office of liquidator.

The Chair will announce the result to the meeting, giving details of the total votes cast in favour of each nomination and the total of votes rejected in whole or in part and the names of creditors and in whose favour they voted and the reasons for the rejection.

If no nominee secures an absolute majority on the first ballot then further votes must be taken (the lowest scoring nominee dropping out) until one nomination secures a majority vote. The Chair may, at any time, put to the meeting a resolution that two nominations act as joint liquidators.

If creditors don't nominate their own choice of liquidator the members' nominee remains in office and acquires full power to act.

Directors/members/creditors may apply to court (s100(3)) about the creditors' choice within seven days of that person's appointment for an order either:

–   Directing that the person nominated as liquidator by the company shall be liquidator instead of, or jointly with, the person nominated by the creditors.

–   Appointing some other person to be liquidator instead of the person nominated by the creditors.

The liquidator must give a statement to the Chair that he is a qualified IP who is willing to act.

The liquidator must notify the creditors of his appointment within 28 days.

The creditors may then establish a liquidation committee of not more than five persons.

Creditors then agree the terms of the remuneration of the liquidator or resolve to defer consideration of the matter (if there is a liquidation committee then the committee will decide).

The Chair may allow any other resolution he thinks appropriate.

The meeting may be adjourned for up to three weeks. It may also be suspended for up to one hour.

The Chair must ensure that minutes of the meeting are kept.

The liquidator must notify the Registrar of Companies of his appointment within 14 days and must take steps to advertise his appointment.

The appointment must be advertised in the London Gazette and the liquidator may also advertise the appointment in such other manner as he thinks fit (r4.106).

1.3   Meeting held before resolution to wind up

In certain cases, for example if the members' meeting is adjourned but the creditor's has already be called in anticipation of the passing of a resolution to wind up the company, the Insolvency (Amendment) Rules 87 say that the resolutions of the creditors are valid, but will only come into effect on the passing of the resolution to liquidate the company by the members (r4.53A).

2 The Statement of Affairs

Section overview

The Statement of Affairs must be produced by the directors of the company on the prescribed form. It details the company's assets and liabilities and should be made up to a date not more than 14 days before the passing of the resolution to wind up. The directors must deliver a copy of the Statement of Affairs to the Registrar of Companies within seven days of the creditors' meeting.

2.1 Content of the Statement of Affairs

The Statement of Affairs must show:

▶ Particulars of the company's assets, debts and liabilities
▶ The names and addresses of the company's creditors
▶ The securities held by them respectively
▶ The dates when the securities were respectively given
▶ Such further or other information as may be prescribed.

Failure to comply with any of the above duties renders the director guilty of an offence and liable to a fine (s99(3)).

Where the directors' Statement of Affairs laid before the meeting fails to state the company's affairs at the date of the meeting, the procedure is (r4. 53B):

▶ The director chairing the meeting, or another person with knowledge of the relevant matters, should make an oral or written report to the meeting 'on any material transactions relating to the company occurring between the date of the making of the statement of affairs and that of the meeting' (r4.53B(I)).

▶ Any such report should be recorded in the minutes of the meeting (r4.53B(2)).

Where the directors make the statement under s99, reasonable and necessary expenses of preparation may be paid out of the company's assets either before or after the commencement of winding-up. Any such payment is an expense of the liquidation. If payment is made before commencement the director presiding at the creditors' meeting must inform the meeting of the payment and the recipient. The liquidator may make the payment himself but must give any liquidation committee seven days' notice of his intention to make it. The liquidator can only make a payment to himself or his associate with the approval of the creditors, liquidation committee or the court (r4.38).

Copies of the Statement of Affairs should be given to both the members' and creditors' nominee as liquidator forthwith on appointment and to all creditors and contributories within 28 days.

2.2 Preparation of Statement of Affairs

The Statement of Affairs must be produced on the prescribed form, Form 4.17 for compulsory liquidations, Form 4.18 for insolvent members' voluntary liquidation, and Form 4.19 for creditors' voluntary liquidations.

The format for a Statement of Affairs is shown below.

ESTIMATED STATEMENT OF AFFAIRS
FOR ABC LTD AS AT X.X.00

	Notes	Book Value £	Realisable Value £
Assets specifically pledged	1		
Assets		X	X
Less amounts due to charge holder			(X)
			X/(X)
Assets not specifically pledged	2		
Assets		X	X
Total assets available for preferential creditors			X
Preferential creditors	3		(X)
Surplus/deficiency as regards preferential creditors			X
Prescribed part	4		(X)
Assets available for floating charge holder			X
Floating charge holder	5		(X)
Surplus/deficiency			X/(X)
Prescribed part carried down			X
Unsecured creditors	6		(X)
Total surplus/ deficiency as regards creditors			X/(X)
Issued and called up share capital			(X)
Estimated deficiency as regards members			X

2.3 Notes to the Statement of Affairs

1 **Assets specifically pledged**

    This is where the company has given some form of security to a creditor for the advance of funds or purchase of an asset. This will include:

    ▶ Assets pledged as fixed charge assets ie freehold property, goodwill
    ▶ Assets subject to HP agreements
    ▶ Debts subject to a factoring agreement

    The sums owed to the charge holder should appear under this heading and the net deficiency or surplus carried down.

Definition

Fixed charge: a charge over assets of the company which are ascertained and definite, or capable of being ascertained and defined.

2 **Assets not specifically pledged**

    These are all other assets of the company not dealt with above. This will include:

    ▶ Book debts
    ▶ Motor vehicles
    ▶ Stock
    ▶ Plant and machinery
    ▶ Office equipment.

    It may be necessary to adjust asset realisable values to take into account bad debt provisions, obsolete assets etc.

3   **Preferential creditors**

These creditors are paid in priority to other creditors. They include:

▸   All holiday pay owed to employees.

▸   Any wages due at the date of insolvency (accruing in four months prior to insolvency) to a maximum claim per employee of £800.

4   **Prescribed part**

Where the floating charge is created on or after 15 September 2003 a prescribed part of the net property must be paid to ordinary unsecured creditors (s176A). The net property is calculated by taking floating charge realisations and deducting costs and preferential creditors. The prescribed part is calculated as follows:

▸   50% of the first £10,000 of the net property, plus
▸   20% of the balance

up to a maximum prescribed part of £600,000.

Any administrative costs incurred in making the prescribed part payment are deducted from the prescribed part itself (r12.2(2)).

There are three situations where the prescribed part rules will not apply:

(a)   Where the net property is under £10,000 in value and the liquidator believes that the costs of making the distribution outweigh the benefits.

(b)   Where the net property is £10,000 or more and the liquidator applies to court for an order that the prescribed part rules should not apply. The grounds of the application is that the costs of making the distribution would outweigh the benefits. This would be useful where, for instance, there are a large number of unsecured creditors each owed a relatively small amount.

(c)   Where the liquidator proposes a CVA or s895 CA 06 Scheme of Arrangement, the terms of the CVA or Scheme can dissapply the prescribed part rules. Obviously, the unsecured creditors will only vote in favour of such a proposal if they believe it to be in their best interests to do so.

5   **Floating charge holders**

A bank may hold a floating charge over the assets of the company. The floating charge ranks after the claims of the preferential creditors but before the ordinary unsecured creditors.

Definition

Floating charge: this is a charge over a class of assets both present and future, which change from time to time in the ordinary course of business. The company is free to carry on the business in the usual way in relation to those assets (until crystallisation occurs).

6   **Unsecured creditors**

These are the normal creditors' claims. It will also include employee claims for redundancy and notice pay and any shortfall owed to charge holders. Any claims above preferential limits will also rank as unsecured.

Definitions

Book value: The value of the assets shown in the accounts at the date of insolvency.

Estimated realisable value: What the assets are likely to realise when sold.

Exam hints

Always show your workings. Easy marks are always available for showing full workings and assumptions.

Try to keep to a layout similar to that shown and leave plenty of space. This makes it easier to read and mark. Marks are always available for presentation.

The net property is that which would have been available for floating change holders.

2.4 Fixed charge over book debts

There are clear advantages to a lender if a valid fixed charge over book debts can be created.

(1)   Book debts may be one of the only assets which are readily realisable by a receiver – a welcome source of liquidity which can be used to make an early distribution to the lender.

(2)   Fixed charge assets are not subject to:

–   the claims of preferential creditors, or

–   the prescribed part rules which apply to floating charges created on or after 15 September 2003.

The 1979 case of *Siebe Gorman v Barclays Bank* – a case concerning Barclays Bank's standard form of debenture – held that is was possible to create a valid fixed charge over debtors.

The hall mark of a floating charge is that the company remains free to deal with the class of assets which are subject to the charge (see *Re Yorkshire Woolcombers*). To establish a charge over debtors as fixed therefore it was and is necessary for the chargee to demonstrate that they have created a sufficient degree of control over the debts. In order to do so bank security documentation usually provided:

▶   That the company could not assign or factor the debts without the consent of the chargee,

▶   And that the proceeds of the debt when received were to be paid into a particular bank account, and could not be withdrawn without the chargee's consent. In practice, of course, the bank allowed the company to make withdrawals from the account so that it could meets its liabilities and continue to trade in the usual way although the bank reserved the right to block the account by the giving of notice. This is the 'blocked account' referred to by Lord Millett in his judgement in the *Brumark* case.

Lenders who were not clearing banks could still require the borrower to seek consent before factoring or assigning the debt but were clearly not in a position to provide ordinary banking facilities to borrowers and therefore could not use the 'blocked account' device in their debentures. In *Re New Bullas Trading* concerning 3i's debenture the court held that it was possible to create a fixed charge over the debt itself and a floating charge over the debtor proceeds.

Since *Siebe Gorman* the fixed charge over book debts became an established and accepted feature of banking security documentation.

The *Brumark* case (Agnew v Commissioner of Inland Revenue)

This was a Privy Council hearing of a New Zealand appeal case. The decision was handed down on 5 June 2001. The Privy Council is the highest court of appeal for some commonwealth jurisdictions and is analogous to the House of Lords. Its decisions are not technically binding on UK courts but are clearly persuasive. Most writers on the subject believed from the outset that Lord Millett closely argued judgement in the case would be followed by UK courts.

The judgement makes it clear that a ban on assigning and factoring is insufficient to render a charge on debts a fixed charge. Moreover 'blocked account' provisions in a debenture won't make a charge fixed either unless the account was *actually* operated as a blocked account, (ie. the company could not make payments out of the account without specific bank authorisation for each payment).

The type of provision approved in *Re New Bullas Trading* and which was almost identical to the term of the debenture which was the subject of the *Brumark* litigation, could not create a fixed charge either. This is because it makes no commercial sense to distinguish between the debt itself and its proceeds. A fixed charge on debts and a floating charge on proceeds are in reality a single floating charge.

The principle which underlies the *Brumark* decision is that whether a charge is fixed or floating is a matter of law – not a matter of looking at the label the parties attach to the charge in the debenture. Book debts are part of the circulating capital of the business and are a class of assets constantly changing as new debts are created and old ones received. To that extent debtors are the natural subject of a floating charge.

Aftermath of the *Brumark* decision

It is fair to say that banks initially reacted defensively to the decision – reluctant to concede that their fixed charges over debtors were in reality floating, and equally reluctant to pursue cases through the higher appellate courts and thereby run the risk that a precedent would be set indicating the *Brumark* does indeed represent the state of UK law on this issue. In a number of cases, debtor realisations were banked and remained undistributed pending an authoritative UK decision on the issue.

This impasse was broken by the Spectrum case law. *Re Spectrum Plus Ltd* (2004) (judgement in the High Court handed down on 15 January 2004). The case confirmed the *Brumark* decision in essential respects i.e. that charges over book debts where the company remains free to make withdrawals from a 'blocked account' of debtor proceeds are properly categorised as floating even if the debenture labels them as fixed.

The chargees appeal:

Re Spectrum Plus Ltd (2004) (judgement in the Court of Appeal handed down on 26 May 2004).

▶   The Court of Appeal declined to follow the decision of the Privy Council in *Brumark* and instead followed its own previous judgement in *Re New Bullas Trading*.

▶   In terms of judicial precedent the Court of Appeal stated that it is bound by its own previous decisions whereas decision of the Privy Council were only of persuasive authority.

▶   However the court expressed the view that the House of Lords would probably overrule *Re New Bullas Trading* in the event that Spectrum was appealed to that higher court.

The long awaited decision of the House of Lords of *Spectrum plus* was published on 30 June 2005 and essentially overruled the Court of Appeals previous decisions in *Re New Bullas Trading* so that existing charges over book debts in standard form will be interpreted as creating a floating charge over debts.

The decision does not prevent:

▶   the factoring of debts

▶   nor the creation of a fixed charge over a specific debt by assignment.

As *Siebe Gorman* and *Re New Bullas* Trading have proven to be wrongly decided there is a clear concern that cases stretching back over the last 25 years will have to be re-visited and debtor realisations clawed back from fixed chargees. However:

▶   HM Revenue and Customs and the Redundancy Payment Service have issued a press release stating that they will not challenge pre- 5 June 2001 distributions on the basis that they were made on a mistaken view of the law.

▶   *Re BHT (UK) Ltd (2004)*. In this case a liquidator applied to the court seeking an order for the repayment of debtor proceeds by a debenture holder (under a, now probably invalid, fixed charge over book debts) on the basis that the debenture holder had been unjustly enriched. The court rejected the application on the basis that the company had not suffered any loss. The only loss suffered was by the preferential creditors who were not parties to the action (presumably because of the views set out in the above press release).

If you are uncertain in the exam whether to treat book debts as a fixed or floating charge asset, you should clearly state what assumptions you have made in determining the treatment of book debts in your answer. If the exam question states that the bank has a valid fixed charge over book debts, you may assume that this is so and treat the book debts as a fixed charge asset. Otherwise, treat it as a floating charge asset and state clearly why you are doing this (ie following decision in *Spectrum Plus Ltd (2004)*).

Interactive question 1: Watson Biofuels Ltd

The directors of Watson Biofuels Ltd have requested the assistance of your principal in connection with a creditors' voluntary liquidation of the company. The meetings of members and creditors have been convened for 2 March 2010.

Following a meeting with the company's finance director you have obtained the following information:

▶ The company trades from freehold premises in Nottingham. The premises were acquired in 2003 for £220,000. Since the acquisition the company has extended the premises, at a cost of £56,000 and the property has recently been valued at £395,000. The property is subject to a mortgage with Satby Bank plc, who hold a fixed charge over the property, in the sum of £180,000.

▶ The company has total trade debtors of £115,000. The director advises you that one customer has recently entered liquidation owing the company £34,000. A dividend is not expected to be received in respect of this debt. A provision of 15% of the remaining book debts is considered prudent.

▶ The company's records show:

	£
Stock	80,000
Plant and machinery	24,000
Vehicles	76,000
Fixtures, fittings, office equipment	12,000

The director believes that, in liquidation, the stock could be sold to a competitor for 70p in the pound. The remaining assets would be sold at public auction. Auctioneers advise that such a sale would be likely to achieve 60% of the book values of the assets.

▶ Trade creditors are recorded in the books at £753,000.

▶ The company has ordinary, fully paid up share capital of £35,000.

▶ HM Revenue and Customs are owed the sum of £48,000 in respect of VAT accruing over the last 11 month period of trading and £21,500 in respect of PAYE/ NIC over the same period.

▶ Employee details are as follows:

– The company employs 23 members of staff, all of whom earn in excess of £200 per week.

– Four weeks' wage arrears are owed totalling £54,000.

– Holiday pay owing has been calculated totalling £39,800.

– Entitlement to redundancy pay has been calculated in the sum of £64,000 and pay in lieu of notice of £39,600.

▶ The company has a trading overdraft of £42,000 with Barwest Bank plc. The overdraft is secured by way of a floating charge over the company's assets which was created on 10 October 2005.

Requirement

Draft the Statement of Affairs as at 2 March 2010 to be presented at the meetings of members and creditors. Show all workings and assumptions.

See **Answer** at the end of this chapter.

3   The Deficiency account

Section overview

The Deficiency account reconciles the last set of accounts with the position shown in the Statement of Affairs. It explains why a once profitable company now appears insolvent or why an insolvent company has now become more insolvent.

3.1   Format for a Deficiency account

A pro forma for a Deficiency account is shown below:

ABC LTD IN LIQUIDATION
DEFICIENCY ACCOUNT FOR THE PERIOD
X.X.00 TO X.X.01

	Notes	
Balance on profit and loss account	1	X
Less assets written down in Statement of Affairs	2	(X)
Less items arising on insolvency	3	(X)
Balancing figure attributable to loss in the period	4	(X)
Deficit to creditors per Statement of Affairs	5	(x)
Share capital write off	5	(X)
Deficit to members per Statement of Affairs	5	(X)

3.2   Notes to the Deficiency account

1   **Balance on profit and loss account**

▶   This figure is taken from the last audited balance sheet (if available) or management accounts.

▶   If a credit (positive) balance, begin with a positive figure.

▶   If a debit (negative) balance, begin with a negative figure.

▶   If this figure is not available, use net assets instead.

2   **Assets written down in Statement of Affairs**

▶   This section details the difference between the book values and estimated to realise values of all assets shown in the Statement of Affairs.

▶   If assets have increased in value, add this figure instead.

3   **Items arising on insolvency**

▶   These represent known items which have arisen as a result of the insolvency only and have added to the liabilities of the company.

▶   These will include:

   –   Pay in lieu of notice
   –   Redundancy
   –   Damages for breach of contract
   –   Termination payments on a lease

4   **Balancing figure attributable to the loss in the period**

This will be the balancing figure on the statement.

5   These figures are taken straight from the Statement of Affairs.

Interactive question 2: Deficiency account

You have been asked to prepare a Deficiency account for a s98 meeting of creditors to be held on 1 September 2010. The last statutory accounts relate to the year ended 31 January 2010 and these show accumulated profits at this date of £8,500.

The company's books and records are up to date but do not show the following claims which will arise on the liquidation of the company:

▶ Breach of contract	£52,000
▶ Redundancy pay, pay in lieu of notice	£36,700

Extracts from the Statement of Affairs are as follows:

	Book Value £	Estimated to Realise £
Freehold property	185,000	240,000
Book debts	98,000	40,000
Plant and machinery	72,000	21,000
Fixtures and fittings	24,000	8,500
Stocks	63,000	29,000
Motor vehicles	80,000	32,000

The estimated total deficiency to creditors as at 1 September 2010 is £280,200 and the estimated total deficiency to members is £330,200.

Requirement

Prepare a Deficiency account for the period 1 February 2010 to 1 September 2010. Show all workings and assumptions.

See **Answer** at the end of this chapter.

4   The liquidation committee

Section overview

The creditors at the s98 meeting, or any subsequent meeting if they think fit, may appoint a committee of not more than five persons to exercise the functions conferred upon it by the Act (s101(1)). The minimum number of members is three (r4.152(2)).

4.1   Eligibility for membership

Any creditor of the company (other than one whose debt is fully secured) is eligible to be a member providing:

▶   He has lodged a proof and

▶   His proof has neither been wholly disallowed for voting purposes, nor wholly rejected for purposes of distribution or dividend.

Companies are eligible but must act through a representative. The representative must hold a letter of authority signed on behalf of the company. A proxy form held by the representative qualifies as such a letter of authority, unless of course, it says to the contrary. The chair of meetings of the committee can ask to see the letter of authority and can exclude the representative if it appears that the authority is deficient. Body corporates or bankrupts may not act as representatives. No person may act for more than one member of the committee nor may they act as both representative and member in their own right (r4.159(4) and (5)).

4.2 Procedure for establishment

Potential members must agree to act. (In the case of a company the representative gives consent – unless the letter of authorisation, or proxy form, contains a statement to the contrary) (r4.153(3).)

The minimum number of persons (three) must have agreed to act (r4.153(4)).

The liquidator issues a Certificate of Due Constitution in Form 4.47. The committee does not come into being and cannot act until this time. If the Chair of the meeting was not the liquidator then the Chair would have to give notice to the liquidator of the establishment and membership of the committee as soon as reasonably practicable.

Amended certificates must be issued if others agree to act later.

Certificates and any amended certificates must be filed with the registrar of companies.

By s101(2) if a committee is established the company may, either at the meeting at which it was resolved to wind-up or subsequently in general meeting, appoint such number of persons as they think fit to act as members of the committee, not exceeding five. By s101(3) however creditors may veto any or all of the appointments. The members could in this case apply to the court which could appoint other members to act on the committee in place of those vetoed by the creditors.

4.3 Functions of the committee

The committee has a number of functions.

▶ Sanctioning the exercise of certain powers of the liquidator:

These are powers which can't be exercised by the liquidator unless he obtains sanction of committee, court or creditors.

They are:

– Pay any class of creditors in full (but the order of priority can't be altered)
– Make compromises or arrangements with creditors
– Compromise claims against contributories or debtors of the company
– Power to bring legal proceedings under ss213, 214, 238, 239, 242, 243 or 423 IA

In a voluntary liquidation all other powers can be exercised without sanction.

The liquidator must get consent before exercising the power. Purported ratification post-exercise of the power by the committee will be ineffective. Court **can** ratify the exercise of such a power without consent where assumption of the power was in the best interests of the creditors.

▶ To supervise the conduct of the liquidation:

The liquidator has a duty to report to the committee all such matters as appear to him to be of concern to them. To this end the committee can insist the liquidator report to it, on all matters which concern it (r4.155).

The liquidator need not comply with any request for information where it appears to him that:

– The request is frivolous or unreasonable

– The cost of complying would be excessive, having regard to the relative importance of the information

– There are not sufficient assets to enable him to comply.

If the committee came into existence more than 28 days after the appointment of the liquidator, the liquidator must report to them in summary form what actions he has taken since his appointment, and shall answer all questions put to him on the conduct of the winding-up to date.

Members joining the committee after its establishment are only entitled to reports in summary form of matters previously arising.

These rules do not limit the committee's (or members') general power to have access to the liquidation records, or to seek explanations.

By r4.168 the liquidator shall, as and when directed by the committee, send a written report to every member of the committee setting out the position generally as regards the progress of the winding-up and matters arising in connection with it, to which he considers the committee's attention should be drawn.

In the absence of directions by the committee – not less often than once in every six months but not more than once every two months.

4.4 Meetings

These are held when and where determined by the liquidator (r4.156(1).

First meeting must be held within three months of the liquidator's appointment, or three months of the establishment of the committee, whichever is the later (r4.156(2).

Subsequent meetings must be called on a member's request within 21 days of the request, or for a specified date where the committee has previously resolved that a meeting be held on that date (r4.156(2).

Seven days' notice of the venue must be given. Members may waive notice at the meeting, or before it.

The Chair of the meeting will be the liquidator or a person nominated by him to act. Such a person must be a qualified IP, or an employee of the liquidator or his firm who is experienced in insolvency matters (r4.157).

A meeting of the committee is duly constituted if due notice of it has been given to all the members, and at least two creditor members are present or represented (r4.158).

Each member has one vote and resolutions are passed when a majority of members present or represented have voted in favour (r4.166).

Every resolution passed shall be recorded in writing either separately or as part of the minutes of the meeting. The record is signed by the Chair and kept with the records of the liquidation.

The rules contain provision for postal resolutions of the committee (r4.167). The liquidator sends a copy of the proposed resolution to every member (or designated representative). This copy is set out in such a way that the recipient can indicate agreement or dissent from each resolution on which a decision is sought.

A member may, within seven business days from the date of the liquidator sending out a resolution, require him to summon a meeting of the committee to consider the matters raised by the resolution.

In the absence of such a request, the resolution is deemed to have been passed by the committee if and when the liquidator is notified in writing by a majority of the members that they concur with it.

Copies of such resolutions and a note that the committee's concurrence was obtained are kept with the records of the liquidation.

4.5 Member's expenses

The liquidator shall defray out of the assets, in the prescribed order of priority, any reasonable travelling expenses directly incurred by members of the liquidation committee or their representatives in respect of their attendance at the committees meetings or otherwise on the committee's business (r4.169).

Where the meeting of the liquidation committee is held immediately after the s98 meeting and the travelling expenses of the creditor (to and from that meeting) have been reimbursed from the company's assets as an expense of attending the liquidation committee meeting, it has been held that this is not appropriate. These expenses should not come out of the company's assets as they were not incurred directly in respect of the attendance of a liquidation committee meeting.

4.6 Vacating office

A member of the committee may resign by notice in writing delivered to the liquidator (r4.160).

A creditor's membership will automatically terminate if:

▸ A member becomes bankrupt (in which case he is replaced by his trustee).

▸ Compounds or arranges with his creditors.

▸ He fails to attend or be represented at three consecutive meetings of the committee (which can resolve at that third meeting that this rule is not to apply).

▸ (In the case of a creditor) he ceases to be or is found never to have been a creditor (r4.161(3)).

A member can be removed by resolution of a meeting of creditors of which at least 14 days' notice has been given. If the member is a contributory removal is by resolution of a meeting of contributories and again 14 days' notice is required.

If the total number of remaining members has not fallen below three then the liquidator and the remaining creditor members may agree that the creditor vacancy need not be filled.

Otherwise appointment is by the liquidator with the concurrence of both the new creditor member and a majority of the other creditor members.

Alternatively, appointment is by a resolution of a meeting of creditors called on 14 days' notice. If the liquidator is not present at this meeting the Chair will report to him that the appointment has been made.

If there is a vacancy for a contributory member, the liquidator and remaining contributory members may simply agree not to fill the vacancy providing the total number of members does not fall below three.

Otherwise appointment is by the liquidator with concurrence of a majority of the contributory members and of the new member or alternatively by a meeting of contributories called on the giving of 14 days' notice.

4.7 Committee members' dealings

R4.170 applies to:

▸ Any member of the committee
▸ Any member's representative
▸ Any associate of the above (an 'associate' being defined by s435)
▸ Any person who has been a member of the committee at any time in the last 12 months.

The rule states that such persons may not enter into any transaction whereby he:

▸ Receives out of the company's assets any payment for services given or goods supplied in connection with the administration

▸ Acquires any asset forming part of the estate

▸ Obtains any profits from the administration.

There are three exceptions to this rule:

▸ Prior leave of court.

▸ Subsequent leave of court applied for without under delay where:

– Transaction entered into as a matter of urgency
– Transaction entered into pursuant to a pre-commencement contractual obligation.

▸ With the prior sanction of the liquidation committee which must be satisfied after full disclosure of the circumstances that the person will be giving full value. No committee member interested in the transaction may vote to sanction it.

The court has the power (on application of any interested party) to set aside any transactions in contravention of the rule and make consequential orders including that the person contravening the rule accounts for any profit obtained and compensates the estate for any resultant loss.

The court will not make such orders in respect of an associate or representative who entered into a transaction with no reason to suppose that in doing so he would be in breach of the rule.

5 SIP 15 – Reporting and providing information on their functions to committees in insolvencies

Section overview

SIP 15 sets out required practice and guidance to office holders when reporting to creditor committees. It covers compulsory liquidations, CVL's, bankruptcies, administrations, administrative receiverships and voluntary arrangements. A good knowledge of the SIP is required for the JIEB exam.

The SIP gives a brief review of the rules on reporting to committees. These are contained:

▶ Liquidation – r4.155, r4.168.
▶ Bankruptcy – r6.152, r6.153.
▶ Administration – r2.52, r2.53.
▶ Administrative receivership – r3.32, r3.33.

The SIP then provides guidance notes which should be issued to members of the creditors' committee for each of the formal insolvency procedures. The information may be given in some other suitable format.

All guidance notes have sections dealing with:

▶ Introduction – brief explanation of the insolvency procedure and the purpose of the liquidation committee.

▶ The functions of the committee:
  – Control of office holder's powers
  – Acts requiring notice to the committee
  – Office holder's remuneration
  – Expenses and disbursements
  – Taxation of costs
  – Review of office holder's security.

▶ Office holder's obligations to the committee.

▶ Office holder's accounts.

▶ Establishment of the committee.

▶ Membership of the committee.

▶ Proceedings of the committee – quorum, chairman, meetings, venue, voting rights, records of meetings etc.

▶ Confidentiality of documents.

▶ Charges for copy documents.

▶ Expenses of committee members.

▶ Dealings by committee members and others.

▶ The security of the office holder.

Interactive question 3: Sussex Garden Supplies Limited

Sussex Garden Supplies Limited (SGS) was placed into creditors' voluntary liquidation on 10 February 2010. A creditors' committee was formed at the s98 meeting and the following creditors were appointed to the committee:

▶ Sarah Gray
▶ Medway Plants Limited represented by Bill Pearson
▶ AD Limited represented by Tom Day
▶ Paul O'Grady
▶ Bob Farthing.

You ascertain the following information about the committee members:

1 Sarah Gray is a creditor of the company and is owed £800. Before SGS entered into liquidation Sarah was in discussions with the directors to purchase some plant and machinery. She now wishes to purchase the plant and machinery from the liquidator.

2 Medway Plants Limited submitted a retention of title claim which has now been settled thus eliminating all of its claim in the liquidation.

3 Bob Farthing has requested, as a committee member, to inspect the liquidator's records and in particular he is interested in reviewing the papers regarding investigations carried out into the directors' activities.

4 Tom Day has not attended the last three committee meetings.

5 Paul O'Grady has submitted the following expenses claim:

	£
Travelling expenses (including £16 for attending the s98 meeting)	94
Compensation for loss of earnings	193

Requirement

Draft a note to the liquidator explaining how the above matters should be dealt with.

See **Answer** at the end of this chapter.

Summary and self-test

Summary

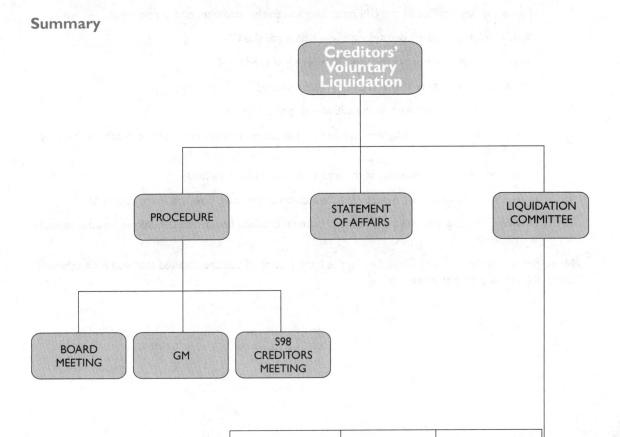

Self-test

Answer the following questions.

1   What are the main characteristics of a creditors' voluntary liquidation?

2   How many days' notice of the GM must be given to the members of the company?

3   What resolutions will be put before the members at the GM?

4   What will invalidate a proxy for the s98 meeting of creditors?

5   Whose responsibility is it to accept or reject a proxy?

6   What matters are dealt with at the s98 meeting of creditors?

7   If a liquidator is appointed by the members, what are his powers prior to the creditors' meeting being held?

8   When should the first meeting of the liquidation committee be held?

9   In respect of resolutions passed by the liquidation committee, how are votes counted?

10   In what circumstances will a creditor's membership of the liquidation committee be automatically terminated?

Now, go back to the Learning Objectives in the Introduction. If you are satisfied that you have achieved these objectives, please tick them off.

Answers to self-test

1   No declaration of solvency, directors swear a Statement of Affairs.
     Insolvent liquidation.
     Creditors have control of the liquidation.

2   14 days' notice if private company, 21 days' notice if public company AGM.

3   Special resolution to wind up the company as a creditors' voluntary liquidation.
     Ordinary resolution to appoint a liquidator.
     Ordinary resolution to agree terms of liquidator's remuneration.

4   Proxy will be invalid if it is:

     ▶   Lodged after the time stated in the notice of the meeting.
     ▶   Incorrectly completed in a material way.
     ▶   Not signed by the principal or a person authorised by them.

5   It is the responsibility of the Chair of the s98 meeting (a director of the company).

6   Present the Statement of Affairs and an explanation thereof to the creditors.
     Invite creditors to ask questions.
     Provide details of the GM.
     Appoint a liquidator.
     Appoint a liquidation committee.
     If no committee, agree liquidator's remuneration.
     Pass any other resolution chair deems appropriate.
     May adjourn meeting for up to three weeks.

7   S166 – the members' choice of liquidator cannot exercise the powers conferred under the Act
     except to:

     ▶   Take control and custody of the company's property
     ▶   Dispose of goods of a wasting nature
     ▶   Do all things necessary to protect the company's assets.

8   Within three months of the liquidator's appointment or three months of the establishment of the
     committee, whichever is the later (r4.156(2)).

9   Each member has one vote and resolutions are passed when a majority of members present or
     represented have voted in favour (r4.166).

10   If the member becomes bankrupt (he will be replaced by his trustee).
     If he compounds or arranges with his creditors.
     If he fails to attend or be represented at three consecutive meetings of the committee.
     If he ceases to be, or is found never to have been a creditor (r4.161).

Answers to interactive questions

Interactive question 1: Watson Biofuels Ltd

WATSON BIOFUELS LTD
ESTIMATED STATEMENT OF AFFAIRS
AS AT 2 MARCH 2010

	Notes	Book Value £	Estimated to realise £
Assets subject to fixed charge			
Freehold property		276,000	395,000
Less Satby Bank plc			(180,000)
			215,000
Assets subject to floating charge			
Trade debtors	1	115,000	68,850
Stock	2	80,000	56,000
Plant and machinery	3	24,000	
Vehicles	3	76,000	
Fixtures, fittings, office equipment	3	12,000	67,200
			192,050
Less: Preferential creditors			
Holiday pay	4		(39,800)
Wage arrears	4		(18,400)
			58,200
Net property			133,850
Less: Prescribed part	5		(29,770)
Assets available for floating charge holder			104,080
Less: Barwest Bank plc			(42,000)
			62,080
Prescribed part			29,770
Fixed charge surplus			215,000
Assets available for unsecured creditors			306,850
Less: Unsecured creditors			
Trade creditors		753,000	
HM Revenue and Customs	6	69,500	
Wage arrears	4	35,600	
Redundancy	4	64,000	
Pay in lieu	4	39,600	
			(961,700)
Deficit as regards creditors			(654,850)
Share capital			(35,000)
Deficit as regards members			(689,850)

Note: This statement does not include the costs of liquidation.

WORKINGS

(1)   *Trade debtors*

	£
Outstanding	115,000
Less known bad debt	(34,000)
	81,000
General provision @15%	(12,150)
	68,850

(Since the *Brumark* case, book debts are no longer classed as a fixed charge asset. However, in the exam, if the examiner tells you there is a 'valid fixed charge over book debts', you can accept that at face value and treat it as a fixed charge asset. If in doubt, state clearly any assumptions made and why you are treating book debts in the manner which you have chosen.)

(2)   *Stock*

Value £80,000 @ 70p in pound = £56,000.

(3)   *Other assets*

	£
Plant and machinery	24,000
Vehicles	76,000
Fixtures, fittings, office equipment	12,000
	112,000 @ 60% = £67,200.

(4)   *Employee claims*

Wage arrears – up to four months' arrears may be claimed preferentially, up to a maximum preferential claim per employee of £800.

	£	
23 employees @ £800	18,400	preferential claim
	35,600	unsecured claim
	54,000	

Holiday pay – all preferential without limit.

Redundancy, pay in lieu of notice – unsecured claim.

(5)   *Prescribed part*

As the floating charge was created after 15 September 2003 the prescribed part rules will apply.

Net property (floating charge realisations less preferential creditors) is £133,850.

	£
10,000 x 50%	5,000
123,850 x 20%	24,770
133,850	29,770

(6)   *HM Revenue and Customs:*

Crown debts no longer have preferential status.

Interactive question 2: Deficiency account

Deficiency account for the period 1 February 2010 to 1 September 2010

	£	£
Balance per profit and loss account		8,500
Less: Amounts written off assets per Statement of Affairs		
Freehold property (negative figure because property has increased in value)	(55,000)	
Book debts	58,000	
Plant and machinery	51,000	
Fixtures and fittings	15,500	
Stocks	34,000	
Motor vehicles	48,000	
		(151,500)
Less: Amounts arising on liquidation		
Breach of contract	52,000	
Redundancy, pay in lieu of notice	36,700	
		(88,700)
Estimated trading loss 01/02/10 to 01/09/10 (balancing figure)		(48,500)
Share capital		(50,000)
Total deficiency to members		(330,200)

	£	£
Balance per P & L		8,500
Add asset gains in SofA - Freehold Property		55,000
Less assets written down in Sof A		
Book Debts	58,000	
Plant & Mach	51,000	
Fix + F/H	15,500	
Stocks	34,000	
Motor Vehicles	48,000	
		(206,500)
Less Amounts arising on insolvency		
Breach of Contract	52,000	
Redundancy, pay in lieu of notice	36,700	
		(88,700)
Estimated Losses in the Period		(48,500)
		(280,200)
Deficit to Creditors per SofA.		
Share Capital		(50,000)
Total deficiency to Members		(330,200)

Interactive question 3: Sussex Garden Supplies Limited

1   Sarah Gray:

By r4.170(2)(c) Sarah, as a member of the committee, is prevented from acquiring any assets of the company.

However, she can apply to court for leave to continue with the transaction (r4.170(3)), or she can obtain sanction of the creditors' committee. She will have to disclose all circumstances of the transaction and show that she is paying full value for the plant and machinery. Sarah will not be allowed to take part in the committee's decision on this matter.

2   Medway Plants Limited:

Only creditors are eligible to act on the creditors' committee therefore Medway Plants Limited ceases to be a member of the committee automatically upon ceasing to be a creditor (r4.161(3)).

Providing at least three members remain on the committee, the vacancy does not need to be filled.

The liquidator should consult the remaining creditors on the committee to ascertain whether the majority want to have the vacancy filled (r4.163(2) & (3)).

If the committee want the vacancy to be filled the liquidator must either seek a written resolution or convene a committee meeting to approve a new creditor member being co-opted.

A meeting of creditors can be convened, on 14 days' notice, to consider filling the vacancy.

3   Bob Farthing:

A committee member has the right to inspect the liquidator's financial records (Reg 10(4) Insolvency Regulations 1994).

If the liquidator considers documents forming part of the records to be confidential he may decline to allow it to be inspected by a committee member (r12.13(2)). A committee may apply, as an aggrieved person, to the court for an order overruling the liquidator (s168(5) IA).

A report on the conduct of directors is not available for inspection by the committee *Re W & A Glaser (1994) BCC 199*.

There is no obligation on the liquidator to make other records available to the committee.

Here, Bob Farley should be allowed access to the financial records, however, information regarding investigations into director's conduct should be considered confidential and wouldn't be available for inspection.

4   Tom Day:

Any member of the liquidation committee who has not attended for three consecutive meetings will be automatically dismissed (r4.161). Tom Day will no longer be a member of the committee and he should be advised as such.

It is possible for the committee to override the automatic termination, however this must be done at the third meeting and it does not appear to have happened here.

Providing that more than three members remain on the committee the vacancy need not be filled.

5   Paul O'Grady:

Reasonable travelling expenses for attending committee meetings may be claimed, however expenses for attending the s98 meeting should not be paid.

Claim for loss of earnings is not an allowable expense and should be rejected.

6

Compulsory liquidation

> > > > > > > > > > > > > > >

Contents

Introduction

Learning objectives

▶ Identify the main features of a compulsory liquidation

▶ Identify the grounds for compulsory liquidation

▶ Understand the procedure to follow to place a company into compulsory liquidation

▶ The provisional liquidator – who may be appointed, functions and powers

▶ The special manager – who may be appointed, functions and powers

Working context

In a work environment you may be asked to advise a client on how they may seek to recover a debt, this may include the presentation of a petition to wind up the company. It is therefore important to understand the procedures to be followed. Or you may be asked to assist your principal when acting as a liquidator in a compulsory liquidation.

Stop and think

What is a compulsory liquidation? How does it differ from voluntary liquidation? Why should a creditor be able to force a company to be wound up? Who is the Official Receiver? What is his role? When is it appropriate to appoint a provisional liquidator? Why is a special manager required? What does he do?

Examination context

Compulsory liquidations are regularly tested in the JIEB examinations. The grounds for compulsory liquidation have not been examined in any detail in past JIEB papers however the way in which it can be proved that a company is insolvent and the procedure to follow to place a company into compulsory liquidation and the effects of a petition being presented or a winding-up order being made have been tested on numerous occasions and should therefore be learnt in detail. The appointment of a special manager or a provisional liquidator have also been tested on a number of occasions. The creditors' committee in a compulsory liquidation appear regularly as a test question.

Exam requirements

Past exam questions to look at include:

2008	Question 2(c)
2007	Question 1(d)
2006	Question 1(c)
2002	Question 2(c)
1999	Question 4
1998	Question 1
1998	Question 5(b)
1997	Question 1
1996	Question 4
1994	Question 5
1993	Question 3
1992	Question 4

1 Grounds for compulsory liquidation

Section overview

▶ A compulsory liquidation is a court process. It commences with the presentation of a petition to wind up the company compulsorily. The Official Receiver (OR) is appointed liquidator. The legislation is contained mainly in s117 to s162 and Part 4 of the Rules.

▶ A compulsory liquidation is deemed to commence at the date of the presentation of the petition rather than the date of the winding-up order.

1.1 Grounds for presenting a winding-up petition

The grounds for the winding-up of a company by the court are set out in s122(1).
These are:

▶ The company has by special resolution resolved that the company be wound up by the court.

▶ Being a public company which was registered as such on its first incorporation, the company has not been issued with a certificate under s761 CA 06 (public company share capital requirements) and more than a year has expired since it was registered.

▶ It is an 'old public company'.

▶ The company does not commence its business within a year from its incorporation or suspends its business for a whole year.

▶ The number of members is reduced below two (but note that private companies may now be single member companies).

▶ The company is unable to pay its debts.

▶ At the time at which a moratorium for the company under s 1A comes to an end, no voluntary arrangement approved under Part 1 has effect in relation to the company.

▶ The court is of the opinion that it is just and equitable that the company should be wound-up.

1.2 Special resolution for winding-up by the court

This should be distinguished from the special resolution passed by a company under s84 (1)(b) where it resolves to wind up voluntarily. A compulsory liquidation has a number of disadvantages when compared to a MVL:

▶ Greater involvement of the court
▶ Involvement of the OR
▶ Generally greater expense and delay
▶ Secretary of State fees calculated as a percentage of payments into the Insolvency Services Account.

However, the members of a company may prefer a compulsory liquidation where they believe that the conduct of the management requires a thorough investigation. The OR has a duty under s132 to investigate the affairs of the company and has the power to apply for the public examination of the directors and others under s133. Also, only in compulsory liquidation is the court likely to apply under s218 to direct the liquidator to refer *prima facie* criminal conduct to the Secretary of State.

1.3 Inability to pay debts

There are four ways in which it can be proved that a company is unable to pay its debts (s123):

▶ A creditor (by assignment or otherwise) to whom the company is indebted in a sum exceeding £750 then due has served on the company by leaving it at the company's registered office, a written demand (in the prescribed form) requiring the company to pay the sum so due.

▶ The company has for three weeks thereafter neglected to pay the sum or to secure or compound for it to the reasonable satisfaction of the creditor (s123(1)(a)).

If in England and Wales execution or other process issued on a judgement decree or order of any court in favour of a creditor of the company is returned unsatisfied in whole or in part (s123(1)(b)).

If it is proved to the satisfaction of the court that the company is unable to pay its debts, as they fall due (s123(1)(e)).

A company is also deemed unable to pay its debts if it is proved to the satisfaction of the court that the value of the company's assets is less than the amount of its liabilities, taking into account its contingent and prospective liabilities (s123(2)).

For a debt to warrant a statutory demand, it must be due and payable at once. It cannot merely be prospective or dependant on a contingency (Re European Life Assurance Society 1869). It must not be disputed on material grounds (Re Richbell Strategic Holdings Ltd 1997).

The form of statutory demand is prescribed by Schedule 4 to the Rules.

It must state the amount of the debt and the consideration given for it (or if no consideration the way in which the debt arose) (Rule 4.5).

It must be signed by or on behalf of the creditor, and must be dated (Rule 4.4).

It must be left at the registered office of the company (s123(1)(a) IA).

21 clear days (ie excluding the day of service of the demand and the day of presentation of the petition) must be given for the company to pay the debt (Re Lympne Investment Ltd 1972) eg a notice served on 1 March should not find a petition issued earlier than 23 March.

For the statutory demand to be satisfied, payment must have been made or secured to the reasonable satisfaction of the creditor in the 21 days following service.

In respect of a judgement debt under s123(1)(b) the court may order that a winding-up petition be stood over upon the company's undertaking to apply to have the judgement against it set aside, where there appears to be a reasonable prospect of that application being successful. A winding-up order however will not be refused if a judgement is under appeal unless a stay of execution has also been granted.

Under s123(1)(e) the court will presume that a company is unable to pay its debts where it cannot pay its debts as they fall due (the 'commercial insolvency' test). Alternatively under s123(2) the court can consider whether the value of the company's assets are less than the amount of its liabilities, taking into account its contingent and prospective liabilities, (the 'balance sheet insolvency' test).

Case law suggests that a company will be held to be 'unable to pay its debts' if:

▶ Its acceptances have been dishonoured (Re Globe New Patent Iron and Steel Co. (1875)).

▶ It has informed a judgement creditor that it has no assets on which to levy execution (Re Flagstaff etc Co. of Utah (1875)).

▶ It persistently fails or neglects to pay its debts until forced to do so (Re A Company (1986)).

▶ The petitioner has demanded payment of a sum due without success (Stephen, Petitioner 1884).

Generally a petitioner is entitled as of right to a winding-up order where he or she has made out the ground.

It is no defence for the company to argue that it has not been given sufficient time to pay. However:

▶ Where a petition is founded on s122(1)(f) and s123(1)(a) 21 clear days must be given.

▶ It is an improper use of the court to present a petition on the basis of a debt which has never been demanded and for which no opportunity to repay has been given (Re A Company (1983)).

That the company has no assets from which the petitioning creditors debt can be paid is not a defence, or that a debenture holder as a secured creditor will take all available assets.

1.4 Just and equitable grounds

Unlike an application under ground (f) applications under this ground very much involve the exercise by the court of its discretion in deciding whether it would be just and equitable to grant the petition.

The court will not order a winding-up under this head if there are no obstacles in the way of voluntary winding-up ie the court must be persuaded there are good reasons why its intervention is required.

This would be the usual ground under which a contributory would petition for a winding-up order. A single shareholder may petition.

Circumstances in which the court will make an order include:

▶ Where the main object of the company has failed (*Re German Date Coffee Company*).

▶ Where the company is a 'bubble', ie there is no *bona fide* intent on the part of the directors to carry on business in a proper manner.

▶ Where there is a deadlock in management.

▶ Where a person has been excluded from management.

▶ Where the company was formed to carry out a fraud or to carry on illegal business.

   Example: A company formed to carry on a business which infringes the Betting, Gaming and Lotteries Act 1963 (*Re International Securities Corporation*).

1.5 Voluntary liquidations

The voluntary winding-up of a company does not bar the right of any creditor or contributory to have it wound-up by the court (s116). However, s124(5) provides that 'the court shall not make a winding-up order on the petition unless it is satisfied that the voluntary winding-up cannot be continued with due regard to the interests of the creditors or contributories'.

S195 is relevant here providing that the court may:

▶ As to all matters relating to the winding-up of a company, have regard to the wishes of the creditors or contributories (as proved to it by any sufficient evidence).

▶ If it thinks fit, for the purpose of ascertaining those wishes, direct meetings of the creditors or contributories to be called, held and conducted in such manner as the court directs, etc.

A creditor would apply for compulsory liquidation by petition in the usual way. There is no need to give grounds in the petition for why a compulsory winding-up should be substituted for the existing voluntary winding-up.

If the voluntary winding-up is a creditors' voluntary winding-up this is *prima facie* evidence that the company is unable to pay its debts.

The Official Receiver attached to the court may petition for the voluntary winding-up to be replaced by a compulsory winding-up.

Directors of the company should not do so as they act by the voluntary liquidator. The voluntary liquidator should be present at any hearing of the petition and can appear by counsel to provide assistance to the court but should not press a view one way or another.

Contributories would be unlikely to apply for displacement of a voluntary winding-up, and by s116 IA would only be successful if they could show that their rights would be prejudiced by a voluntary liquidation.

The creditors may apply for the company to be wound up compulsorily.

It is perhaps difficult to see why creditors would seek a compulsory liquidation when a voluntary liquidation is already in operation. Perhaps:

▶ To get their own nominee appointed as liquidator instead of the liquidator appointed at the meeting of creditors (called pursuant to s98).

Note: By r4.63 IR 1986 a resolution is passed at that meeting by a 'majority (in value) of those present and voting (in person or by proxy) in favour of the resolution'. So generally the majority creditors will get their choice of liquidator, but the directors or members of the company may themselves be the majority creditors, or the creditors' nominee even if acceptable to all the creditors may have insufficient funds to investigate fully circumstances which suggest that serious offences may have been committed.

▶   To instigate a thorough investigation into the affairs of the company and the conduct of the directors.

1.6   Receivership

A court is not precluded from making a winding-up order because the company is in receivership, however, the fact that a company is in receivership is not conclusive evidence that it is unable to pay its debts within s122(1)(f). It is strong evidence of a company's inability to pay debts unless a Statement of Affairs has been lodged showing a likely surplus of assets for both secured and unsecured creditors.

2   Who may present a winding-up petition?

Section overview

A winding-up petition may be presented by either the company, the directors, any creditor(s) (including any contingent or prospective creditor(s)), contributory or contributories or by all of these parties, together or separately s124(1).

2.1   The company

The company will normally prefer to resolve in general meeting to wind up voluntarily, this being generally a quicker and cheaper procedure. The membership as a whole however, may feel that a compulsory liquidation is required so that an extensive investigation of the affairs of the company may be conducted.

2.2   The directors

The directors will normally have a strong reluctance to petition the court for compulsory winding-up where the voluntary procedure is available.

2.3   Any creditor or creditors

A compulsory liquidation is usually initiated by a creditor's petition.

Secured creditors will normally rely on their security, so therefore unsecured creditors are the more usual petitioners.

As explained earlier a creditor will need to show that his or her debt is:

▶   Liquidated, and not disputed on substantial grounds.

▶   If this is the case the creditor will normally be entitled as of right to an order. However, s195 gives the court a wide discretion to dismiss the petition where a majority of the creditors by value are opposed to the making of a winding-up order.

Under s195:

▶   If the company is solvent the court will consider the views of both creditors and contributories.

   However, if only a contributory opposes the petition it will usually be granted (*Re Comburn Petroleum Products Ltd*).

▶ If the company is insolvent the court will consider the views of only the creditors, as the contributories have no interest in the winding-up.

Where there are different classes of creditors the wishes of those particularly interested will be given the most weight.

The court might refuse the petition of the unsecured creditor, for instance, where opposed by secured creditors in circumstances where there was no reasonable prospect of the unsecured creditors receiving anything.

S125(1) provides that 'the court shall not refuse to make a winding-up order on the grounds only that the company's assets have been mortgaged to an amount equal to or in excess of those assets, or that the company has no assets.

S195 provides the court with a discretion that it does not fetter the court to the wishes of the majority of the creditors. Although the court will usually make an order in accordance with the wishes of the majority it does not have to do so.

2.4 Contributory or contributories

A 'contributory' is a person liable to contribute to the assets of the company in the event of it being wound-up. By s74 this includes:

▶ Present members of the company.

▶ Past members in certain circumstances (eg where was a member within 12 months of the winding-up).

Conditions for a contributory to petition:

S124(2) '... a contributory is not entitled to present a winding-up petition unless either:

▶ The number of members is reduced below two (remember this is plcs only).

▶ The shares in respect of which he is a contributory, or some of them, either were:

– Originally allotted to him, or have been held by him, and registered in his name, for at least six months during the 18 months before the commencement of the winding-up, or

– Have devolved on him through the death of a former holder.

The purpose of s124(2) is to prevent some one from acquiring a share with the sole purpose of petitioning to wind-up the company.

A shareholder whose calls are in arrears can petition providing that he/she pays into court the amount of the arrears (*Re Diamond Fuel Co*).

2.5 The Secretary of State

The Secretary of State can petition under s1035 CA 06 where it is in the public interest following a report of inspectors. Also, under s72 of the Financial Services Act 1986 where an 'authorised person' or 'appointed representative' is unable to pay his debts or where the court considers it just and equitable.

2.6 The Official Receiver

'Where a company is being wound-up voluntarily in England and Wales, a winding-up petition may be presented by the Official Receiver attached to the court as well as by any other person authorised in that behalf under the other provisions of this section...

... but the court shall not make a winding-up order on the petition unless it is satisfied that the voluntary winding-up cannot be continued with due regard to the interests of the creditors or contributories' (s124(5)).

The court will need to be satisfied on the balance of probabilities (*Re J. Russel Electronics Ltd*).

2.7 Administrative receiver, administrator and supervisor of a CVA

An administrative receiver has the power to petition in Schedule 1 as does an administrator.

A supervisor of a CVA has the power to petition in s7(4)(b).

3 The petition

Section overview

The petition must be in one of the forms specified in the Insolvency Rules 86. A contributory's petition must specify the grounds on which it is presented and the nature of the relief sought (r4.22(1)).

3.1 Content of a petition (Form 4.2)

The petition should contain the following information.

▶ The name of the company.

▶ The date of the company's incorporation.

▶ The address of the company's registered office.

▶ The share capital of the company.

▶ The principal objects for which the company was formed.

▶ The ground or grounds upon which the petition is presented.

▶ A statement as to whether, in the opinion of the petitioner, the EC Regulations apply.

▶ Whether, if the Regulations do apply, the proceedings are main, secondary or territorial proceedings.

3.2 Procedure

▶ The following should be delivered to the Court office:

   – Petition.

   – Three copies of the petition (and sufficient copies to give to any voluntary liquidator, administrator or supervisor of a CVA if appropriate) (r4.7(3)). (Copies of the petition are required to give to:

      ▶ Petitioner/ petitioners' solicitor

      ▶ For service on the company

      ▶ For exhibiting to the affidavit of service

      ▶ For exhibiting to the affidavit verifying the petition (this will be the court's copy of the petition and is usually stamped 'filed')).

   – The court fee (£190).

   – An affidavit verifying that the statements made in the petition are true or true to the best of the deponent's knowledge, information and belief (r4.12).

   – Receipt for the deposit (currently £715) payable on presentation of the petition.

   – An SAE, if the petition has been posted to the court office and a covering letter

▶ The court will now endorse the date, time and place of the hearing on the petitions. This is crucial, as this will become the date of 'presentation of the petition', and the date of commencement of winding-up.

Date + time of presentation is the date of commencement.

These will then be sealed with the court seal and given a number by the court. This is the number of the court's file and should be quoted on all correspondence. The petition will be dated. The petitions will be handed back to the petitioner/petitioner's solicitors for filing.

▶ The petition must be served at the company's registered office, as last notified to the Registrar of Companies. If there is no registered office, it should be served at the company's principal or last known place of business.

At least 14 days before the hearing date the petition should be served on any director or other officer or employee of the company, or with any person who acknowledges himself to be authorised to accept service.

If no such person to be found it can simply be deposited at the registered office, etc. in such a way that it is likely to come to the notice of a person attending the office.

The petition must also be served on any administrator, liquidator under a voluntary winding-up, receiver or supervisor of a voluntary arrangement (if relevant).

Service in the way provided above may for one reason or another prove impossible, in which case application may be made to the court for an order that service be made in some other way.

The petitioner/petitioner's solicitor, or other person actually serving the petition, should make an affidavit of service specifying the manner in which service was accomplished (r4.9).

The petitioner, etc. will also (unless this was done on presentation of the petition for issue) file an affidavit verifying the contents of the petition.

▶ Unless the court otherwise directs every petition must be advertised in the London Gazette not less than seven business days:

– Before the hearing of the petition
– After the petition has been served on the company.

It is not necessary to advertise a petition in a local newspaper although this may be felt desirable.

The court has a discretion to extend or abridge the time limits.

Advertisement is notice to all the world of the presentation of the petition.

(If a second petition, therefore, is issued after the advertisement of the first petition, it will be dismissed and the second petitioner will be left to pay his own costs.)

▶ Every director, contributory or creditor is entitled to a copy of the petition from the petitioner or his solicitor within two days of requiring the same on payment of the appropriate fee.

3.3 Before the hearing of the petition

The company in respect of whom the petition has been presented may:

▶ Apply (by motion plus affidavit) for an injunction restraining the petitioner from advertising (and hence as such advertisement is a pre-condition for the making on order, from securing the winding-up of the company) the petition.

Grounds on which injunction might be obtained:

– Debt genuinely disputed.
– Company is able to pay its debts.
– Company has a counter claim or set-off which would extinguish debt.

▶ Apply for a stay of any other proceedings against the company. Again the application is made by motion.

The application is made to the court which is dealing with the winding-up proceedings.

Exception: If the proceedings which are sought to be stayed are in the High Court (in which case the application is to the High Court).

▶ Apply for the staying of execution in respect of any judgement against the company.

Note: Once a winding-up order has been made any execution against the company will be void. By s129 the commencement of the winding-up is deemed to be the date of the presentation of the petition.

▶ Apply for the appointment of a provisional liquidator. (See Rules 4.25 – 4.31 IR 1986) This is a crucial area for the JIEB examiner.

▶ Apply for sanction of disposition of the company's property.

Under s127 'In any winding-up by the court any disposition of the property of the company, and any transfer of shares or alteration in the status of the company's members made after the commencement of the winding-up is, unless the court otherwise orders, void'.

The purpose of the section is to avoid the improper dissipation of the company's assets in a compulsory liquidation.

The problem with it is that it paralyses the company's trading.

If a winding-up order is likely to be made (which will, of course, retrospectively take effect from the date of presentation of the petition) the company may wish to apply to the court for sanction to enter into transactions otherwise void under s127 , ie to continue running their business.

3.4   Steps to be taken pre-hearing by the petitioner

File (if not done already) an affidavit verifying petition.

File an affidavit of service of petition.

Advertise the petition in the London Gazette.

Send copies of the petition to any interested party who requests one, and who pays a fee.

At least five days before the hearing file a Certificate of Compliance with the Rules relating to service and advertisement.

Prepare a list of all of the name and addresses of the persons who have given notice of their intention to appear at the hearing of the petition and of their respective solicitors.

If the petitioner wishes to withdraw the petition (eg debt has now been paid) then:

▶ Petition not yet served – petitioner must lodge with the court a request to withdraw the petition. Registrar will then give leave for petition to be withdrawn.

▶ Petition has been served – petitioner must apply to the court for leave to withdraw petition.

▶ Petition has been served and advertised – petitioner must apply at the hearing of the petition for withdrawal. Some other creditor may wish to be substituted as petitioning creditor at the hearing. If not then the usual order is for the petition to be dismissed.

3.5   Steps to be taken by other parties

By r4.16(1) every person who intends to appear on the hearing of a petition must give the petitioner notice of his intention to do so.

3.6   The hearing

The court must not refuse to make order merely because:

▶ All company's assets have been mortgaged to an amount equal to, or in excess of, the value of those assets

▶ Company has no assets (s125(1)).

A petitioner on the 'company unable to pay its debts' ground is entitled to an order if the ground is made out.

S195 – The court may have regard in all matters relating to winding-up (ie including whether to make an order or not) to the wishes of creditors or contributories.

Notes:

(1)   The court is not bound to acquiesce to wishes of majority.

(2)   The court will have regard to value of each creditor's debt (or contributory's shareholding).

(3)   The opposition of connected parties will not be given as much weight as views of independent creditors (eg *Re. Holiday Stamps Ltd 1984*).

(4)   The wishes of creditors, etc. are normally expressed by their appearance at the hearing.

S124(5) – If a voluntary liquidation is in place an order will only be made if the voluntary liquidation cannot be continued with due regard to the interests of creditors and contributories.

The court may adjourn the hearing, this is not the same as dismissal of the petition.

An adjournment will not normally be granted merely to give the creditor company time to pay the debt.

It may be granted where:

▶   Company needs time to instruct solicitors and counsel.

▶   Company states intention of disputing the debt.

▶   Company states intention of applying for the judgement which forms the basis of the petition to be set aside.

▶   Petitioner consents (eg where petitioner needs time to consider proposals for payment of the debt made by the creditor company).

▶   Adjournment sought by non-petitioning creditors.

The court may substitute petitioner. By r4.19(2) the court may substitute as petitioner, on terms which it thinks just, any creditor or contributory who in the court's opinion, would have a right to present a petition and who wants to prosecute the petition.

The Court might do this where the original petitioner:

▶   Has served a defective statutory demand for payment under s122(1).
▶   Has failed to advertise the petition within the time prescribed.
▶   Consents to withdraw his or her petition.

Following the substitution order:

▶   The petition should be amended to give name of new petitioner and particulars of his/her debt.
▶   A fresh affidavit verifying the amended petition should be prepared and served on the company
▶   It is not necessary for the amended petition to be re-advertised.

The court may dismiss the petition or make the winding up order.

3.7   Effect of the winding-up order being made

No action or proceeding shall be proceeded with or commenced against the company or its property, except by leave of the court and subject to such conditions as the court may impose and

The company must forthwith forward a copy of the order to the Registrar of Companies. (s130)

The official receiver, by virtue of his office becomes liquidator of the company. (s136(2))

3.8   Post hearing

The Official Receiver will receive a notice of the making of the winding-up order and copies of the order from the court.

Official Receiver must serve copy orders on:

▶   The company at its registered office
▶   The registrar of companies.

Official Receiver will advertise the order in:

▶ The London Gazette
▶ and may also be advertised in such other manner as the OR thinks fit.

Official Receiver will write to the following (notifying them of making of order) where appropriate:

▶ Directors and company secretary of the company
▶ Court enforcement officer
▶ Public utilities
▶ Bank
▶ Company's professional advisers
▶ Company's landlords
▶ Debtors of company
▶ Any IP in place
▶ The company's creditors.

Under s131 the Official Receiver has a discretion to demand one or more Statements of Affairs.

The following persons may be required to provide a statement (s131(3)).

▶ Past/present officers of the company.

▶ Promoters of the company (who were so involved in the year before the winding-up order).

▶ Past/present employees/sub-contractors who are in the opinion of the Official Receiver capable of giving the information required.

▶ Past/present employees/officers of a corporate director of the company.

S131(2) details the required content of the statement of Affairs:

▶ Particulars of the company's assets and liabilities.
▶ The names and addresses of the company's creditors.
▶ The securities held by them respectively.
▶ The dates when the securities were given (for s239 preferences and s245 floating charge purpose).
▶ Such further or other information as may be prescribed or as the Official Receiver may require.

The Official Receiver sends notice to each person (called a 'deponent') he requires to provide statement (r4.32(2)).

The notice must state (r4.32(4)):

▶ Names and addresses of others required to provide statement.

▶ Time within which statement must be delivered.

▶ Penalties for non-compliance.

▶ That deponent has a statutory duty under s235 to provide information and attend on Official Receiver when required.

The statement must be delivered in 21 clear days (s131(4)) unless:

▶ Official Receiver extends time.
▶ Official Receiver having refused to extend, the court does.
▶ Official Receiver releases deponent from obligation to provide statement.
▶ Official Receiver having refused to release, the court does.

The statement must be in the prescribed form, (Form 4.17) and must be verified by affidavit (r4.33(1)).

The Official Receiver may require affidavits of concurrence with a statement from any other potential s131 deponent:

▶ Such affidavits may be qualified
▶ Must be delivered to Official Receiver with copy
▶ Official Receiver files affidavit of concurrence with court.

Where a deponent is unable to prepare statement himself the Official Receiver may:

▶ Employ person(s) to assist in preparation of statement.

▶ Authorise deponent to employ person(s) to assist in preparation making an allowance payable out of the company's assets for the payment of that persons expenses.

S131(7) 'if a person without reasonable excuse fails to comply with any obligation imposed under this section, he is liable to a fine and for continued contravention to a daily default fine'.

Interactive question 1: Bell Engineering Limited

Fred Jones is owed £1,900 by Bell Engineering Limited in respect of supplies made to the company. Fred has sent a number of letters to the company requesting payment however, despite the company acknowledging that the debt is due, payment has not been forthcoming.

Requirement

Write a note, to form the basis of discussions at a forthcoming meeting with Fred, detailing how Fred may present a petition for the compulsory winding up of Bell Engineering Limited and the procedure to be followed to have the company wound up.

See **Answer** at the end of this chapter.

4 First meeting of creditors

Section overview

▶ The OR has a duty to decide whether to call meetings of the company's creditors and contributories in order to choose an insolvency practitioner to become liquidator of the company in place of the OR (s136).

▶ The OR has 12 weeks following the date of the granting of the winding-up order to decide whether to call such meetings.

▶ If he decides not to call such a meeting he must give notice of this to the Court, the company's creditors and contributories s136 (5)(b).

▶ One quarter, in value, of the company's creditors can require the OR to call such a meeting. The meeting must be called within three months of the requisition.

4.1 Procedure for calling first meetings of creditors and contributories

The meetings being called by the OR must be held within four months from the date of the winding-up order (r4.50).

Notice of the meetings must be given to the court and:

▶ Every creditor known to the OR in respect of the creditors' meeting, and

▶ Every person appearing to be a contributory of the company, in respect of the contributories meeting.

The notices must be filed at court immediately after fixing the venue. Creditors and contributories must be given at least 21 days' notice of the meetings.

The notices issued should contain details of the time and date by which proofs and proxies must be lodged in order for individuals to be entitled to vote at the meeting. This should not be more than four days before the date of the meeting.

In addition, details of the meeting may also be advertised in such manner as the OR thinks fit.

4.2   Matters to be dealt with at the meetings

The business of the meetings is, in the main, the same as that to be dealt with at a s98 meeting of creditors (see Chapter 5).

Both meetings may nominate a liquidator.

If the creditors' meeting nominates a liquidator – then this person is appointed as such.

If the creditors' meeting does not nominate a liquidator, then the contributories choice will become liquidator.

If both meetings nominate different people, then the creditors' choice will be appointed as liquidator subject to the right of objection to the court.

Any creditor or contributory can object to the appointment but such an objection must be made within seven days of the liquidator's appointment. The court can make such order as it thinks fit.

If neither meeting nominates a liquidator, the OR must consider making an application to the Secretary of State for a liquidator to be appointed in his place (s137(2)). In such a circumstance the Secretary of State has the discretion whether to appoint a liquidator or not.

4.3   Reports by OR

At least once in the period after the making of a winding-up order, the OR must report to creditors and contributories with respect to the proceedings and the state of the company's affairs. A copy of the report must also be filed at court r4.43.

If a Statement of Affairs has been lodged in the proceedings, a summary of this must be included within the report to creditors and contributories r4.45(1).

5   The provisional liquidator

Section overview

Before the making of a winding-up order the petitioner, the company, any creditor or contributory or The Secretary of State may apply for the appointment of a provisional liquidator (PL). The OR or any other fit person qualified to act as an IP in relation to the company may be appointed. The normal function of a PL is to preserve the assets and records of the company until the hearing of the petition.

5.1   Procedure to follow to appoint a PL

The proposed provisional liquidator (if not the OR) and the OR must be notified of the application to appoint a PL (r4.25(3)).

The application must be supported by an affidavit stating (r4.25(2)):

▶   The grounds on which it is proposed a PL should be appointed.

▶   If some person other than the OR is proposed to be appointed, that the person is qualified to act as an IP in relation to the company and has consented to act.

▶   Whether or not the OR has been informed of the application and been provided with a copy of the application.

▶   Whether, to the applicant's knowledge, a CVA is in force or an administrator or administrative receiver is acting in relation to the company, or a liquidator has been appointed for its voluntary winding up.

▶   The applicant's estimate of the value of assets in respect of which the provisional liquidator is to be appointed.

Copies of the application and affidavit must be sent to the OR who may attend the hearing and make any representations he thinks appropriate.

Where an appointment is made the court shall forthwith give notice to the OR (r4.25A(1)) and to the PL (where he is not the OR).

The court shall send three copies of the appointment to the PL who must send one to the company and one to the Registrar of Companies.

If the OR is to be appointed PL, before an appointment is made, the applicant must deposit with the OR a sum to cover the OR's remuneration and expenses as PL.

5.2 Grounds for appointment of a PL

The court is likely to appoint a PL where:

▶ It can be shown that the company's assets are at risk
▶ It is not in the public interest for the company to continue trading
▶ To preserve a business until its financial affairs can be brought into order.

5.3 Duties of the PL

The normal duties of a PL is to preserve the company's assets and records. The court order appointing the PL must specify the duties to be carried out by him. As an officer of the court the provisional liquidator also has a duty to act with the utmost good faith and acts in the interests of the company, not the creditor who petitioned for his appointment.

The PL must provide security, which must not be less than the value of the assets under his control.

5.4 Effect of appointment of PL

On appointment of a PL, no proceedings can be commenced or continued against the company except with the leave of the court. Within 21 days of appointment, the directors are required to furnish the OR with a Statement of Affairs.

5.5 Powers of the PL

The PL only has those powers which are granted by the order appointing him. The powers given to liquidators in Schedule 4 of the Act are not specifically given to a PL.

A PL has no power to continue trading. If the company is still trading then either the court order should state that he has the power to trade or a special manager should be appointed under s177 .

The PL can apply to the court however if further powers are required.

It would be usual for the following powers and functions to be applied for:

▶ To take possession of, collect and get in all property and assets (of whatever nature) to which the company is or appears to be entitled, including the books and records of the company.

▶ To do all things which may be necessary or expedient for the protection of the company's assets.

▶ To bring or defend any action or other legal proceedings in the name and on behalf of the company.

▶ To conduct such investigations and obtain such information as may be required to enable a liquidation to proceed in a speedy and efficient manner.

▶ To employ such accountants, lawyers and other persons and to do all things which are necessary or which the provisional liquidators may consider expedient in connection with the above.

▶ To open or maintain such bank accounts as they consider expedient and to authorise payments out of the company's bank account in connection with the performance of the functions and exercise of the powers of the provisional liquidators.

▶ To carry on the business of the company including to employ, retain or dismiss any employees of the company.

▶ To do all other things incidental to the performance of the functions and powers of the provisional liquidator.

5.6 PL's remuneration

The PL's fees are payable out of the company's assets in the usual way and with the same priority as any other liquidator's fees.

5.7 Termination of appointment

The appointment of a PL may be terminated by the court (r4.31) This includes discharge where the Court makes an administration order.

If the petition is dismissed a PL's appointment will terminate and also on the making of a winding-up order.

The application for termination could be made by the PL, the petitioner, a creditor, a contributory, the company itself or the Secretary of State or any person who under any enactment could present a petition.

On termination the Court may give such directions as it thinks fit with respect to accounts of a PL's administration or any other matter.

6 The special manager

Section overview

Where a company has gone into liquidation or a provisional liquidator has been appointed, the court may appoint any person (need not be an IP) to be the special manager of the business or property of the company to assist the provisional liquidator in the management of the company by taking charge of the day to day affairs (s177). It is usual for an IP or an expert in another field to be appointed.

6.1 Procedure for appointment

Application for the appointment may be made by the liquidator or provisional liquidator, where it appears that the nature of the business or property of the company, or the interests of the company's creditors or contributories or members generally, require the appointment of another person to manage the company's business or property.

The application must be supported by a report:

▶ Setting out the reasons for the application

▶ Including an estimate of the value of the assets in respect of which the special manager is to be appointed.

6.2 Powers of the special manager

The special manager will have such powers as may be given by the court. The powers are usually limited to exclude the making of decisions which could be deferred until after the appointment of the liquidator.

The court order will specify the duration of the appointment which may be extended even after the winding-up order.

6.3 Duties of the special manager

The special manager must:

▶ Give security – based on the value of the assets in respect of which he is appointed.

▶ Prepare and keep accounts showing details of his receipts and payments – these must be prepared for each three month period since appointment and produced to the liquidator for approval.

6.4 Remuneration

The remuneration of the special manager will be fixed from time to time by the court.

Acts of the special manager are valid notwithstanding any defect in his appointment or qualifications.

6.5 Termination of appointment

The appointment of the special manager will terminate if:

▶ The winding-up petition is dismissed.
▶ The provisional liquidator is discharged with no winding-up order being made.
▶ The liquidator is no longer of the opinion that the employment of a special manager is necessary.
▶ Creditors request the liquidator to apply to court for the dismissal of the special manager.

Interactive question 2: Chapple Engineering Ltd

You have been approached by solicitors acting for Tool Hire Limited. They advise you that 11 days ago they issued a statutory demand for £115,000 against Chapple Engineering Limited to which there has been no response. They intend to present a winding up petition against Chapple Engineering Limited as soon as the 21 day limit expires.

Since the statutory demand was issued, Tool Hire Limited has been unable to contact the directors of Chapple Engineering Limited, even though they are aware that the company is continuing to trade. The solicitors are concerned that assets are being removed from the company and diverted to other companies controlled by the directors. They intend to apply for the appointment of yourself as provisional liquidator immediately following the presentation of the winding up petition.

Requirement

Prepare a memo for use at a meeting to be held with the solicitors for Tool Hire Limited covering the following points:

(i) Who may be appointed as a provisional liquidator and what grounds are commonly stated in the application as the reason for appointment?

(ii) What are the duties of a provisional liquidator and with which statutory requirements must he comply?

(iii) Who should be notified of the application for the appointment of a provisional liquidator and what documents should be prepared before the court hearing?

(iv) What would you expect to be contained in an order for the appointment of a provisional liquidator?

(v) In relation to a special manager, briefly explain:

    (a) Who may be appointed to that office
    (b) The role of a special manager
    (c) What defines the powers of a special manager and how would these normally be restricted?

See **Answer** at the end of this chapter.

Summary and self-test

Summary

Compulsory liquidation – Summary of the procedure

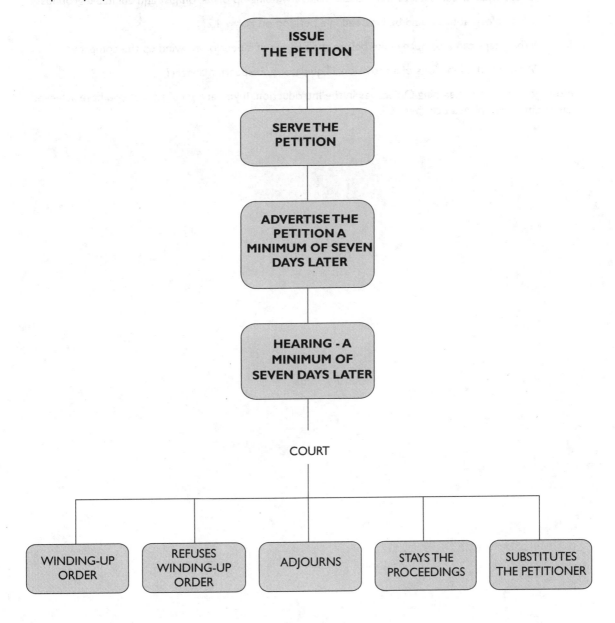

Self-test

Answer the following questions.

1   What type of resolution is required to be passed by the members when resolving to wind up a company compulsorily?

2   What are the ways in which it can be proved that a company is unable to pay its debts per s123?

3   Under what circumstances will a court make a winding-up order on just and equitable grounds?

4   What information should be included in a petition on Form 4.2?

5   What steps can a company take before the hearing of a petition to wind up the company?

6   What are the functions of a provisional liquidator and special manager?

Now, go back to the Learning Objectives in the Introduction. If you are satisfied that you have achieved these objectives, please tick them off.

Answers to self-test

1   Special resolution.

2   ▶   Unsatisfied statutory demand.

   ▶   Unsatisfied judgement debt.

   ▶   Proved to the satisfaction of the courts that the company is unable to pay its debts as they fall due (commercial insolvency test).

   ▶   The value of the company's assets are less than the amount of its liabilities, taking into account its contingent and prospective liabilities (balance sheet test).

3   Where main objects of the company have failed.
    Where the company is a bubble.
    Where there is a deadlock in management.
    Where a person has been excluded from management.
    Where the company was formed to carry out a fraud or to carry on an illegitimate business.

4   Name of the company.

    Date of the company's incorporation.

    Address of the company's registered office.

    Share capital of the company.

    Principal objects for which the company was formed.

    The ground or grounds upon which the petition is presented.

    A statement as to whether, in the opinion of the petitioner, the EC Regulations apply.

    Whether, if the Regulations do apply, the proceedings are the main, secondary or territorial proceedings.

5   Apply for an injunction restraining the petitioner from advertising the petition.
    Apply for a stay of any other proceedings against the company.
    Apply for the staying of execution in respect of any judgement against the company.
    Apply for the appointment of a provisional liquidator.
    Apply for the sanction of any disposition of the company's property.

6   Function of a provisional liquidator – to preserve the company's assets and records until a liquidator is appointed.

    Function of a special manager – to assist the provisional liquidator in the management of the company by taking charge of the day to day affairs of the company.

Answers to interactive questions

Interactive question 1: Bell Engineering Limited

As a creditor of the company Fred may present a winding up petition against the company on the ground that the company is unable to pay its debts (s122 (1) (f)).

Fred can show that the company is unable to pay its debts as they fall due (commercial insolvency test) by:

1   Serving a written demand (in the prescribed form) on the company requiring them to pay the sum due. The debt must be liquidated and not disputed on substantial grounds and must be in excess of £750. If the company fails to pay the sum due or secure or compound for it to the reasonable satisfaction of Fred, the company will be deemed unable to pay its debts.

2   Fred could obtain judgement on the debt, if execution of that debt is returned unsatisfied in whole or in part, the company will be deemed unable to pay its debts.

Or, Fred could prove, to the satisfaction of the court that the value of the company's assets is less than the amount of its liabilities, taking into account its contingent and prospective liabilities (balance sheet test).

The procedure to be followed by Fred is as follows:

1   Deliver to the court office:

   ▶   Petition and three copies.

   ▶   Court fee £190.

   ▶   Affidavit verifying that the statements made in the petition are true to the best of the deponent's knowledge and belief.

   ▶   Receipt for the deposit (currently £715) payable upon presentation of the petition.

   ▶   An SAE if the petition is posted to the court and a covering letter.

2   Serve the petition at the company's registered office at least 14 days before the hearing date set by the court.

3   Advertise the petition in the London Gazette not less than seven days

   ▶   Before the hearing of the petition
   ▶   After the petition has been served on the company.

4   File affidavit verifying service of the petition.

5   At least five days before the hearing file a Certificate of Compliance with the Rules relating to service and advertisement.

6   Prepare a list of all of the names and addresses of the persons who have given notice of their intention to appear at the hearing of the petition and their representative solicitors.

   At the hearing the court has the discretion to:

   ▶   Make the order
   ▶   Adjourn the hearing
   ▶   Substitute the petitioner
   ▶   Dismiss the petition.

Interactive question 2: Chapple Engineering Ltd

Memo format

(i)　The Official Receiver or any other fit person qualified to act as a licensed IP in relation to the company may be appointed as a provisional liquidator.

The grounds are likely to be:

▶　　Preservation of the company's assets, or
▶　　Public interest, or other reasonable grounds.

(ii)　The duties of the provisional liquidator are stated in the order of appointment.

The principal duty is to safeguard the property of the company.

As an officer of the court the provisional liquidator also has a duty to act with the utmost good faith and acts in the interest of the company, not the creditor who petitioned for his appointment.

The only statutory requirement is the provision of security, which must be not less than the value of the assets under the control of the provisional liquidator. Other requirements are imposed by the court, not statute.

(iii)　Persons to be notified are:

▶　　The proposed provisional liquidator, if not the OR
▶　　The Official Receiver.

Documents to be prepared before the hearing include:

▶　　The winding up petition.

▶　　An affidavit in support of the application to appoint a provisional liquidator.

▶　　A consent to act by the proposed provisional liquidator.

▶　　A draft order of appointment to be prepared by the solicitor in conjunction with the proposed provisional liquidator, which would include the powers required by the provisional liquidator.

(iv)　Contents of the order

The order would contain the following provisions:

▶　　That one or more named insolvency practitioners are appointed (joint) provisional liquidator(s).

▶　　That any act required or authorised to be done by a provisional liquidator may be done by any one of them in a joint appointment.

▶　　That no disposition of the company's assets by the provisional liquidator(s) in the carrying out of their duties under the order shall be avoided by virtue of the provision of s127.

▶　　That the provisional liquidator(s) may apply to the court for further orders as may be necessary or appropriate.

▶　　That notice of the order be given to the company as soon as reasonably practicable.

▶　　That the provisional liquidator(s) shall have the following powers and functions in relation to the company:

1　　　To take possession of, collect and get in all property and assets (of whatever nature) to which the company is or appears to be entitled, including the books and records of the company.

2　　　To do all things which may be necessary or expedient for the protection of the company's assets.

3　　　To bring or defend any action or other legal proceedings in the name and on behalf of the company.

4   To conduct such investigations and obtain such information as may be required to enable a liquidation to proceed in a speedy and efficient manner.

5   To employ such accountants, lawyers and other persons and to do all things which are necessary or which the provisional liquidator(s) may consider expedient in connection with the above.

6   To open or maintain such bank accounts as they consider expedient and to authorise payments out of the company's bank account in connection with the performance of the functions and exercise of the powers of the provisional liquidator(s).

7   To carry on the business of the company including to employ, retain or dismiss any employees of the company.

8   To do all other things incidental to the performance of the functions and powers of the provisional liquidator.

(v)   Appointment of a special manager:

Anyone may be appointed (need not be a qualified IP), but usual to be an IP or an expert in another field.

To assist the provisional liquidator in the management of the company by taking charge of day to day affairs.

Stated in the court order as requested by the provisional liquidator.

The powers are usually limited to exclude the making of decisions which could be deferred until after the appointment of the liquidator.

7

Liquidators' investigations

> > > > > > > > > > > > > >

Introduction

Learning objectives

▶ Understand why a liquidator investigates the affairs of an insolvent company ☐

▶ State the statutory requirements re submission of directors' reports under CDDA ☐

▶ State the form that a liquidator's investigation will take following the guidance given by SIP 2 ☐

▶ Understand the difference between a disqualification order and a disqualification undertaking ☐

▶ Be aware of the content of SIP 4 ☐

▶ Identify the statutory duties introduced by CA 06 ☐

Working context

You may be asked to assist your principal by carrying out a review of the company's books and records. It is important to know what you are seeking to achieve when conducting such a review. You may also be asked to complete a directors' return under CDDA. It is therefore important that you understand the statutory regulations regarding such returns and what matters should be reported when completing the returns.

Stop and think

Why does a liquidator investigate the affairs of an insolvent company? What powers does a liquidator have to obtain information regarding the company? What does it mean when a director is disqualified? What is he disqualified from? What constitutes undesirable conduct?

Examination context

The completion of directors' returns and liquidator's investigations are both topics which are regularly tested in the JIEB exam. It is important to know both the statutory requirements regarding CDDA as well as the content of SIP 4, understanding the matters which the disqualification unit will take into account when assessing the conduct of a director. The most important grounds for disqualification in terms of the JIEB exam is the unfitness ground dealt with in s6 CDDA 1986 and s7 CDDA 1986. (S8 CDDA 1986 of the Act provides for disqualification following a BERR investigation on the application of the Secretary of State. This should be outside the remit of the exam and hence is not mentioned in the notes). You should also be aware of Disqualification Undertakings which were introduced in April 2001 via the Insolvency Act 2000.

Liquidator's investigations requires a knowledge of SIP 2. Listing the basic practical points outlined will be relevant to questions regarding wrongdoing by the directors.

Exam requirements

Past exam questions to look at include:

2007	Question 4
1999	Question 1
1998	Question 1(c)
1997	Question 4(c)(ii)
1995	Question 3
1991	Question 4

1 Liquidators' investigations

Section overview

The liquidator in a voluntary liquidation, unlike the OR in a compulsory liquidation, does not have a statutory duty to carry out an investigation into the affairs of an insolvent company. He must however, investigate the affairs of the company in order to ascertain the assets and liabilities of the company, determine whether any transactions may be set aside and identify any rights of action against third parties. This will also enable the liquidator to fulfil his duty to report on the conduct of the directors under Company Directors Disqualification Act 1986 (CDDA). SIP 2 provides guidance to the liquidator when carrying out an investigation into the affairs of the insolvent company.

1.1 Duty of OR to investigate

Under s132(1) the OR in a compulsory liquidation has a statutory duty to investigate:

▶   If the company has failed, the causes of failure.
▶   Generally the promotion, formation, business dealings and affairs of the company.

The OR must make such report, if any, to the court on the outcome of his investigations as he thinks fit. If a report is made it may be used as evidence in any proceedings.

Pursuant to s132 the OR will:

▶   Make an inspection at the company's premises, if necessary
▶   Take custody of deeds, books, records and the company's seal
▶   Call the principal director for an interview.

1.2 Public examination

If the OR wishes to obtain further information he has the power to apply to the court for the public examination of (s133(1)):

▶   Past and present officers of the company.
▶   Any liquidator, administrator, receiver or manager of the company.
▶   Any person who has taken part in the promotion, formation or management of the company.

Past and present officers would normally include all directors (by whatever name called) including directors who have held office in the last three years, the company secretary, other senior officials and employees and the company's professional advisers.

One half, in value, of the company's creditors or three-quarters, in value, of the company's contributories may require the OR to apply for a public examination.

A public examination takes place in court. The following people may attend and ask questions:

▶   Official Receiver
▶   Liquidator of the company (if any)
▶   Special manager (if any)
▶   Any creditor who has tendered a proof
▶   Contributory.

If a person fails to attend their public examination without a reasonable excuse they will be in contempt of court. The punishment for non-attendance may be the issue of a warrant for their arrest, or seizure of the person's books, papers, records, money or goods in their possession.

2 SIP 2 A liquidator's investigation into the affairs of an insolvent company

Section overview

The objective of SIP 2 is to set out a minimum procedure in carrying out the duty to investigate the affairs of the company (whether there are assets or not). This is so creditors can be confident that the duty has been discharged.

2.1 Procedure for the investigation

The liquidator should ascertain the location and safeguard and list the company's books, records and other accounting information.

The liquidator should carry out an analytical review based on the initial information available, in order to determine whether a more detailed investigation is required. This initial review should include:

▶ Inviting creditors of the company to bring to his attention any matters of concern.

▶ Question officers of the company and other senior officials as to the company's affairs, including the reasons for the company's failure and the location of the company's books and records.

▶ Compare Statement of Affairs with the last audited, filed or management accounts in order to identify material movements in fixed and current assets.

▶ Review books, records and minutes for the last six months to identify unusual and exceptional transactions.

▶ Identify possible rights of action against third parties.

Where the liquidator believes there are grounds for further investigation or possible actions, he should discuss the matter with the liquidation committee in order to ascertain their views. Funding issues should also be discussed with the committee.

If there is no committee, the liquidator should seek the views of the creditors, either by correspondence, a creditors' meeting, or discussions with the major creditors.

It is not the duty of a liquidator to investigate criminal conduct, but if it should come to his notice that any past or present officer (or member) of the company may have been guilty of an offence in relation to the company for which he is criminally liable, then the liquidator should report the matter. In a compulsory winding-up it should be reported to the OR and in a voluntary winding-up to the Secretary of State.

2.2 Rights of action by company or liquidator

Potential actions which may be taken by the liquidator include the following:

S76	Redemption or purchase of own shares.
S127	Avoidance of property dispositions etc.
S128	Avoidance of attachments etc.
S150, s165	Uncalled capital.
S212	Misfeasance.

Wrongful Trading, Fraudulent Trading and Misfeasance (see Chapter 8).

Voidable Transactions, ie preferences, transactions at an undervalue, s423 transactions defrauding creditors, extortionate credit transactions (see Chapter 8).

S76. This is an action against directors and/or shareholders where:

▶ A company has acquired its own shares within one year of commencement of winding-up and

▶ Has made a permissible capital payment (ie. capital has not been maintained).

Part 17 CA 2006 – This is in relation to uncalled share capital.

S847 CA 2006 – Unlawful distribution to members.

S190 CA 2006 – Directors entering into contracts with own company.

Ss197–214 CA 2006 – Unlawful loans to Directors.

2.3 Investigative powers of the liquidator

The principal powers of an office holder (including an administrative receiver) are derived from ss234–236.

▶   S234 enables an office holder to apply to court for an order requiring any person who has in their possession or control any property, books, papers or records to which the company appears to be entitled, to pay, deliver, convey, surrender or transfer such property to the office holder forthwith – or should this now be as seen as reasonably practicable? Or within such period as the court thinks fit.

   In doing this, if the office holder seizes or disposes of property which is not actually the property of the company, but at the time he had reasonable grounds for believing it could be seized or disposed of, the office holder will not be liable for any loss or damage resulting from it.

▶   S235 provides the company's officers and employees with a duty to provide information concerning the company and its promotion, formation, business, dealings, affairs or property. The office holder may require such information to be given at any time as is reasonable.

   The person supplying the information may also be required to attend on the office holder to provide this information as the office holder may reasonably require.

▶   S236 enables the court to summon before it, on the application of the office holder, any relevant person (to include any officer, any person known or suspected to have in their possession property or any person the court thinks is capable of giving information about the company's promotion, formation, business, dealings and affairs).

   The court can also require such a person to submit an affidavit containing an account of any dealings with the company or to produce any books, papers or other records in his possession or under his control relating to the company.

   If the person fails to appear it can issue a warrant for their arrest, requiring them to comply and for the seizure of any books, papers, records, money or goods in that person's possession.

3 Disqualification of directors

Section overview

The Company Directors Disqualification Act 1986 (CDDA) provides a number of grounds under which a disqualification order may be made.

3.1 The grounds for a disqualification order

▶   **S2 CDDA 1986**

   Where a person is convicted of an indictable offence in connection with the promotion, formation, management or liquidation of a company, or with the receivership or management of a company's property.

   Maximum disqualification is 15 years (unless under Summary Jurisdiction in which case the maximum is five years).

▶ **S3 CDDA 1986**

Where it appears that a person has been persistently in default in relation to provisions of the companies legislation requiring any return, account or other document to be filed with, delivered or sent, or notice of any matter to be given, to the Registrar of Companies.

Persistent default may be conclusively proved by showing three or more defaults in the five years prior to the hearing.

Maximum disqualification is five years.

▶ **S4 CDDA 1986**

Where it appears in the course of the winding-up of a company that a person:

– Has been guilty of fraudulent trading under s993 CA 2006.

– Has otherwise been guilty while an officer or liquidator of the company or receiver or manager of its property, of any fraud or any breach of duty.

Maximum disqualification is 15 years.

▶ **S5 CDDA 1986**

Where a person has been convicted of three offences of failing to make returns, deposit accounts or send notices or documents to the registrar of companies in the last five years. These offences are summary offences but the conviction itself may be either summary or on indictment.

Maximum disqualification is five years.

▶ **S6 CDDA 1986**

The court shall make a disqualification order when it is satisfied that a person:

– Is or has been a director of a company which has at any time become insolvent (whether while they were a director or subsequently).

– Their conduct as a director of that company or with other companies makes them unfit to be concerned in the management of a company.

The minimum period for a disqualification order is two years with the maximum being 15 years.

Re Sevenoaks Stationers (Retail)Ltd (Court of Appeal)

– 2–5 years for 'relatively not very serious cases'
– 5–10 years for serious cases not meriting the top bracket
– 10–15 years for particularly serious cases

Re D J Matthews (Joinery Design) Ltd and Another (1988) – Director permitted to continue as director of the family company providing he adopted unlimited liability.

Re Majestic Recording Studios Ltd and Another (1988) – says it is no defence under CDDA 1986 to say that the director left all financial matters to the other directors.

Re Lo-Line Electric Motors Ltd – 'Director' includes 'shadow director'. The case suggests that the conduct must display:

– A lack of commercial probity
– Gross negligence.

However *Re Sevenoaks Stationers* warns against treating such statements as judicial paraphrases of the words in the Statute.

▶ **S8 CDDA 1986**

Where it appears to the Secretary of State that it is expedient in the public interest, following an investigation by inspectors under Companies Act or FSA&M 2000, to apply to the court for a disqualification order.

Maximum disqualification is 15 years.

▶ **S10 CDDA 1986**

Where a court makes an order under s213 Fraudulent trading or s214 Wrongful trading.

Maximum disqualification is 15 years.

3.2 Directors' returns

In the case of an insolvent voluntary liquidation the liquidator must report forthwith to the Secretary of State on the conduct of past or present directors where it appears to him that the conduct of the director makes him unfit to be concerned in the management of a company, s7(3) Company Directors Disqualification Act 1986 (CDDA). SIP 4 provides guidance to office holders re disqualification of directors. The law is contained in CDDA and The Insolvent Companies (Reports on Conduct of Directors) Rules 1996.

3.3 Statutory requirements

The following office holders are required to report on the director's conduct:

▶   Compulsory liquidation – the OR.
▶   Insolvent voluntary liquidation – the liquidator.
▶   Administration – the administrator.
▶   Administrative Receivership – the administrative receiver.

The office holder should make the necessary returns within six months of the relevant date.

The relevant dates are:

▶   Creditors' voluntary liquidation – date of the resolution to wind up.

▶   Members' voluntary liquidation – date when the liquidator formed the opinion that the company was unable to meet its liabilities.

▶   Administrative receivership – date of appointment of the receiver.

▶   Administration – date administration order made by the court.

The office holder is required to file a D1 report for those directors with unfit conduct and a D2 return where an IP makes an interim or final return which does not disclose 'unfitted conduct'. The returns should include all directors and shadow directors who were in office in the three years preceding the relevant date.

The office holder is expected to base his report, or decision that only a return is necessary, on information coming to light in the ordinary course of his work and is not required to carry out investigations specifically for the purpose of fulfilling his duties under the Act.

The Secretary of State must make an application for a disqualification order within two years from the relevant date. The Secretary of State can apply for leave to apply for a disqualification order out of time. Guidelines for the court to exercise its discretion were set out in *Re Probe Data Systems*. The court must consider:

▶   Length of the delay
▶   Reasons for the delay
▶   Strength of the case against the respondent
▶   Degree of prejudice that would be caused to the respondent by the length of the delay.

3.4 Terms of a disqualification order

A person shall not, without the leave of the court:

▶   Be a director of a company, act as a receiver of a company's property or in any way, whether directly or indirectly, be concerned or take part in the promotion, formation or management of a company.

▶   Act as an insolvency practitioner.

Acting in contravention of a disqualification order is an offence (s13 CDDA) and such a person will become jointly and severally liable for the company's debts.

3.5   SIP 4 Guidance

SIP 4 Disqualification of directors (England and Wales).

SIP 4 provides further guidance to IPs on the submission of disqualification reports to the Secretary of State and work they are required to undertake.

SIP 4 states that if an IP has not found any 'unfitted' conduct within six months or if the information is insufficient to make a decision, they should make an interim return. If they later find any adverse conduct then an adverse report can be submitted.

The SIP states that preferably all reports should be submitted within one year given that the application must be submitted to court within two years.

Liquidators do not have to carry out any specific investigations into directors' conduct – they can base the return on information coming to light in the ordinary course of their investigations.

The liquidator should be aware that the matters of unfitness set out in Schedule 1 to the CDDA are not exhaustive and other matters considered relevant should be included in the return.

IPs shouldn't take a pedantic view of isolated technical failures but should form an overall view of directors' conduct.

In the report itself the IP should:

▶   Avoid defamation.
▶   Include copies of accounts and reports to creditors' meetings where relevant.
▶   Give specific examples of instances of unfitted conduct where possible.
▶   IP should avoid disclosure of contents of report to outsiders.

The Dear IP letter no 36 reminds IPs that a D1 report should be submitted with:

▶   A copy of the Statement of Affairs
▶   Last two sets of audited accounts (and any draft management accounts subsequently prepared)
▶   Questionnaires completed by directors.

Matters that the disqualification unit look at include:

▶   Directors' misconduct:

   –   Loans to directors to purchase shares in the company
   –   Personal benefits obtained by the directors
   –   Directors' criminal convictions
   –   Misfeasance/breach of duty
   –   Misapplication of funds
   –   Voidable transactions.

▶   Prejudicing creditors:

   –   Transactions at an undervalue
   –   Preferences
   –   Extortionate credit transactions
   –   Dishonoured cheques
   –   Deposits accepted for goods/services not supplied
   –   Delaying tactics
   –   Retention of crown monies to finance trading.

▶   Miscellaneous:

   –   Overvaluing assets in the accounts to obtain loans etc

   –   Misconduct in relation to the operation of a factoring account

   –   Breach of CA 1985, 1989 and 2006 provisions regarding the keeping of statutory books and preparation of accounts

   –   Responsibility for the insolvency

- Responsibility for non delivery of paid for goods and services

- Responsibility for preferences

- Responsibility for non compliance with s98 (calling of creditors' meetings where voluntary winding-up)

- Responsibility for non compliance with various IA 1986 requirements.

3.6 Disqualification undertakings

S5 to s8 of the Insolvency Act 2000 introduced a regime of disqualification undertakings into the CDDA 1986.

A disqualification undertaking is where the Secretary of State accepts an undertaking by any person that for a period of time (specified in the undertaking document) they will not be a director of any company, act as a receiver of a company's property or in any way, whether directly of indirectly, be concerned or take part in the promotion, formation or management of a company and will not act as an IP.

The minimum and maximum periods for undertakings are as per a normal disqualification order.

The Secretary of State may accept an undertaking from a person instead of applying for, or proceeding with an application for, a disqualification order.

Following the giving of a disqualification undertaking the court may:

▶ Reduce the period for which the undertaking is to be in force
▶ Provide for it to cease to be in force.

An application for variation must be made to the court by the person subject to the disqualification undertaking (s8A(1)).

Interactive question: Furnish Productions Ltd

Your principal was appointed liquidator of Furnish Production Limited on 11 January 2010 following a winding up order which was made on 10 December 2009.

The company's sales director has attended the OR's office for an interview and has provided some information regarding the company's affairs but denied all knowledge of any financial matters. The company's remaining directors have ignored the OR's requests for further information.

Requirements

(a) What powers does the liquidator have to assist him in his investigations into the company's affairs?

(b) As a result of the directors' actions a Disqualification Order has been applied for. The sales director has asked that he be allowed to make a Disqualification Undertaking instead. Explain the effects of a disqualification order and how a disqualification undertaking differs from this.

See **Answer** at the end of this chapter.

4 Directors' duties

Section overview

The Companies Act 2006 introduced a statutory statement of directors' duties which is generally accepted as replacing existing common law and equitable duties and changed the rules regarding directors' conflicts of interest.

4.1   Statutory duties

With effect from 1 October 2007 the CA 06 introduced the following statutory duties:

▶   **To act within powers** This means that a director must act in accordance with the company's constitution and must only exercise his powers for their proper purpose (s171 CA 06).

▶   **To promote success of the company** This requires a director to act in the way he considers, in good faith, would be most likely to promote the success of the company for the benefit of the members as a whole (s172 CA 06).

▶   **To exercise independent judgement** Directors must exercise their powers independently of third party instructions (s173 CA 06).

▶   **To exercise reasonable skill, care and diligence** A director owes a duty to the company to exercise the same standard of care, skill and diligence that would be exercised by a reasonably diligent person with:

  –   The general knowledge, skill and experience that may reasonably be expected of a person carrying out the same functions as the director in relation to that company (an objective test)

  –   The general knowledge, skill and experience that the director actually has (a subjective test) (s174 CA 06).

Three further duties were introduced as from 1 October 2008:

▶   **To avoid conflicts of interest** This requires a director to avoid situations where he has or could have a direct or indirect interest conflicting with the company's interests. The duty is not infringed if the situation cannot reasonably be regarded as likely to give rise to a conflict of interest or where permitted, the matter is authorised by the directors. Only 'independent directors' should vote on the authorisation. This represented a change from the previous law whereby shareholders can authorise conflicts (s175 CA 06).

▶   **Not to accept benefits from third parties** This duty prohibits the acceptance of benefits (including bribes). Shareholders will be able to authorise the receipt of benefits but the board may not. The duty is not infringed by the acceptance of a benefit which cannot reasonably be regarded as likely to give rise to a conflict of interest (s176 CA 06).

▶   **To declare interest in proposed transactions or arrangements** The director must declare an interest in any proposed transactions or arrangements with the company to the board before the company proceeds (s177 CA 06).

4.2   S172 CA 06 Duty to promote the success of the company

This is what has been called 'enlightened shareholder value'. In fulfilling this duty the director must have regard (among other things) to:

▶   The likely consequences of any decision in the long-term.
▶   The interests of the company's employees.
▶   The company's relationships with suppliers, customers and others.
▶   The impact upon the environment.
▶   The company's reputation in relation to business conduct.
▶   The need to act fairly between members.

This duty to promote the success of the company broadly replaces the duty of the directors to act in the best interests of the company.

4.3   S177 CA 06 Duty to declare an interest in a proposed transaction or arrangement

If a director of a company is in any way, directly or indirectly, interested in a proposed transaction or arrangement with the company, he must declare the nature and extent of that interest to the other directors.

The declaration may (but need not) be made at a meeting of the directors or by notice to the directors in accordance with:

▶   S184 CA 06 notice in writing.
▶   S185 CA 06 general notice.

Any declaration required by this section must be made before the company enters into the transaction or arrangement.

If the declaration proves inaccurate or incomplete a further declaration must be made.

A declaration of interest is not required where:

▶   The director is not aware of the transaction or arrangement in question.

▶   If it cannot reasonably be regarded as likely to give rise to a conflict of interest.

▶   If the other directors are already aware of it.

▶   It concerns terms of his service contract that have been or are to be considered by a meeting of the directors or by a committee of the directors appointed for the purpose under the company's constitution.

The new law applies to transactions or arrangements entered into by a company on or after 1 October 2008, s317 CA 85 will continue to apply to those entered into before that date.

4.4   Breach of duty – civil consequences

There are a number of consequences if the duties are breached:

▶   Payment of damages compensation where the company has suffered a loss
▶   Restoration of the property
▶   Account of profits
▶   Rescission.

In addition, the members can sue the directors on behalf of the company using the 'derivative claims' procedure.

Summary and self-test

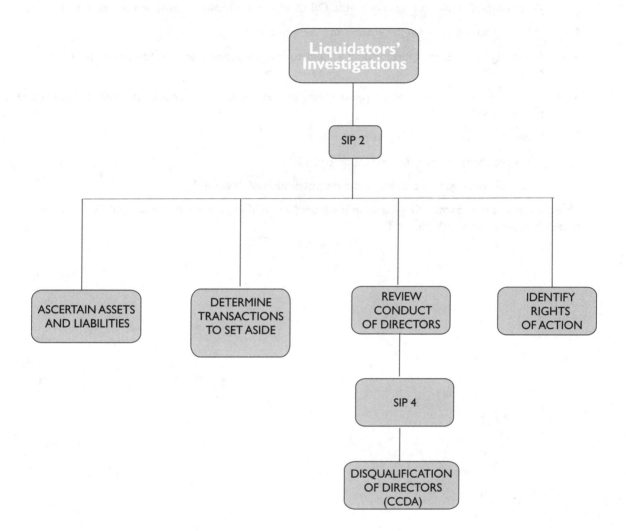

Self-test

Answer the following questions.

1   Why does a liquidator in a CVL carry out an investigation into the affairs of the company?

2   What duty does the OR in a compulsory liquidation have to investigate the affairs of the company?

3   What value of creditors may require the OR to apply for a public examination of a director?

4   Who may attend a public examination and ask questions?

5   According to SIP 2, what form should a liquidator's investigation into the affairs of an insolvent company take?

6   Within how many months of the relevant date should a liquidator submit a return on the conduct of the directors?

7   In respect of whom should a return be made?

8   What are the terms of a disqualification order?

9   Which SIP gives guidance to IPs re the disqualification of directors?

Now, go back to the Learning Objectives in the Introduction. If you are satisfied that you have achieved these objectives, please tick them off.

Answers to self-test

1 Ascertain the assets and liabilities of the company.
   Determine whether any transactions may be set aside.
   Review the conduct and decisions of the directors.
   Identify any rights of action against third parties.

2 Under s132, the OR has a duty to investigate:

   ▶ If the company has failed, the causes of failure
   ▶ Generally, the promotion, formation, business, dealings and affairs of the company.

   The OR must make a report to Court on the outcome of his investigations as he thinks fit.

3 One half, in value, of the company's creditors may require the OR to apply for a public examination.

4 The OR
   Liquidator of the company (if any)
   Special manager (if any)
   Any creditor who has tendered a proof
   Contributory

5 The liquidator should ascertain the location and safeguard and list the company's books, records and other accounting information.

   The liquidator should carry out an analytical review based on the initial information available, in order to determine whether a more detailed investigation is required. This initial review should include:

   ▶ Inviting creditors of the company to bring to his attention any matters of concern.

   ▶ Question officers of the company and other senior officials as to the company's affairs, including the reasons for the company's failure and the location of the company's books and records.

   ▶ Compare Statement of Affairs with the last audited, filed or management accounts in order to identify material movements in fixed and current assets.

   ▶ Review books, records and minutes for the last six months to identify unusual and exceptional transactions.

   ▶ Identify possible rights of action against third parties.

   Where the liquidator believes there are grounds for further investigation or possible actions, he should discuss the matter with the liquidation committee in order to ascertain their views. Funding issues should also be discussed with the committee.

6 The liquidator should make the return within six months of the relevant date.

7 All directors and shadow directors who were in office in the three years preceding the relevant date.

8 A person shall not, without leave of the court:

   ▶ Be a director of a company, act as a receiver of a company's property or in any way, whether directly or indirectly, be concerned with or take part in the promotion, formation or management of a company.

   ▶ Act as an IP.

9 SIP 4

Answer to interactive question

Interactive question: Furnish Productions Ltd

(a)   The liquidator has the following powers to obtain information from the directors and other parties (solicitors, accountants, senior employees) who he believes holds relevant information:

(i)   **S234** enables an office holder to apply to court for an order requiring any person who has in their possession or control any property, books, papers or records to which the company appears to be entitled, to pay, deliver, convey, surrender or transfer such property to the office holder forthwith, or within such period as the court thinks fit.

In doing this, if the office holder seizes or disposes of property which is not actually the property of the company, but at the time he had reasonable grounds for believing it could be seized or disposed of, the office holder will not be liable for any loss or damage resulting from it.

(ii)   **S235** provides the company's officers and employees with a duty to provide information concerning the company and its promotion, formation, business, dealings, affairs or property. The office-holder may require such information to be given at any time as is reasonable.

The person supplying the information may also be required to attend on the office holder to provide this information as the office holder may reasonably require.

(iii)   **S236** enables the court to summon before it, on the application of the office holder, any relevant person (to include any officer, any person known or suspected to have in their possession property or any person the court thinks is capable of giving information about the company's promotion, formation, business, dealings and affairs). This is known as a private examination.

The court can also require such a person to submit an affidavit containing an account of any dealings with the company or to produce any books, papers or other records in his possession or under his control relating to the company.

If the person fails to appear it can issue a warrant for their arrest, requiring them to comply and for the seizure of any books, papers, records, money or goods in that persons possession

The liquidator can also ask the OR to apply to the court under s133(1) for the public examination of:

▸   Past and present officers of the company.
▸   Any liquidator, administrator, receiver or manager of the company.
▸   Any person who has taken part in the promotion, formation or management of the company.

Past and present officers would normally include all directors (by whatever name called) including directors who have held office in the last three years, the company secretary, other senior officials and employees and the company's professional advisers.

One half, in value, of the company's creditors or three-quarters, in value, of the company's contributories may require the OR to apply for a public examination.

A public examination takes place in court. The following people may attend and ask questions:

▸   Official Receiver
▸   Liquidator of the company (if any)
▸   Special manager (if any)
▸   Any creditor who has tendered a proof
▸   Contributory.

If a person fails to attend their public examination without a reasonable excuse they will be in contempt of court. The punishment for non-attendance may be the issue of a warrant for their arrest, or seizure of the person's books, papers, records, money or goods in their possession.

(b)   The terms of a disqualification order are that a person (the director disqualified) shall not, without the leave of the court:

    (i)   Be a director of a company, act as a receiver of a company's property or in any way, whether directly or indirectly, be concerned or take part in the promotion, formation or management of a company.

    (ii)   Act as an IP.

Acting in contravention of a disqualification order is an offence (s13 CDDA) and such a person will become jointly and severally liable for the company's debts.

A disqualification undertaking was introduced by ss5–8 of the IA 2000.

The Secretary of State may accept an undertaking instead of applying for, or proceeding with an application for, a disqualification order.

The undertaking states that the person, for a period of time (specified in the undertaking document), will not be a director etc of any company and will not act as an IP.

Acceptance of an undertaking generally results in avoiding costs of proceedings and a reduced tariff of the disqualification period.

8

Antecedent
transactions

> > > > > > > > > > > > >

Introduction

Learning objectives

▶ Identify requirements of the relevant legislation with regards to antecedent transactions ☐

▶ Learn relevant section numbers and relevant time periods with regards to possible courses of action ☐

Working context

You may be asked to review the books and records of an insolvent company to identify possible rights of action against third parties or to provide evidence to support a claim against the directors of the company. It is important therefore to be able to identify when an antecedent transaction, for example a preference or transaction at an undervalue, has taken place and to understand what rights the liquidator has in respect of challenging such transactions.

Stop and think

Why is a liquidator concerned with transactions which have occurred prior to his appointment? Why is it appropriate that certain transactions should be overturned? Who will benefit from action being taken by the liquidator?

Examination context

Antecedent transactions are examined in nearly every JIEB paper. It is important to be able to identify when an antecedent transaction has occurred and to be able to show an understanding of the main features of the rules. Fraudulent and wrongful trading are often examined in the same question together with the disqualification of directors (see Chapter 7). The question will often describe a series of transactions entered into by the directors and the candidate will be required to identify the statutory provisions breached and to list practical investigative steps to be taken by the liquidator before bringing an action.

Exam requirements

Past exam questions to look at include:

2008	Question 4
2007	Question 1(c)
2004	Question 4
2003	Question 5(d)
2002	Question 5
2001	Question 2
2000	Question 4
1999	Question 2(a)
1998	Question 4
1997	Question 4
1996	Question 2(a)
1996	Question 5(c)
1995	Question 3
1994	Question 1
1993	Question 2
1992	Paper I, Question 1(d)
1990	Paper II, Question 1(a)

1 Antecedent transactions

Section overview

▶ Whilst investigating the affairs of an insolvent company the liquidator must identify any rights of action which the liquidator or the company may have against third parties and consider whether any transactions may be set aside under the provisions of the Insolvency Act 1986.

▶ Certain transactions may be set aside if they fall within certain time limits and may result in funds being recovered for the benefit of creditors.

▶ Actions which the liquidator may take are as follows:

Transaction at an undervalue	s238
Preference	s239
Extortionate credit transaction	s244
Avoidance of floating charges	s245
Transactions defrauding creditors	s423
Fraudulent trading	s213
Wrongful trading	s214
Misfeasance	s212
Re-use of a company name	s216

1.1 Transactions at an undervalue s238

A transaction at an undervalue is where there has been a gift (or other transaction with no consideration) or, the value received by the company is significantly less in money or money's worth than it ought to have received.

The company must have been insolvent at the time of, or become insolvent as a result of, the transaction taking place (as per s123 – see Chapter 6 for details). Where the recipient of the transaction is a connected person, insolvency is presumed.

The transaction must have taken place at a relevant time (see section 2 below).

There is a defence where the transaction was entered into in good faith, and it was carried out for the purpose of the company's business, and there were reasonable grounds for believing it would benefit the company.

This section applies when a company enters administration, a resolution for the voluntary winding-up of the company is passed or an order for winding-up is made by the court. Application is made to court by the liquidator or administrator.

The court can make such order as it thinks fit for restoring the position to what it would have been if the company had not entered into that transaction. However, the court will not prejudice any interest in property which was acquired in good faith and for value (s241(2)).

The alternative remedy of misfeasance under s212 may apply. This is because the company's directors have breached their fiduciary or other duties. In this case an order to repay, restore or account, or to make a personal contribution towards the company's assets can be made against the directors.

In certain, limited, circumstances the granting of security could be attacked as a transaction at an undervalue, however this would more ordinarily be construed as a preference (Hill v Spread Trustee).

Definition

Transaction: includes a gift, agreement or arrangement s436.

1.2   Preference s239

A preference is a transaction where:

▸   The person preferred must be a creditor, guarantor or surety.

▸   The company must 'do anything' or 'suffer anything' to be done which puts that creditor, guarantor or surety in a better position in the event of insolvent liquidation than they would otherwise have been in.

▸   The company must have been influenced by a desire to prefer (presumed if the parties are connected).

M C Bacon 1990 – the word 'desire' is subjective ie. the company must actually wish to improve the position of the creditor etc.

The company must have been insolvent at the time of, or become insolvent as a result of, the preference taking place.

The preference must have taken place at a relevant time (see below).

Either a liquidator or administrator can apply to court for the position of the company to be restored to what it was prior to the transaction.

1.3   Extortionate credit transaction s244

An extortionate credit transaction is where:

▸   The company is or has been a party to a transaction involving the provision of credit to the company, and

▸   Having regard to the risk undertaken by the giver of the credit the terms of the agreement require grossly exorbitant payments to be made, or otherwise grossly contravenes the ordinary principles of fair dealing.

It is assumed by the court that transactions are extortionate and it is therefore left to the defence to prove that this is not the case.

The provision of credit must have taken place at a relevant time (see below).

The liquidator or administrator can apply to the court to have:

▸   The whole or part of any obligation created by the transaction set aside.

▸   The terms of the agreement varied or to vary the terms on which any security is held for the purposes of the transaction.

▸   Any person who is or was a party to the transaction pay to the office holder any sums paid to that person by virtue of the transaction by the company.

▸   Any person surrender to the office holder any property held by him as security for the purposes of the transaction.

▸   Accounts to be taken between any persons.

1.4   Avoidance of floating charges s245

A floating charge on the company's undertaking or property is invalid except to the extent of the aggregate of any fresh consideration given for it.

The creation of the floating charge must have been within the relevant time period (see below).

If a liquidator or administrator is able to prove that a floating charge is invalid, the assets covered by the charge can be claimed, security free, for the benefit of the estate.

S245 does not have retrospective effect *(Mace Builders (Glasgow) v Lunn)*. The acts of an Administrative receiver pre-winding-up remain valid where the AR was appointed under a floating charge which has now been invalidated under s245.

Interactive question: Painters Ltd

You were appointed liquidator of Painters Limited at a s98 meeting of creditors held on 10 February 2010. You have completed your initial review of the company's books and records and the following information has come to light:

(i)   On 11 November 2009 the company sold a substantial amount of stock with a book value of £75,000, to B Green Limited for £28,000. A search of B Green Limited shows that the finance director is Anne Green, the wife of the managing director of Painters Limited.

(ii)   The company sold a large piece of equipment in October 2009 for a substantial sum of money. The funds received were used to settle the debt owed to Barbery Supplies Limited in full. Initial enquiries suggest that the equipment was sold at full value.

(iii)   The company owed the sum of £56,000 to Satby Bank plc by way of the company's trading overdraft. The overdraft was secured by a floating charge over the assets of the company which was created on 13 April 2009.

Requirement

What action, if any, could you take as liquidator and what would be the likely outcome? Give your reasoning.

See **Answer** at the end of this chapter.

1.5   Transactions defrauding creditors s423

This is where the company has transacted and caused a 'gift' to be made (ie no consideration received), or received 'significantly less' consideration under the transaction than it ought to have done.

There has to be an intention to either prejudice the interests of the victim (ie the persons taking the action under s423) or to put the assets beyond the reach of the claimants or potential claimants.

There is no relevant time in respect of transactions under s423. It will also apply where the company was solvent at the time it transacted as there is no reference to insolvency in the definition.

The court can order restoration as under s238 or under s212 an action can be taken for misfeasance against the directors of the company.

1.6   Fraudulent trading s213

This section applies if:

▸   In the course of winding-up of a company it appears that any business of the company has been carried on with intend to defraud creditors of the company or creditors of any other person or for any fraudulent purpose (s213(1)).

▸   The court, on the application of the liquidator, may declare that any persons who were knowingly parties to the carrying on of the business (in that way) are to be liable to make such contributions to the company's assets as the court thinks proper (s213(2)). This is a civil offence.

▸   Under s993 CA 06 there is a criminal offence for fraudulent trading. The section says:

–   Anyone convicted of fraudulent trading can be fined and/or imprisoned. Maximum sentence is ten years. The fine is unlimited.

–   This applies whether or not a company is being/has been wound up.

The civil offence is set out under s213 itself. It states that the perpetrators can be required to make a personal contribution to the company out of their personal assets at such rate as the court thinks proper.

The actions/omissions of directors which give rise to the charge of fraudulent trading need not have been conducted in the course of the winding-up.

If a company is not being wound up at all – civil liability cannot flow under s213. It might flow as regards the members in an action against the directors for breach of duty, or from the creditors in an action in tort, but not under s213.

S213 is not limited to insolvent liquidations.

In *R v Kemp* it was held that a single act intended to defraud potential creditors can give rise to a claim of fraudulent trading. It need not be a chain of multiple acts; one fraudulent act will do.

By *Re L Todd (Swanscombe) Ltd* – VAT evasion is within the definition.

Some actual element of dishonesty must be proved (*Re Patrick and Lyon Ltd*).

Dishonesty is assessed on a subjective basis – not 'would the reasonable director know he was party to fraudulent trading, but did **this** particular director know.'

Re William C Leitch Bros Ltd (1932) – Dishonesty will be proved where:

▶ Directors knew there was no reasonable prospect of creditors ever receiving payment, but
▶ Continued to carry on business and incur debts.

So even on this basis it is a good defence if a director can say he genuinely believed 'the clouds will roll away and the sunshine of prosperity will shine upon them again and disperse the fog of their depression', even if this belief is totally unreasonable (*Re White and Osmond (Parkstone) Ltd (1960)*).

R v Grantham 1984 – The court reviewed the authorities and told that there will be fraudulent trading where:

▶ The defendant realised there was no reason to believe funds would become available to pay debts, and
▶ There was dishonesty involving real moral blame.

S213 is difficult to prove. The Cork Committee felt that law was held in disrespect and contempt.

Directors are not the only persons who may be liable under the section, eg:

▶ Creditors could be liable: *Re Gerald Cooper Chemicals Ltd (in liquidation) 1978*.

▶ A Holding Company could be liable: *Re Sarflax 1979*.

▶ The phrase 'anyone knowingly a party' will extend to shadow directors (s251), senior employees (those who are part of executive decision making), administrative receivers and administrators.

1.7   Wrongful trading s214

Wrongful trading is where a director (or shadow director) of a company in insolvent liquidation, at some time before the commencement of the winding-up of the company, knew or ought to have concluded that there was no reasonable prospect that the company would avoid going into insolvent liquidation.

The court may declare that the director is to be liable to make such contributions to the company's assets as the court thinks proper. *Re Produce Marketing* – it was held that the purpose of s214 is compensatory rather than penal. The measure of liability is thus the amount by which the company's assets have been depleted by the directors' conduct. Punitive awards should not be made.

There is a defence to wrongful trading – that the person took every step with a view to minimising the potential loss to the company's creditors as he ought to have taken.

Unlike fraudulent trading, wrongful trading is not available in a member's voluntary winding-up.

Wrongful trading is a civil matter and is often easier to prove than fraudulent trading as the liquidator only needs to show that the directors ought to have realised that the company was insolvent rather than having to prove actual knowledge and fraudulent intent as is the case for fraudulent trading.

s214(4) defines the standard as that of 'a reasonably diligent person' having both:

▶ General knowledge, skill and experience that can be reasonably expected of a person carrying out the same functions as that director.

▶ And the general knowledge, skill and experience that the director has (this is an additional subjective test).

▶ *Re Produce Marketing*: 'Knowledge' includes all matters which the directors should have found out given reasonable diligence and a level of general skill appropriate to their experience. On this basis the directors were liable for losses incurred after the date on which audited accounts should have been filed.

So if you have higher than 'reasonable' standards you are expected to apply them.

Case law suggests that in deciding when the directors 'ought to have concluded' courts will look at:

▶ When statutory accounts should have been filed.

▶ The date of the auditors qualifying the accounts.

▶ The time when it became clear that the company could no longer pay its debts as they fell due, ie:

   – Writs and summonses were issued.
   – Suppliers refused to continue to supply.
   – Other evidence of creditor pressure.

The onus is on the director to prove that he took every step to minimise the loss to creditors. This would include:

▶ Consulting with bankers early.

▶ Preparing up to date management accounts and ensuring prompt filing of statutory accounts.

▶ Consulting professional advisers.

▶ Making cash payments to avoid dissipation of assets.

▶ Avoiding last ditch hazardous action to save the business.

▶ Avoiding making supplies to creditors who may exercise a right of set off.

▶ Refine the company's overheads. Deal only in cash.

▶ Document any decision to continue to trade, supporting the decision with reference to ongoing trading.

▶ Avoid taking new credit.

▶ Resignation is not an appropriate step.

Taking steps to initiate insolvency proceedings may limit liability under s214.

The following is a checklist of matters to pursue to ascertain whether or not an action should be brought against directors:

▶ Check the management accounts of the company at various dates, to identify when the company became insolvent in the cash-flow sense and / or the balance sheet.

▶ Look at the legal files and discover whether or not any winding-up petitions were presented, or statutory demands served which may demonstrate that the company was unable to pay debts that had fallen due.

▶ Check the minute books and any other memoranda to ascertain whether the directors considered the solvency or otherwise of the company.

▶ Send a questionnaire to all directors asking their views on the reasons for the failure of the company.

Interview the directors to ascertain their understanding of the position at various times. Bearing in mind s214, matters to consider include:

- The individual qualifications of each director.

- Whether individual directors knew that the company was insolvent.

- Whether they ought to have known that the company was insolvent, given their level of skills, and their individual functions.

- What action the director took or ought reasonable to have taken with requisite degree of diligence to minimise the loss to creditors.

- What extent the director took and heeded professional advice.

In addition to what extent did they:

- Make cash payments to avoid dissipation of assets.
- Avoid last ditch hazardous action to save the business.
- Avoid making supplies to creditors who may exercise set off.

As with any court action:

- Sanction – compulsory liquidation – of the liquidation committee or the OR on behalf of the Secretary of State. No sanction necessary in a CVL.

- Consider the costs of bringing such an action (especially in light of the *Leyland Daf* decision, which says the liquidator will not be able to collect costs of unsuccessful action out of realisations).

- Take appropriate legal advice.

- Consider whether the prospect of an action could be used as negotiating weapon in discussion with individual directors.

And in addition consider:

- Assess the ability of the directors to meet any liability, if a claim is successful.

- Consider awaiting the results of any director disqualification proceedings, which the BERR may bring. This may provide ready evidence.

Insolvency (Amendment) Rules 2008 amended r4.218(1)(a) to make it clear that the costs of an action whether or not successful could be claimed by a liquidator.

1.8 Misfeasance s212

The OR, liquidator or any creditor or contributory can bring an action for misfeasance. If a contributory (shareholder) wishes to bring an action they need the sanction of the court before they commence.

Action under s212 may be brought against:

- Officers or ex-officers of the company (this would include directors and the company secretary).

- Liquidators, administrators, administrative receivers. (The provision against administrators appointed post 15/09/03 is contained in Sch B1 para 75 IA.)

- Persons who are or have been involved in the promotion, formation or management of the company.

Misfeasance is either:

- Misapplying, retaining or becoming accountable for any money or other property of the company.

- Being guilty of any misfeasance or breach of any fiduciary or other duty in relation to the company. A breach of 'fiduciary or other duty' by a director might involve:

    - An unlawful loan made by a company to a director of itself or its holding company.

    - A director entering into a contract with his or her own company and failing to notify the board of directors at the next board meeting (ss182–187 CA 06) or to seek prior approval for the contract in general meeting where it is a substantial property transaction (s190 CA 06).

► Any action by a director or shadow director that is not in the best interests of the company as a whole will be a breach of their 'fiduciary duty'.

The court may compel the person in relation to whom the application is being made to:

► Make restitution (repay, restore or account), or

► To compensate the company by making a personal contribution towards the assets of the company. This is not a punitive award.

1.9 Re-use of company names s216

The rules are designed to deal with the abuse of directors running a company into insolvent liquidation, leaving unpaid creditors, only to set up a new similar business trading under a similar name.

s216 provides that anyone who was a director or shadow director of a company in the twelve months ending with the day before it went into insolvent liquidation is prohibited, for a period of five years from being:

► A director of a company known by a prohibited name, or

► In any way concerned, directly or indirectly in the promotion, formation or management of such a company or in the carrying on of business under a prohibited name.

Definition

A **prohibited name:** Any name by which the liquidating company was known in the last 12 months or which is so similar to such a name that it suggests an association with the liquidating company.

S216(3) itself provides for two exceptions to the general rule:

► Sanction of the court.
► Such circumstances as may be prescribed. (These are set out in the rules (see later).)

Breach of these provisions is a criminal offence, and the offending director could be liable to a fine and/or imprisonment (s216(4)).

Where a person breaches the prohibition by being involved in management, or is willing to act on the instructions of a director subject to s216, that person may be held personally responsible for 'relevant debts'. This civil liability is joint and several with the company and anyone else who is liable for those debts (s217).

Definition

Relevant debts: All liabilities for the period during which the person was involved in management or was acting on instructions as the case may be (s217(3)).

Exceptions to the rule in s216 (Rules 4.226–4.230):

S216 allows the court to grant leave as an exception to the prohibition in that section. The court can ask the liquidator or former liquidator for a report on the circumstances in which the company became insolvent and the degree of the applicant's responsibility for its doing so (r4.227).

The rules then go on to set out three circumstances where an 'old name' can be used without having to apply to the court for sanction.

First excepted case (r4.228) – a director of an insolvent company which goes into insolvent liquidation is permitted to act as a director of a company with a prohibited name where that company acquires the whole or substantially the whole of the business of the insolvent company, provided that certain notice requirements are complied with. (Such a person may also carry on business under a prohibited name other than by way of a company.)

Notice must be published in the Gazette and given to all creditors whose name and address are known to the director or could be ascertained by him on making reasonable enquiries. The prescribed notice must be given before the company enters into insolvent liquidation (for example, where it is in administration or administrative receivership and may go into liquidation later). In cases where the company is not in insolvent liquidation, notice can be given where the director of the insolvent company is already a director of the acquiring company. Notice must always be given however before a director acts in such a way that would be prohibited by s216.

The effect of the rule is that, although the person concerned may act as a director of the acquiring company before the notice is issued, the prohibited name cannot be used until after the notice has been given and published.

The notice to creditors must be in Form 4.73 and must state:

▶ The name and registered number of the insolvent company.

▶ The name of the director or shadow director.

▶ That it is his intention to act (or, where the company has not entered liquidation, to act or continue to act) in all of the ways specified in s216(3) in connection with the carrying on of the business of the insolvent company.

▶ The prohibited name, or where the company has not entered liquidation, the name under which the business is being or will be carried on which would be prohibited in the event that the company goes into liquidation.

Second excepted case (r4.229) – This exception covers applicants who are seeking court sanction for use of a prohibited name (provided that they made their application within seven days of liquidation) while they are waiting for their application to be heard. This temporary relaxation of the rule applies from the day the company goes into insolvent liquidation until the earlier of:

▶ Six weeks, or
▶ The day the court disposes of the application.

Third excepted case (r4.230) – this applies where the company in question has been known by the name for the 12 months consecutive to the failed company going into liquidation. Such a company must not have been dormant at any time during that period of 12 months for the exception to apply.

From 1 October 2009 the rules relating to similar names were amended. Companies House will only register the new name if the existing company consents to the name being registered. This could have implications where an IP sells a business to a new company which intends to be registered with a similar name to the insolvent company's name, for example, if the old company is called John Smith Limited and the directors of the new company wish to call it John Smith (UK) Limited,

The insolvent company and any other group companies with similar names would have to consent to the registration of the new name.

2 Relevant time periods

Section overview

Action may only be taken if the transactions have occurred within a relevant time period.

A summary of the relevant time periods are provided below:

*S.238/239
States date
at which decision
was taken to enter
into transaction*

Provision	Relevant Time	Is insolvency required at the Transaction date	Is insolvency presumed
Transaction at undervalue – unconnected person	2 years	Yes	No
Transaction at undervalue – connected person	2 years	Yes	Yes
Preference – unconnected person	6 months	Yes	No
Preference – connected person	2 years	Yes	No (but the 'desire to prefer' will be)
Extortionate credit transactions – unconnected or connected person	3 years	No	N/A
S245 – unconnected person	12 months	Yes	No
S245 – connected person	2 years	No	N/A

Notes to the Table:

- **Relevant Time** – in the case of transactions at an undervalue, preferences and s245 these time periods are calculated back from 'the onset of insolvency' (s240(1)(a)).

- **'Insolvency' at Transaction Date**

  This is demonstrated by the usual s123 means.

  The company must either have been insolvent at the time or become so as a result of the transaction.

- The onset of insolvency is (s240(3)):

  - In liquidation, the date of the commencement of liquidation, which is:

    - In a compulsory liquidation – the date of the presentation of the petition.

    - In a voluntary liquidation – the date of the resolution to wind up (unless liquidation follows conversion from administration in which case it is the date the company entered administration).

  - In administration, the date of onset of insolvency depends on how the administration was initiated:

    - If by the court, the date of the application to court is taken.

    - If out of court, the notice of intention to appoint an administrator is taken or, if there is no qualifying floating chargeholder (and therefore no need to serve a notice of intention to appoint) the date of appointment of the administrator is taken.

- In the case of extortionate credit transactions the time period is calculated back from the day on which the administration order was made or the company went into liquidation (s244(2)).

> ▶ A company is in liquidation when (s247):

  - In a compulsory liquidation – the court makes an order to wind up.
  - In a creditors' voluntary liquidation – the date of the resolution to wind up the company.

Note: You should ensure that you do not mix up these rules with the rules in personal insolvency.

Definitions

Connected person: A person is connected with a company if (s249):

▶ He is a director or shadow director of the company or an associate of such a director or shadow director.

▶ He is an associate of the company.

Associate: A person is an associate of an individual if that person is the individual's husband or wife or civil partner, or is a relative, or the husband or wife or civil partner of a relative, of the individual or the individual's husband or wife or civil partner (s435).

A person is an associate of any person with whom he is in partnership, and of the husband or wife or civil partner or a relative of any individual with whom he is in partnership.

A person is an associate of any person whom he employs or by whom he is employed.

A person in his capacity as trustee of a trust is an associate of another person if the beneficiaries of the trust include, or the terms of the trust confer a power that may be exercised for the benefit of, that other person or an associate of that other person.

A person is an associate of another company:

If the same person has control of both, or a person has control of one and persons who are his associates, or he and persons who are his associates, have control of the other, or

If a group of two or more persons has control of each company, and the groups either consist of the same persons or could be regarded as consisting of the same persons by treating (in one or more cases) a member of either group as replaced by a person of whom he is an associate.

A company is an associate of another person if that person has control of it or if that person and persons who are his associates together have control of it.

References to husband or wife include former husband or wife and a reputed husband and wife and references to a civil partner include a former civil partner.

Summary and self-test

Summary

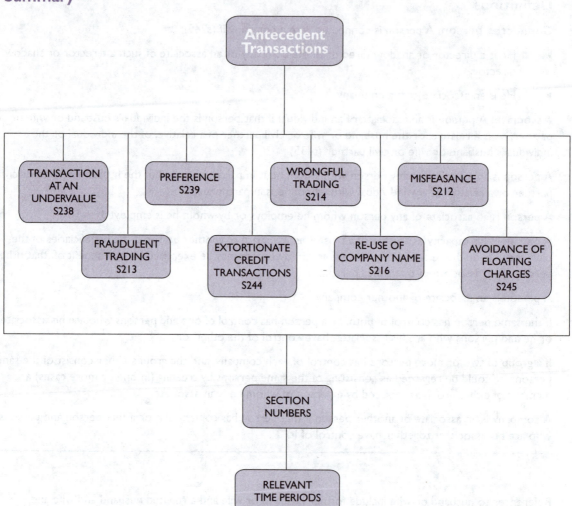

Self-test

Answer the following questions.

1   What is the definition of a transaction at an undervalue?

2   What is a relevant time for a transaction to be challenged as an extortionate credit transaction?

3   What is the definition of a preference?

4   What are the main differences between an action for fraudulent and wrongful trading?

5   What is wrongful trading?

6   Who may be found guilty of fraudulent trading?

7   What steps should a director take to avoid a claim of wrongful trading?

8   Give an example of behaviour by a director that may be construed as a misfeasance.

9   What is a prohibited name?

10   What are the restrictions imposed by s216?

Now, go back to the Learning Objectives in the Introduction. If you are satisfied that you have achieved these objectives, please tick them off.

Answers to self-test

1   A transaction at an undervalue (s238) is one where there has been:

▶   A gift (where no consideration has been received by the company) or

▶   The value received by the company is significantly less in money or money's worth than it ought to have received.

The company must have been insolvent at the time of the transaction, or rendered insolvent due to it (where recipient of the transaction is a connected party, insolvency is presumed).

The transaction must have taken place at a relevant time, within two years of the commencement of the winding-up.

There is a defence, that the transaction was entered into in good faith, it was carried out for the purpose of the company's business and there were reasonable grounds for believing it would benefit the company.

2   The relevant time for an extortionate credit transaction is three years, whether the parties are connected or unconnected.

3   The person preferred must be a creditor, guarantor or surety. The company must have been influenced by a desire to put that creditor, guarantor or surety in a better position in the event of insolvent liquidation than they would otherwise have been. (The desire to prefer is assumed if the parties are connected.)

The preference must have been given at a relevant time, within six months of the onset of insolvency (or two years where the parties are connected).

The company must have been insolvent at the time of the preference or rendered insolvent by it.

4

Fraudulent trading s213	Wrongful trading s214
Also a criminal offence – s993 CA 06	Not criminal offence
Civil liability	Civil liability – compensatory orders
Subjective test	Objective test minimum
Actions against any persons who are a party to the fraud	Action against directors and shadow directors only
Applies in solvent and insolvent liquidations	Applies only in insolvent liquidations

5   Where the company has gone into insolvent liquidation and at some time before the commencement of the winding-up of the company the director knew or ought to have concluded that there was no reasonable prospect that the company would avoid going into insolvent liquidation, the director may be found guilty of wrongful trading under s214.

There is a defence that the director took every step with a view to minimising the loss to creditors.

6   Any persons who were knowingly parties to the carrying on of the company's business in a fraudulent way may be found guilty of fraudulent trading. This means that directors are not the only parties who may be liable, creditors, shadow directors, senior employees, administrative receivers and administrators may also be found liable.

7   Steps to take to avoid a claim for wrongful trading include:

-    Consulting with bankers early.

-    Preparing up to date management accounts and ensuring prompt filing of statutory accounts.

-    Consulting professional advisers.

-    Making cash payments to avoid dissipation of assets.

-    Avoiding last ditch hazardous action to save the business.

-    Avoiding making supplies to creditors who may exercise a right of set off.

-    Refine the company's overheads. Deal only in cash.

-    Document any decision to continue to trade, supporting the decision with reference to ongoing trading.

-    Avoid taking new credit.

-    Resignation is not an appropriate step.

8   Misapplying, retaining or becoming accountable for any money or other property of the company.

Being guilty of any breach of fiduciary or other duty, ie:

-    An unlawful loan made by a company to a director of itself or its holding company.

-    A director entering into a contract with his own company and failing to notify the board of directors at the next board meeting or failing to seek prior approval for the contract in general meeting where it is a substantial property transaction.

9   A prohibited name is any name by which the liquidating company was known in the last 12 months or which is so similar to such a name that it suggests an association with the liquidating company.

10   S216 provides that anyone who was a director or shadow director of a company in the 12 months ending with the day before it went into insolvent liquidation is prohibited, for a period of five years, from being:

-    A director of a company known by a prohibited name

-    In any way concerned, directly or indirectly in the promotion, formation or management of such a company or in the carrying on of business under a prohibited name.

Answer to interactive question

Interactive question: Painters Ltd

(i) Sale of stock to B Green Limited:

This could be challenged as a transaction at an undervalue s238. In order to be successful the liquidator would have to show:

- ▶ The value received by the company was significantly less in money or money's worth than it ought to have been.

- ▶ The company was insolvent, or became insolvent as a result of the transaction taking place (where transaction is with a connected person insolvency is presumed).

- ▶ The transaction took place at a relevant time.

Here, stock with a book value of £75,000 has been sold for £28,000. This appears to be considerably less than it was worth, however, further enquiries would need to be made to confirm the valuation of the stock at the date of sale. It may have become obsolete or have been damaged during storage and its low value would then be appropriate.

Because B Green Limited is a connected company (the director's wife is a director of B Green Ltd), insolvency at the date of the transaction is presumed.

The relevant time for a connected party transaction is within two years of the onset of insolvency. Here the transaction took place on 11 November 09 which was within three months of the commencement of the liquidation.

There is a defence, that the transaction was entered into in good faith and was carried out for the purpose of the company's business and there were reasonable grounds for believing that it would benefit the company. The liquidator would have to interview the directors to see if the defence applies in this case.

If the action is successful the court can make an order restoring the position to what it would have been if the transaction had not been entered into.

The liquidator could also take an action against the directors for misfeasance (s212). They could be ordered to make a personal contribution towards the company's assets.

(ii) Sale of asset and repayment of debt to Barbery Supplies Limited:

This could be challenged as a preference under s239. In order to be successful the liquidator would have to show:

- ▶ The person preferred must be a creditor, guarantor or surety.

- ▶ The company must 'do anything' or 'suffer anything' to be done which puts that creditor, guarantor or surety in a better position in the event of insolvent liquidation than they would otherwise have been in.

- ▶ The company must have been influenced by a desire to prefer (presumed if the parties are connected).

- ▶ The transaction must have taken place at a relevant time.

Here, the debt owed to Barbery Supplies Limited has been paid in full.

The liquidator must show that the company 'desired' to prefer Barbery Supplies Limited. The companies do not appear to be connected so desire will not be presumed. Desire could be refuted if Burbery Supplies Limited had made a demand for repayment, or threatened to take action for the recovery of their debt or if other creditors were repaid in full at that time.

The relevant time for a preference to an unconnected company is within six months of the onset of liquidation. This transaction took place within that time.

If successful, the court can make an order restoring the position to what it would have been if the transaction had not occurred.

(iii)   Creation of floating charge:

This could be challenged under s245.

A floating charge on the company's undertaking or property is invalid except to the extent of the aggregate of any fresh consideration given for it.

The creation of the floating charge must have been within the relevant time period. In the case of a charge which is created in favour of a person who is not connected with the company, within 12 months of the onset of insolvency.

If the liquidator is able to prove that the floating charge is invalid, the assets covered by the charge can be claimed, security free, for the benefit of the estate.

Here, the charge was created at a relevant time. The liquidator must make enquiries to see whether fresh consideration has been provided for the loan.

9

The Asset Protection Regime

> > > > > > > > > > > > > > >

Contents

Introduction

Learning objective

To understand the detailed rules in compulsory and voluntary liquidation relating to:

Tick off

▶   Litigation against the company

▶   Execution

▶   Distress

▶   Post commencement dispositions

Working context

At the time that a liquidator is appointed it is likely that a number of the company's creditors will be seeking to recover their debts, for example, the liquidator may be required to deal with a landlord who is attempting to distrain for unpaid rent. It is therefore important to understand the statutory rights of both the liquidator and the creditors in such circumstances.

Stop and think

Why should a creditor be prevented from taking enforcement action against a company in liquidation? What is distress? Why are some post petition dispositions allowed when others are not?

Examination context

This is an important topic which is often tested in the JIEB exam. Whilst it is unlikely that the topics covered in this chapter will be tested in their own right in a question, they often form part of any question relating to the practical aspects of liquidation, for example, matters to be dealt with immediately upon appointment by the liquidator. It is important to understand the rules outlined in this chapter and how matters are dealt with differently in a compulsory and voluntary liquidation.

Exam requirements

Past exam questions to look at include:

1 The Asset Protection Regime

Section overview

▶ The ultimate objective of the statutory provisions making up the asset protection regime is to protect the interests of creditors generally. To this end the rules both:

— Seek to preserve the company's assets (to ensure that as much value as possible is eventually available for distribution) and

— To further the principle of *pari passu* distribution (this is the principle that all creditors of the same class should rank equally in winding-up)

▶ The asset protection regime is stricter and the rules more complex in the case of compulsory liquidation.

1.1 Risks for assets

The assets of a company are at risk of being dissipated either by:

▶ The company voluntarily making dispositions of its assets. An example of this would be directors causing a company to pay off an ordinary unsecured creditor in full, or sell company assets for less than their open market value.

▶ Third parties such as creditors exercising statutory, common law, contractual or other rights against the company's property. Examples of this would include:

— A landlord distraining against the company's property for arrears of rent.

— A creditor who has obtained a judgement against the company levying execution against the assets of the company.

— A creditor alleging ROT rights repossessing stock from the warehouse of the company.

The rules seek to control both of these broad categories of risk to the company's estate. Notice that some of the examples given above may result in a reduction in asset values, whilst others (eg the directors causing the company to pay an unsecured creditor in full) would only breach the *pari passu* principle.

2 Actions or proceedings (litigation) against the company

Section overview

A creditor may seek to take action against the company, for example a creditor seeking to enforce a retention of title claim against the company.

2.1 The position in compulsory winding-up

Between the presentation of the petition and the granting of the winding-up order:

▶ There is no automatic stay of proceedings so creditors can continue with any action against the company.

▶ However, s126(1) allows the company, any creditor or contributory to apply to the court for an order to stay or restrain any action or proceedings against the company.

▶ Where a s126(1) application is made depends on the court in which the litigation is pending:

- If in the High Court or Court of Appeal – application should be made to that court

- If in any other court the application should be made to the court having jurisdiction to wind-up the company.

Post winding-up order:

▶ S130(2) provides that once a winding-up order has been made no action or proceeding shall be proceeded with or commenced against the company or its property.

▶ This provision is also triggered by the appointment of a provisional liquidator.

▶ S130(2) is subject to the leave of the court which can impose conditions. Leave will usually be refused where the dispute can with equal convenience and less delay and expense be decided in the liquidation proceedings themselves (*Re Exchange Securities and Commodities Ltd and Others (1983.*).

▶ It follows that the court's function on applications for leave is to decide where the dispute is best dealt with, rather than to inquire into the merits of the dispute itself.

2.2 The position in voluntary winding-up

S126(1) and s130(2) do not apply. There is no automatic stay on proceedings, and no court discretion. Actions and proceedings against the company may therefore be commenced/continued.

A liquidator may be able to persuade a litigant to take no further steps in relation to an action, whilst the matter is dealt with in the normal course of the winding up. The liquidator has power to compromise claims against the company (sanction of the liquidation committee is required).

Failing which the liquidator (or any creditor or contributory) can apply to the court under s112. The court can exercise any of the powers which it could exercise in winding-up by the court, and this would include staying any proceedings.

3 Execution

Section overview

Execution or attachment refers to the situation where a creditor of a company is seeking to use the enforcement mechanism of the court to obtain repayment of a debt. The court will issue a judgement in respect of the debt if the action is successful and execution is the action taken in respect of the judgement.

S183(3) execution or attachment are completed on the happening of one of the following events:

▶ Against goods by seizure and sale or by the making of a charging order under s1 of the Charging Orders Act 1979.

▶ Attachment of a debt by receipt of the debt.

▶ Against land by seizure, appointment of a receiver or making of a charging order under s1 of the Charging Orders Act already mentioned.

3.1   The position in compulsory winding-up

Execution pre-commencement of winding-up:

A creditor who completes execution prior to commencement may retain the benefit of that execution s183.

Definition

Commencement: A compulsory winding-up is deemed to commence on the date of the petition to wind up the company.

A voluntary winding-up is deemed to commence on the date of the passing of the resolution to wind up (s86).

If execution is not completed by commencement the creditor is not entitled to retain any assets seized and may be required by the liquidator to hand such assets over.

The court has power to set aside the provisions of s183 in favour of the creditor to such extent and subject to such terms as the court thinks fit.

A third party buying goods through an Enforcement Officer's sale will always acquire good title (even if the execution falls foul of s183) providing the third party acted in good faith. The Enforcement Officer refers to the court official whose duty it is to administer the court's enforcement procedures.

S184 imposes a number of duties on the Enforcement Officer. The purpose of these provisions is to facilitate the operation of s183 and to try to ensure that where executions on goods are not 'completed' prior to commencement, that the goods or sale proceeds are preserved for the company and are available to be clawed-back by the liquidator. The duties are as follows:

▶ Where notice is served on the Enforcement Officer that a provisional liquidator has been appointed or a winding up order made the Enforcement Officer shall (on being required to do so) deliver goods and any money seized or received in part satisfaction to the liquidator. The costs of execution are, however, a first charge on goods/monies handed to the liquidator.

▶ Whenever execution is levied in respect of a judgement for £500 or more the Enforcement Officer is to retain the proceeds for 14 days (after deducting his costs). If within those 14 days the Enforcement Officer is notified of the presentation of a petition he must pay the balance to the liquidator.

▶ Again the court has power to set aside the provisions of s183 in favour of the creditor.

Execution post commencement of winding-up:

▶ Under s128(1) any attachment or execution put in force against the estate or effects of the company after commencement is void.

▶ The section makes no mention of any power of the court to give leave, but case law suggests that leave could be given in appropriate circumstances (*The Constellation* 1966). An application could be made to the court by a creditor under s126(1) or s130(2) .

3.2   The position in a voluntary winding-up

S183 and s184 do apply in a CVL as well as in a compulsory liquidation. A creditor will have to complete execution by the date of the resolution to wind up at the latest. However this date will be earlier where a creditor has notice of the GM at which a resolution to wind-up will be passed. SIP 8 points out the usefulness of circulating the notice of the GM with the notice of the s98 meeting so as to bring forward the date by which executions must be completed to the date of that notice.

S128 does not apply in a CVL. Execution could be continued with however the liquidator could apply under s112 to the court for the action to be stayed.

Interactive question: Midland Industries Ltd

You were appointed liquidator of Midland Industries Ltd on 1 September 2009 at a s98 meeting of the company's creditors.

As part of your investigations you discover that one of the company's creditors, B Wilde Ltd, received judgement against Midland Industries Ltd for the non payment of a debt to the value of £19,500. The judgement was given by the court on 18 August 2009.

The Enforcement Officer issued execution against the property of Midland Industries Ltd on 21 August 2009 and sold the goods at public auction on 22 August 2009, receiving a reasonable market value for the goods.

Requirement

What, if anything, can you do in respect of this action by the Enforcement Officer? Include in your answer any references to statutory action you can take and the reasons for taking it.

See **Answer** at the end of this chapter.

4 Distress

Section overview

Distress is the process whereby landlords seek to recover unpaid rent by seizing the company's assets. This is a common law remedy available to landlords and does not require the intervention of the court.

4.1 The position in a compulsory winding-up

Two rules need to be considered when looking at the position of a landlord in a compulsory winding-up.

S128 provides that in a compulsory liquidation distress 'put in force' against the estate or effects of the company after commencement is void. A landlord cannot validly distrain for arrears of rent after the date of petition. (There is no equivalent, therefore, of the rule in bankruptcy which allows a landlord to distrain post-commencement but only for six months rent accrued due pre-commencement.)

A creditor could apply for leave to distrain to the court, despite the fact that the section makes no express references to such applications.

S176 provides that where any person has distrained against the goods or effects of the company in the three months prior to the winding up order goods/effects/sale proceeds are charged for the benefit of the company with the preferential debts of the company to the extent that the company's property is for the time being insufficient for meeting those preferential debts.

The practical effect of the rule is that landlords and others who have distrained during the three month period may be required to surrender the benefit of distress to the liquidator.

S176(3) says that such a creditor would then in turn rank as preferential to the extent of their surrender or payment to the liquidator. The effect of this rule is to constitute this creditor as a separate class of preferential creditor ranking below the general body of 'preferential creditors', but above other unsecured creditors.

Worked example

A landlord takes walking possession of some machinery at a factory on 1 February. A petition is presented on 7 February. The machinery is sold on 14 February. A winding-up order is made on 1 March.

Solution

The distraint is 'put in force' on 1 February.

S128 does not apply as the distraint was put in force prior to the date of the 'commencement'. Therefore the distraint is not void.

S176 will apply, however, as the distraint is within three months of the date of the winding-up order. If the assets of the company are insufficient for the time being to meet preferential claims the liquidator will be able to clawback the proceeds of the sale on 14 February for the benefit of preferential creditors.

The purpose of the overlap between the two rules is therefore to catch distraint commenced prior to the petition date, but not completed until post-petition.

4.2 The position in a voluntary winding-up

Neither s128 nor s176 apply in a CVL.

There is no restriction therefore on distress in a voluntary winding up. (Statutory forms of distress requiring the courts assistance may be affected by s183 and s184).

The liquidator may be able to persuade the distraining creditor to hold off failing which application may be made to the court under s112.

4.3 CRAR

Students should be aware that Part 3 of The Tribunal Courts and Enforcement Act 2007 (entitled 'Enforcement by Taking Control of Goods') abolishes the common law remedy of distress and replaces it with Commercial Rent Arrears Recovery (CRAR). Like distress, CRAR allows recovery of rental arrears by taking possession of goods belong to the tenant to cover the amount of arrears.

At the time of going to print, Part 3 of The Tribunal Courts and Enforcement Act 2007 has not yet come into force and it is not yet clear when it will do so, and so the provisions outlined in this manual remain effective.

5 Post commencement dispositions

Section overview

A disposition will include:

▶ Payments out of the company's bank account
▶ Payments into an overdrawn bank account (*Re Grays Inn Construction*)
▶ Payment to a creditor
▶ Sales of assets for less than their market value

5.1 The position in a compulsory winding-up

S127 states that dispositions of company property made after the date of presentation of petition are void unless the court otherwise orders.

Post petition transfers of shares, or alteration in a members' status, are also void subject to the same proviso.

The rule creates a potentially serious practical problem for the directors of the company. At the time of presentation of the petition it will not be certain whether or not a winding-up order will be eventually made on that petition. If it is made however s127 will operate retrospectively to avoid all post petition dispositions.

S127 may, therefore, have the practical effect of paralysing a company's trading.

S127 does not apply where an administrator petitions the court to bring the administration to an end and simultaneously make a winding up order.

Application may be made to the court by the company itself or by other interested parties such as a creditor or creditors to exempt a transaction or a class of transactions from the effect of s127 should the winding-up order be made. The application should be made prior to the winding up order being made.

The general principle is that transactions will only be validated which are not likely to have the effect of reducing the assets available to the creditors (*Re Grays Inn Construction*).

The following cases illustrate the principle:

▶   In *Re A Company (no 007523 of 1986)* Court refused to validate payments out of company's bank account in the ordinary course of business as the company was making losses and trading on was therefore unlikely to benefit the creditors.

▶   In *Re Web Electrical* Harman J gives three examples of where a validation order may be made.

    –   '... perhaps to enable the company to obtain supplies on a contract which looked profitable. ...

    –   '... to pay wages which would have had to be paid in any event even though above the subrogation level permitted'

    –   '... or in some way properly and responsibly paid out under threat of a winding up petition with a *bona fide* view to the assistance of the company.'

▶   Where a company in compulsory winding up is solvent (eg on a just and equitable petition) the court will usually make an order validating all payments made in the ordinary course of business.

▶   In *SA and D Wright Ltd etc 1992*. The court validated payment of arrears made to a supplier to maintain supplies essential for trading on.

▶   In *Re French's Wine Bar 1987*. The case involved the court validating a sale of leasehold property. If the sale is at arm's length and for value there will not be any prejudice to creditors. Where the contract has been entered into prior to the petition the disposition may be seen as having taken place pre-commencement (even though completion will not take place until after commencement) so that s127 does not apply. However in most cases it will be prudent to apply to the court for sanction in any event.

5.2   The position in a voluntary winding-up

S127 does not apply in a voluntary liquidation.

Summary and self-test

Summary

Asset Protection	Compulsory Winding-up	CVL
Litigation against the company	S126 – between Petition and Order – company/creditor/ contributory can apply for a stay S130 – from the Winding-up Order/Appointment of a Provisional Liquidator – "no action/proceeding shall be proceeded with/commenced", subject to leave of the court	S126 and s130 do not apply – ie actions/proceedings can continue/commence though: ▶ Liquidator can compromise claims (with sanction of the Liquidation Committee) and ▶ S112 applies – the liquidator (or creditor or contributory) can apply to court to request exercise of the powers the court has in compulsory wind-up
Execution	S128 – execution put in force post commencement (petition) is void S183 – Creditor can retain benefit of execution completed prior to commencement S184 – the High Court Enforcement Officer has various duties re handing over monies to a liquidator	S128 doesn't apply though liquidator can apply under s112 as above S183 and s184 do apply though "commencement" is: ▶ Date of resolution ▶ Although, notice of GM can be substituted
Distress	S128 – Distress put in force post commencement (petition) is void S176 – Proceeds of distress from distress completed within three months prior to the Order are subject to the prefs to the extent that the estate is insufficient	S128 and s176 do not apply – ie no restriction on levying distress, though: ▶ If court involvement is required – s183 and s184 apply and ▶ S112 applies as above
Post commencement dispositions	S127 – dispositions of assets post commencement (petition) are void … and any transfer of shares or alteration in the status of the company's members	S127 does not apply. In CVL the members'/creditors' liquidator is in place already S88 – similar provisions re shares/status – void without sanction of liquidator

Self-test

Answer the following questions.

1   S184 deals with the duties of the Enforcement Officer. If the High Court Enforcement Officer receives proceeds exceeding £500 following an execution from sale or payment to avoid sale, for what period must he hold the proceeds?

2   Any disposition of property is void (unless ratified by the court) if it takes place between what dates?

3   How may an execution be completed per s183?

4   The landlord of the trading premises of Barley Wines Ltd took walking possession of some machinery on the company's premises on 8 June 2009. A petition for the compulsory liquidation of the company was presented by a creditor on 15 June 2009. The machinery was sold by the landlord on 18 June 2009 and a winding up order was made on 30 June 2009.

Requirement

Write a letter to the liquidator of Barley Wines Ltd advising him what, if any, action he may take in respect of the action taken by the landlord and specifically whether the machinery or proceeds of sale may be recovered for the benefit of the company's creditors.

5   A creditor wishes to take action against a company in order to recover a debt. He believes that the company may soon be placed into compulsory liquidation but does not know if a petition has been presented or not.

Requirements

(a)   If action is commenced by the creditor, how will he be affected by the compulsory liquidation of the company?

(b)   Would your answer be any different if the company had been placed into creditors' voluntary liquidation rather than compulsory liquidation?

6   You are assisting the directors of ABC Ltd in placing the company into creditor's voluntary liquidation. Notices of the s98 meeting have been posted to all creditors and the meeting is due to be held in one week's time. You have just received notification from the directors that the HM Revenue and Customs have obtained walking possession over a considerable amount of the assets of the company in respect of VAT arrears which have arisen over the last 12 months. They are threatening to remove the assets and sell them at auction next week.

Requirement

What, if anything, may be done in respect of the action taken by HM Revenue and Customs?

7   A winding up petition was presented against Gregg and Sons Ltd on 24 September. The directors were unsure how to react to the petition and carried on trading the company, making a number of payments out of the company's bank account. Your principal was subsequently appointed liquidator of the company and has asked you to review the records of the company.

Requirement

What are the general principles of law regarding payments made by a company after the presentation of a petition to wind up the company has been presented? Give examples of the type of payments which are likely to be validated.

Now, go back to the Learning Objective in the Introduction. If you are satisfied that you have achieved this objective, please tick it off.

Answers to self-test

1   14 days

2   Between the date of the presentation of the petition and the date of the winding up order.

3   Against goods – by seizure and sale or by the making of a charging order.
    Attachment of a debt – by receipt of the debt.
    Against land – by seizure or appointment of a receiver or making of a charging order.

4   Letter format (marks are always awarded for layout and style, these are easy marks to obtain in the exam).

    S128 – landlord cannot validly distrain for arrears of rent after the date of the petition to wind up the company (14 June). Here, landlord distrained on 8 June, prior to the petition, therefore the distraint is valid.

    However, because the distraint is within three months of the date of the winding up order (30 June) s176 will apply. The liquidator has the power to claw back the proceeds of sale for the benefit of the preferential creditors where the assets of the company are insufficient to meet the preferential claims.

    The landlord may be required to surrender the benefit of the distress to the liquidator. He would then rank as preferential to the extent of his surrender or payment to the liquidator. He would form a separate class of preferential creditors, ranking below the general body of preferential creditors but above other unsecured creditors.

5   (a)   A compulsory liquidation has two parts – the presentation of a petition to wind up the company and the making of a winding up order.

          (i)   There is no automatic stay of proceedings after a petition has been presented, so the creditor will be able to continue with any action against the company. However, s126 allows any creditor, the company or any contributory to apply to the court for an order to stay or restrain any action or proceedings against the company.

          (ii)   Once a winding up order is made, no action or proceedings shall be commenced or proceeded with against the company or its property (s130).

          In order to succeed in his action, the creditor must complete his action before the presentation of the petition, or his action may be stayed.

    (b)   In a voluntary winding up s126 and s130 do not apply, there is no automatic stay of proceedings therefore the creditor will be able to continue his action against the company. The liquidator may however persuade the creditor to take no further action or he can apply to court under s112. The court can exercise any of the powers which it could exercise in a winding up by the court, and this would include staying any proceedings.

6   HM Revenue and Customs have a statutory right to obtain walking possession in respect of arrears of VAT. Neither the directors nor the office holder have any authority to prevent them exercising their distraint, however the directors should be advised to talk to HM Revenue and Customs and try to get them to agree to refrain from taking action until after the liquidator has been appointed (the liquidator may then apply to court under s112 for the action to be stayed).

7   S127 states that dispositions of the company's property made after the date of the presentation of a petition are void unless the court orders otherwise.

    Dispositions will include:

    ▶   Payments out of the company's bank account
    ▶   Payments into an overdrawn bank account.

An application to court to validate a payment may be made by the company or other interested parties such as the creditor and should be made prior to the winding up order being made.

The general principle is that transactions will only be validated which are not likely to have the effect of reducing assets available to the creditors *Re Grays Inn Construction*. Payments must be made *bona fide* and in the ordinary course of the company's business and must not prejudice the interests of the ordinary unsecured creditors.

Payments made to a secured or preferential creditor (where in the liquidation they would have been paid anyway) would normally be validated *(Re Clifton Place Garage Ltd 1969)*.

Where the transaction is post the presentation of the petition but does not dissipate the company's assets ie the sale of an asset at full price.

Payments to pay wages which would have to be paid in any event, or payments made under threat of a winding up petition with a *bona fide* view to the assistance of the company *(Re Web Electrical)*.

The court will validate payment of arrears made to a supplier to maintain supplies essential for trading on *(SA and D Wright Ltd)*.

Answer to interactive question

Interactive question: Midland Industries Ltd

This is a voluntary winding up (we know this because of the reference to the s98 meeting of creditors). S128 will not apply, any action taken by the Enforcement Officer will not be automatically void. The liquidator could apply to the court under s112 asking it to void the execution from the commencement of liquidation. It is unlikely that this would be successful as it is a debt validly owed to B Wilde Ltd and to allow them to continue with their legal right of enforcement of a court judgement would not unduly prejudice the company's preferential creditors.

S183 states that if a creditor completes execution prior to commencement he may retain the benefit of that execution and the liquidator will be able to take no action in respect of it. Completion will be by seizure and sale (and the proceeds of sale being passed to the creditor) and commencement is the date of the passing of the resolution to wind up the company.

Here, the liquidation commenced on 1 September. While the goods were sold prior to this on 22 August, the execution is not complete because the Enforcement Officer will not yet have passed the proceeds to the creditor. This is because s184 provides that if execution is levied in respect of a judgement of £1,000 or more, the Enforcement Officer must retain the proceeds for 14 days (ie until 5 September). If, within this time, he is notified that a winding up resolution has been passed, he must pay the balance (after deduction of his costs) to the liquidator. The Enforcement Officer should have been served notice of the members' meeting at which the resolution to wind up was to be passed and this would have had the same effect.

The liquidator should ensure that the relevant notices were issued and if not, serve notice of his appointment on the Enforcement Officer immediately.

10

Proof of debts

> > > > > > > > > > > > > > > >

Contents

Introduction

Learning objectives

▶   Identify which debts are provable and those which are not

▶   Understand the difference between proving for voting and dividend purposes

▶   Understand the duties of an office holder when rejecting a claim

▶   Understand the statutory requirements when making dividend payments to creditors

▶   Learn the priority of payments from funds in the hands of the liquidator

Working context

Dealing with creditors' claims is an important part of the office holder's role. Creditors have to submit proofs of debt in order to vote at s98 meetings of creditors and to rank for dividend payments. It is therefore important to understand the statutory requirements when dealing with creditors' claims.

Stop and think

Why are creditors required to formally claim in a liquidation? Why would the liquidator have to reject a creditor's claim? Why are there detailed rules regarding the payment of funds to creditors?

Examination context

The agreement of creditors' claims and the payment of dividends are popular topics in the JIEB exam, not just in the Liquidations paper. You should know not only the statutory rules but also how to apply them in practice.

Exam requirements

Past exam questions to look at include:

2008	Question 3
2007	Question 1(b)
2007	Question 2(b)
2006	Question 1(a),(b)
2006	Question 2(c)
2004	Question 2
2004	Question 3(d)
2002	Question 3)c), (d), (e)
2001	Question 3(c)
2001	Question 4(c)
2001	Question 5(b)
2000	Question 2
1999	Question 3(b)
1998	Question 1(d)
1998	Question 2
1998	Question 4 (II)
1998	Question 5 (I)(a)
1997	Question 5
1996	Question 1(b)
1996	Question 3(b)
1994	Question 3(b)
1993	Question 1
1993	Question 5(a)
1991	Paper II, Question 2(b)
1990	Paper II, Question 1(b)(2)

1 Provable debts

Section overview

▶ A creditor establishes his right to vote at meetings of creditors and his right to a dividend by submitting a proof of debt form. It is for the liquidator to decide whether or not the creditor has established his right to be treated as a creditor within the provisions of the Act and Rules.

▶ The rules re the treatment of proofs in liquidation are very similar to the rules in bankruptcy.

1.1 Debts for which a creditor can prove

Debts are defined in r13.12, as being:

▶ Any debt or liability to which the company is subject at the date on which it goes into liquidation.

▶ Any debt or liability to which the company may become subject after that by reason of any obligation incurred before that date.

▶ Any interest on the above provable under r4.93(1).

R13.12(2) makes it clear that liabilities in tort are provable, providing the cause of action accrued prior to the company going into liquidation.

R13.12(3) states that it is immaterial whether the debt or liability is:

▶ Present or future
▶ Certain or contingent
▶ Fixed or liquidated or is capable of being ascertained by fixed rules or as a matter of opinion.

Definition

Liability: A liability to pay money or moneys worth (r13.12(4)) including any liability:

▶ Under any enactment
▶ For breach of trust
▶ In contract
▶ In tort
▶ In bailment
▶ Arising out of an obligation to make restitution.

All claims by creditors are provable, whether present or future, certain or contingent, ascertained or sounding only in damages.

1.2 Debts which are not provable

R12.3(2)(b) applies to both bankruptcy and liquidations:

▶ Any obligation arising under a confiscation order made under s1 of the Drug Trafficking Offences Act 1986 or s71 of the Criminal Justice Act 1988.

▶ Certain claims under the Financial Services and Markets Act 2000 are only provable once all other creditors have been paid in full.

2 Proof of debt

Section overview

In a compulsory liquidation the liquidator must send a proof of debt form to every creditor. In a voluntary liquidation the creditor's proof may be in any form.

Definitions

Prove: A creditor who claims (whether or not in writing) is referred to as 'proving' for his debt (r4.73).

Proof: A document by which a creditor seeks to establish his claim.

2.1 Contents of a proof of debt

The contents of the proof are:

▶ The creditor's name and address. *(or co registration no)*

▶ The total amount of his claim as at the date when the company went into liquidation. *date of bankruptcy order in PI.*

▶ Whether or not that amount includes outstanding uncapitalised interest.

▶ Whether or not the claim includes VAT.

▶ Whether the whole or any part of the debt is preferential and if so which part.

▶ Particulars of how and when the debt was incurred by the company.

▶ Particulars of any security held, the date when it was given and the value which the creditor puts upon it.

▶ The name, address and authority of the person signing the proof if other than the creditor himself.

ROT ?

3 Voting rights and proxies

Section overview

Under r4.67 a creditor is only entitled to vote at a meeting of creditors if:

▶ There has been duly lodged a proof of debt

▶ There has been lodged, by the time and date stated in the notice of the meeting, any proxy requisite for that requirement.

3.1 Proving for voting and dividend purposes

These must be distinguished for two reasons:

▶ Future Debts. These need to be discounted in accordance with r11.13 for dividend, but not for voting, purposes.

▶ Unspecified Debts:

– For voting purposes r4.67(3) provides that a creditor shall not vote on such debts unless the Chair agrees to put upon the debt an estimated minimum value. A similar rule applies to bankruptcy, both types of voluntary arrangement, Administration and Administrative Receivership.

CVA £1 or agreed.

– For dividend purposes r4.86 provides that the liquidator **shall** estimate the value of any debt which by reason of its being subject to a contingency or for any other reason does not bear a certain value. This rule also applies in bankruptcy.

A secured creditor is entitled to vote only in respect of the balance of his debt after deducting the value of his security as estimated by him.

In a voluntary liquidation it is at the chairman's discretion to allow a creditor to vote.

Votes are calculated according to the value of the creditor's debt at the date of the meeting.

The creditor bears the cost of proving his own debt. The liquidator may, if he feels it is necessary, require a creditor to verify his proof by affidavit.

A creditor's proof may at any time, by agreement between himself and the liquidator, be withdrawn or varied as to the amount claimed.

3.2 Proxy forms

If a creditor does not wish to attend the meeting in person, he may submit a proxy form giving another person, or the Chair, the power to vote on his behalf. The proxy may be general, allowing the proxy holder to vote at his discretion, or specific, specifying that the proxy holder should vote in a certain way.

Proxies used for voting at any meeting must be retained by the Chair of the meeting.

The proxies may be inspected by persons attending the meeting.

SIP 10 is concerned with the completion of proxy forms.

When sending out proxy forms with notices convening any insolvency meeting no details of any person should be pre completed.

The title of the proceedings may be pre completed together with details of the title and venue for the meeting.

3.3 Admission and rejection of proofs for voting purposes

R4.70 gives the Chair the power to admit or reject a creditor's proof of debt for the purposes of his entitlement to vote. This decision is subject to appeal to the Court by any creditor or contributory.

If the Chair is in doubt whether a proof should be admitted or rejected, he should mark it as objected to and allow the creditor to vote, subject to his vote subsequently being declared invalid if the objection to the proof is sustained.

3.4 Entitlement to vote – contributories

At a meeting of contributories, votes are as at a general meeting of the company, subject to any provisions in the articles affecting entitlement to vote, either generally or at a time when the company is in liquidation (r4.69).

Interactive question: Joseph Jester Ltd

On 16 October 2009, the shareholders of Joseph Jester Ltd passed a Special Resolution to wind up the company because it could not by reason of its liabilities continue its business. The notice convening the creditors meeting under s98 required proxies and proofs of debt to be lodged by 12 noon on 30 October 2009. Joseph Jester Ltd is a subsidiary of Joseph Jester (Holdings) Ltd.

Requirements

You have been asked to advise the Chairman of the meeting on whether the following claims should be admitted for voting purposes and if so, the amount for which they should be permitted to vote.

(a)   Peter Jones trading as Red Brick Materials attended the meeting in person as the sole proprietor of the business, bringing with him a Proof of Debt in the sum of £9,650. No proxy form was lodged.

(b)   James Greig, a partner in Greig & Somers attended the meeting in person bringing with him a Proof of Debt for £6,220 and a general proxy in his favour.

(c)   The landlord of the company's trading premises faxed a special proxy in favour of a nominated insolvency practitioner for his appointment as sole Liquidator, which arrived by 10.30 a.m. on 30 October 2009. This followed the earlier submission of a general proxy in favour of the Chairman of the meeting, together with a Proof of Debt form in the sum of £192,000 representing the 18 years unexpired on the current lease, in addition to arrears of rent of £12,000. The lease provided for no rent reviews even though rental levels were expected to increase throughout the duration of the lease. The trading premises are in very good state of repair, whilst the open market rental is likely to be at least £30,000 per annum which is the rental already contracted for by an incoming tenant.

(d)   Fairbrother Woodsmith Ltd lodged by the stipulated deadline, a general proxy in favour of the Chairman of the meeting, together with a Proof of Debt form in the sum of £15,450 due on a Bill of Exchange. Persons previously liable on the Bill of Exchange include a UK clearing bank.

(e)   Chester Jobb Ltd had issued a general proxy in favour of the Chairman of the meeting, together with a Proof of Debt form in the sum of £26,750. The Proof of Debt form confirmed that Chester Jobb Ltd had obtained a judgement in support of its full debt in August 2009 and had instructed the Court Enforcement officer to levy execution over the company's chattel assets, which was undertaken on 20 October 2009. The value of the unsold chattel assets levied over by the Court Enforcement officer were valued at £21,650.

(f)   Gary Rochester, a shareholder in the company, lodged a Proof of Debt form for £16,000 and attended the meeting in person without lodging a proxy form. His claim, which is disputed by the company, is based upon damages which he believes he has incurred as a result of misleading information given to him by the company when he was asked to subscribe to an additional issue of shares in September 2009.

(g)   Biggins Bank Ltd lodged a Proof of Debt form for £120,000 plus interest at 4% above base rate from 30 June 2009, together with a general proxy in favour of Jim Smith, its local branch manager. The Proof of Debt arises from a 'Letter of Comfort' given to Biggins Bank Ltd in respect of an associated company which has since entered into compulsory liquidation. The 'Letter of Comfort' stated that Joseph Jester Ltd would make arrangements to meet the associated company's commitments to the Bank if the associated company was unable to meet them itself. (NB: base rate is 7½% per annum)

(h)   Samuel Squires Ltd lodged a special proxy in favour of a named insolvency practitioner for his appointment as sole Liquidator and a Proof of Debt form for £58,950 in respect of monies (principal only) lent to Joseph Jester Ltd. Samuel Squires Ltd holds a first legal charge over the freehold property of Joseph Jester (Holdings) Ltd which is valued at £97,000.

(i)   HM Revenue and Customs lodged a Proof of Debt form (but not in the format sent out with the notice convening the meeting) totalling £33,270 of which £16,000 is estimated to rank as preferential. A local VAT officer attended the Meeting of Creditors without a form of proxy having been lodged.

See **Answer** at the end of this chapter.

4 Rules relating to special cases

Section overview

It is often necessary for a creditor's proof to be amended for the purposes of paying a dividend.

4.1 Debts payable in a foreign currency

Amount of the debt must be converted into sterling at the official exchange rate on date when the company went into liquidation.

A company 'goes into liquidation' when it passes a resolution to wind up voluntarily, or the presentation of the petition once a winding-up order is made.

The official exchange rate is the Bank of England mid-market rate (if no such rate, such rate as the court shall determine).

4.2 Discounts (R4.89)

Generally the creditor must deduct any discounts that would have been available to the company but for its liquidation. However discounts for early, immediate or cash settlement do not need to be deducted.

4.3 Payments of a periodical nature (R4.92)

In respect of claims for payments of a periodical nature, eg rent (other than under a formal lease agreement), the creditor proves for amounts due and unpaid up to the date when the company went into liquidation.

Where on the date of the order any payment was accruing due, the creditor claims 'for so much as would have fallen due at that date, if accruing from day to day'.

In respect of claims made by landlords:

▸ Claims for arrears of rent and/or service charge may be admitted in full.

▸ A claim for rent payable in advance for a period 'straddling' the date on which the company went into liquidation should be admitted in full.

▸ Claims for dilapidations and future rent are unspecified and must be estimated (and the landlord will have a duty to mitigate his loss). The House of Lords gave judgement in *Re Park Air Services plc* on 4 February 1999.

The Lords held that the landlord's compensation is measured by reference to the difference between the rents and other payments which the landlord would have received in future, but for any disclaimer and the rents and other sums which the disclaimer would enable the landlord to receive by re-letting.

Though allowance would have to be made for accelerated receipt, this would not be under r11.13. The rationale for this was that the landlord's entitlement was not a right to a future payment, but a present right to immediate payment.

The appropriate discount rate was held to be the yield on gilt-edged securities for an equivalent term from the date of the disclaimer.

4.4   Secured Creditors (R4.88)

Secured creditors can prove in three situations:

▶ The creditor realises the security and proves for the balance.

▶ The creditor proves for the whole debt by voluntarily surrendering his security for the general benefit of creditors.

▶ The creditor estimates the value of the security in his proof and proves for the unsecured balance.

  – If the security is subsequently realised the original valuation is substituted for that shown in the proof (r4.99).

  – If the liquidator disagrees with the value put on the security he can require the security to be realised (r4.98). Terms will be set by the court in default of agreement, if property auctioned – liquidator and creditor can both bid.

▶ If the creditor fails to disclose his security in the proof he must surrender that security.

  Exception – If court provides relief on grounds that the omission 'was inadvertent or the result of honest mistake'.

▶ The creditor can revalue the security given in the proof:

  – With the court's permission in the case of compulsory winding-up if he petitioned or voted with unsecured balance.

  – With either the court's or the liquidator's permission in any other case.

▶ The liquidator may redeem the security at the value given in the proof (costs of transfer will be payable out of the assets). He must give 28 days' notice to creditor. The creditor now has 21 days in which to revalue the security. If the creditor revalues the liquidator can now only redeem at that new price. The creditor can by written notice, force the liquidator to decide in a period of six months whether he will or will not redeem.

4.5   Negotiable Instruments (R4.87)

Proofs in relation to money owed on these must be accompanied by the instrument or a certified copy.

4.6   Double Proof

Where a debt has been guaranteed the creditor and the guarantor (surety) may not both prove in the liquidation of the company for the same debt. The general rule is that the primary creditor should prove in the proceedings.

4.7   Set-off   *allowed*

R4.90 – The rule applies where before the company goes into liquidation there have been mutual credits, mutual debts or other mutual dealings, between the company and any creditor.

R4.90(2) – an account shall be taken of what is due from each party to the other in respect of the mutual dealings and the sums due from one party shall be set-off against the sums due from the other (and only the balance can be proved for).

R4.90(3) – Sums due from the company to the creditor are not however to be included in the account if the creditor had notice that, in a CVL, a meeting of creditors had been summoned under s98, or, in a compulsory winding up, that a petition for the winding-up of the company was pending at the time.

R4.90(4) – Only the balance of the account taken under r4.90(2) can be proved for or needs to be paid to the liquidator.

The Rules that relate to administration and liquidation have been revised and new Rules substituted:

- R2.85 and r4.90

  The substituted Rules are designed to provide greater detail and clarity of meaning for the user to reflect the applicable case law and bring the rule on set-off for liquidation into line with the rule in administration.

The main points to note are:

- 'Mutual dealings' that are not to be included in the set-off account are defined; these include any debt acquired by a creditor by way of an agreement entered into after one of the dates set out in r2.85(2)(e) and r4.90(2)(d). If a creditor acquires, or re-acquires, a debt after one of those dates, as a result of an agreement entered into at an earlier date, then such a debt would be considered a 'mutual dealing' for the purposes of the set-off account.

- Set-off in liquidation proceedings and administration proceedings are harmonised so that all amounts due to and from a company are 'mutual dealings' to be included in, or excluded from, the set-off account, as applicable.

- The provision of a meaning for the term 'sums due' drawing on the definition of 'debts or liability' in r13.12(3):

  - For the purposes of calculating the set-off account, the Rules which relate to the quantification of debts (r2.81, r2.86 to r2.88, r2.105, r4.86, r4.91 to r4.93 and r11.13) are extended to cover debts owed to a company, as well as debts owed by a company. Accordingly, debts owed to the company that are contingent or payable at a future time are to be included in the set-off account and liquidators and administrators will be able to place a value on such debts.

  - R2.78 and r4.83 provide the means of appeal if a mutual third party disagrees with an administrator's or liquidator's valuation of a debt that a third party owes to a company:

  - Where, after the calculation of the set-off account an amount is owed to the company arising from a contingent debt or a debt payable at a future time, such an amount only has to be paid to the liquidator or administrator if and when it becomes due and payable.

Case Law

D H Curtis (Builders) Ltd 1978 – Claims do not have to arise out of contract to be set off against each other.

Lister v Hooson 1908 – Claims must have been incurred in the same right.

Nat. West Bank Ltd v Halesowen Presswork and Assemblies Ltd – Parties may not contract out of r4.90.

Re E J Morel – A creditor must set off rateably against all debts owed (ie against preferential and ordinary debts rateably).

4.8 Foreign tax

Article 39 of the EC Regulations on Insolvency Proceedings 2000 provides that any creditor who has habitual residence, domicile or registered office in a Member State other than the state opening the proceedings, including the tax authorities, shall have the right to lodge claims in insolvency proceedings.

As a result, EU tax is therefore provable. Other foreign taxes are not provable (*Government of India v Taylor*).

4.9 Interest

Pre-commencement interest

R4.93 applies to interest arising before the company went into liquidation.

R4.93 states that where a debt proved in the liquidation bears interest, that interest is provable as part of the debt, except in so far as it is payable in respect of any period after the company went into liquidation.

The rate of interest under s189 is the greater of the rate specified by section 17 of the Judgements Act 1838 on the day on which the company went into liquidation and the rate applicable to that debt apart from the winding-up.

The rate of interest may be challenged under s244 as an extortionate credit transaction.

If the debt is due because of a written instrument and payable at a certain time, interest can be claimed from that time to the date of liquidation.

If the contract itself provides for payment of interest, the contractual rate of interest will apply (unless extortionate).

In all other cases interest will only be payable if the creditor serves a written demand for the payment of interest, stating that interest would be payable from the date of service of demand to the date of payment.

The rate of interest charged is again that in the Judgements Act 1838 unless the demanded rate of interest is lower in which case that will apply.

The rate currently specified in s17 of the Judgements Act 1838 is 8%.

Post commencement interest

S189 provides that interest is payable on any debt proved in the winding up.

S189(2) requires any surplus remaining after the payment of debts proved in the winding up to be applied in the paying of interest on those debts in respect of the period that they have been outstanding since the company went into liquidation. (S 328 (4))

The interest payable under s189 ranks equally even if the debts on which it is payable do not rank equally.

The rate of interest that is payable is the greater of:

▶   The rate specified in s17 of the Judgements Act 1838 on the day the company went into liquidation (currently 8%)

▶   The rate applicable to that debt apart from the winding up.

Late payment of commercial debts

The late Payment of Commercial Debts (Interest) Act 1998 (LPCD) gives businesses a statutory right to claim interest on the late payment of commercial debts by making the entitlement to interest an implied contractual term.

The LPCD applies to contracts for the supply of goods and services where both parties are acting in the course of business. It does not apply to consumer credit agreements, mortgages and charges.

The Act was brought fully into effect on 7 August 2002.

Interest under the LPCD runs from the day following the agreed date of payment, or if no agreed date, from 30 days after the supplier performs their obligation under the contract.

The rate of interest is 8% over the base rate in force on 30 June or 31 December immediately before the day on which the interest starts to run.

The interest will be provable up until the date the company goes into liquidation and the same rules for proving apply.

Parties cannot contract out of the LPCD unless there is a substantial contractual remedy for late payment of the debt.

4.10   Future debts

R4.94 refers to debts which are payable at a future time. These claims can be proved for but are subject to r11.13 in relation to discounting the amount due for the purposes of paying a dividend.

R11.13 provides a formula to calculate the percentage discount as follows:

$$\frac{x}{1.05^n}$$

Where x = amount of the debt

n = decimalised amount of time from the relevant date to the date the debt is due (relevant date is the commencement of liquidation).

4.11 Preferential creditors

Preferential creditors are paid in priority to other creditors out of floating charge assets.

Preferential debts comprise:

▶ All holiday pay without limit

▶ Wage arrears arising in the four months prior to the winding-up subject to a maximum preferential claim of £800.

5 Payment of dividends

Section overview

Whenever the liquidator has sufficient funds in hand for the purpose he shall, subject to the retention of such sums as may be necessary for the expenses of the winding-up, declare and distribute dividends among the creditors in respect of the debts which they have respectively proved (r4.180). The rules relating to the payments of dividends are found in Part II of the Rules.

5.1 Notice of intended dividend

The liquidator shall give notice of his intention to declare and distribute a dividend to all creditors whose addresses are known to him and who have not proved their debts (r11.2).

The notice must state a last date for proving (not more than 21 days from that of the notice) and that the liquidator will declare a dividend within four months from the last date for proving.

5.2 Final admission/rejection of proofs

The liquidator must, within seven days from the last date of proving, deal with every creditor's proof. If the liquidator wishes to reject a creditor's proof he should prepare a written statement detailing the reasons for rejecting the creditor's claim and send it to the creditor as soon as reasonably practicable (r4.82(2)).

5.3 Appeal against decision on a proof

If a creditor is dissatisfied with the liquidator's decision with respect to his proof, he may apply to the court for the decision to be reversed or varied (r4.83). The application must be made within 21 days of his receiving the statement sent under r4.82(2).

▶ The court will fix a venue for the application to be heard and notice must be sent by the applicant to the creditor who lodged the proof (if it is not himself) and to the liquidator

▶ On receipt of the notice the liquidator must file in court the relevant proof and his statement under r4.82(2)

▶ After the application has been heard and determined the proof will be returned to the liquidator by the court, unless it has been wholly disallowed.

5.4   Declaration of dividend

Within the four month period the liquidator must proceed to declare the dividend.

Where the liquidator has declared a dividend, he shall give notice of the dividend and of how it is proposed to distribute it; and a notice given under this subsection shall contain such particulars with respect to the company, and to its assets and affairs, as will enable the creditors to comprehend the calculation of the amount of the dividend and the manner of its distribution.

R11.6(2) provides a list of details which should be included in the notice of the dividend:

▶   Amounts realised from the sale of assets, indicating (so far as is practicable) amounts realised from the sale of assets.

▶   Payments made by the office holder in the administration of the insolvent estate.

▶   Provision, if any, made for unsettled claims and funds, if any, retained for particular purposes.

▶   The total amount to be distributed and the rate of dividend.

▶   Whether and if so when, any further dividend is to be expected.

R4.182 – in the calculation and distribution of a dividend the liquidator shall make provision:

▶   For any debts which appear to him to be due to persons who, by reason of the distance of their place of residence, may not have had sufficient time to tender and establish their proofs.

▶   For any debts which are the subject of claims which have not yet been determined.

▶   For disputed proofs and claims.

Liquidator may distribute property in specie (r4.183):

▶   This is where it cannot be readily or advantageously sold.
▶   Specific sanction of the liquidation committee is required.

5.5   Rights of creditors

A creditor who has not proved his debt before the declaration of any dividend is not entitled to disturb, by reason that he has not participated in it, the distribution of that dividend or any other dividend declared before his debt was proved, but

▶   When he has proved that debt he is entitled to be paid, out of any money for the time being available for the payment of any further dividend, any dividend or dividends which he has failed to receive.

▶   Any dividend or dividends payable under paragraph (a) shall be paid before that money is applied to the payment of any such further dividend (r4.182(2)).

R4.182(3) states no action lies against the liquidator for a dividend, but if the liquidator refuses to pay a dividend the court may, if it thinks fit, order him to pay it and also to pay, out of his own money interest on the dividend, at the rate for the time being specified in section 17 of the Judgements Act 1838, from the time it was withheld, and the costs of the proceedings in which the order to pay is made.

5.6   Unclaimed dividends

The liquidator must pay any unclaimed dividends into the Insolvency Services Account.

6 Rules of priority

Section overview

The Insolvency Act lays down the order of priority of payments from monies coming into the hands of the liquidator.

6.1 Order of payment

The order for payment of debts is as follows:

▸ The expenses of the winding-up, including the liquidator's remuneration (s115).

▸ The preferential debts, as defined by s386 and s387, and Schedule 6 (s175).

▸ Any preferential charge on goods distrained that arises under s176(3).

▸ The company's general creditors.

▸ Interest on creditors' claims outstanding for the period after the company went into liquidation (s189(3)).

▸ Any debts or other sums due from the company to its members as members, eg dividends or profits (s74(2)(f)).

▸ The members generally, in accordance with their respective rights and interests (s107).

Secured creditors are, in principle, entitled to be paid out of the proceeds of their security ahead of all other claims. However, remember that if the security is by way of a floating charge, the preferential debts in the liquidation must be paid first under s175(2)(b).

An Administrative Receiver appointed after the commencement of the winding-up will be liable to pay the liquidation expenses out of any assets subject to a floating charge before making any payment to the preferential creditors or the charge holder (unless the uncharged assets are sufficient to pay them in full) *Re Barleycorn Enterprises Ltd 1970*.

The statutory order for the application of assets cannot be varied by contract, except in the case of some arrangements in the financial markets.

R4.218 sets out the order of priority of the expenses of the liquidation.

Summary and self-test

Summary

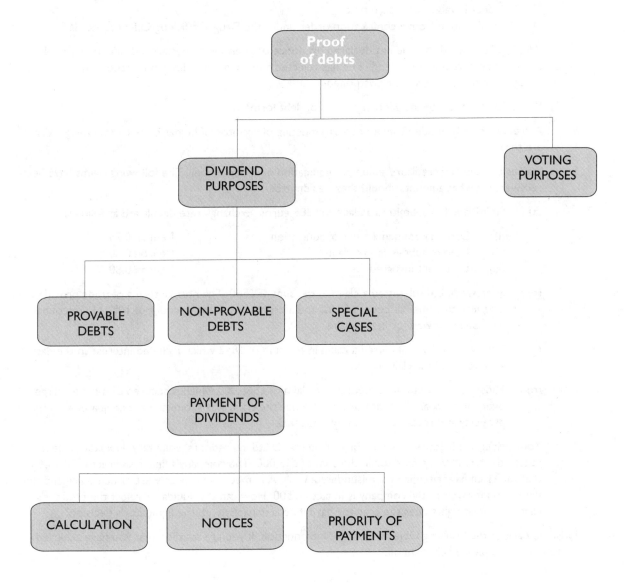

Self-test

Answer the following questions.

1   Which of the following is a provable debt?

    A   A fine imposed for a driving offence
    B   A claim for maintenance under Child Support Act 1991
    C   A debt payable at a future time
    D   An obligation from a confiscation order under the Drug Trafficking Offences Act 1986

2   Within what period after he has declared his notice of intention to declare a dividend may an IP cancel or postpone that dividend, if he has rejected a proof and application is made to the court for his decision to be reversed or postponed?

3   What details should be included in a proof of debt form?

4   A creditor is only entitled to vote at a s98 meeting of creditors if he has done certain things. What are they?

5   Staines Ltd entered creditors' voluntary liquidation on 9 September. The following claims have been received, for what amounts should they be admitted?

    (a)   Petit Blanc has submitted a claim for 385 euros. Exchange rate details are as follows:

(i)	Date of commencement of liquidation	1 euro:£0.75
(ii)	Date of submission of claim	1 euro:£0.60
(iii)	Date debt incurred	1 euro:£0.80

    (b)   Sportswide Ltd submitted a claim in the sum of £560. The normal terms of trade provided for a regular customer discount of 15% and a prompt payment discount of 10%. No discounts have been allowed for in the claim.

    (c)   J Brown Ltd have submitted a claim in the sum of £842 which included interest to the date of submission of the claim of £42.

    (d)   Midshires Bank Ltd have submitted a claim of £560,000 which is secured by a fixed charge over the company's trading premises. Since the claim was submitted the liquidator sold the property and received the sum of £385,000.

6   Your principal, Mr Jones, is liquidator of Fine Foods Ltd in creditors' voluntary liquidation. He has received a claim from a creditor in the sum of £15,000. The company's financial director advises you that the claim has arisen from a misunderstanding. A number of invoices were issued twice and the true amount owed to the company is in fact £8,500. How can the liquidator reject the creditor's claim and what rights does the creditor have if he is unhappy with the liquidator's decision?

Now, go back to the Learning Objectives in the Introduction. If you are satisfied that you have achieved these objectives, please tick them off.

Answers to self-test

1   C   A debt payable at a future time

2   Within four months from last date of proving.

3   The following details should be included in a proof of debt form (r4.75):

▶   The creditor's name and address

▶   The total amount of his claim as at the date when the company went into liquidation

▶   Whether or not that amount includes outstanding uncapitalised interest

▶   Whether or not the claim includes VAT

▶   Whether the whole or any part of the debt is preferential and if so which part

▶   Particulars of how and when the debt was incurred by the company

▶   Particulars of any security held, the date when it was given and the value which the creditor puts upon it

▶   The name, address and authority of the person signing the proof if other than the creditor himself.

4   Under r4.67, a creditor is only entitled to vote at a meeting of creditors if:

▶   There has been duly lodged a proof of debt

▶   There has been lodged, by the time and date stated in the notice of the meeting, any proxy requisite for that requirement.

5   (a)   Claim should be converted into sterling at the official exchange rate on the date the company went into liquidation.

385 euros @ £0.75/euro = £288.75

(b)   All regular discounts should be deducted but not a prompt payment discount.

£560 x 15% = £84 discount should be applied.

Accept claim for £560 – £84 = £476

(c)   Interest cannot be claimed for any periods after the company has entered liquidation. The claim for interest should be rejected.

Accept claim £842 – £42 = £800

(d)   A secured creditor can only claim for any unsecured balance of their claim. The sale proceeds should be deducted.

Accept claim £560,000 – £385,000 = £175,000

6   If the liquidator wishes to reject a creditor's proof he should:

(a)   Prepare a written statement detailing the reasons for rejecting the creditor's claim and send it to the creditor forthwith (r4.82(2)).

(b)   If the creditor is dissatisfied with the liquidator's decision they may appeal to the court within 21 days from receiving the statement (r4.83).

(c)   The court will fix a venue for the application to be heard and notice must be sent by the applicant to the creditor who lodged the proof (if it is not himself) and to the liquidator.

(d)   On receipt of the notice the liquidator must file in court the relevant proof and his statement under r4.83(4).

(e)   After the application has been heard and determined the proof will be returned to the liquidator by the court, unless it has been wholly disallowed.

Answer to interactive question

Interactive question: Joseph Jester Ltd

(a)   As an individual creditor there is no requirement for a form of proxy to be lodged.

Providing there is no reasonable doubt over the identity of Peter Jones, his vote should be admitted by the Chairman in the sum of £9,650.

(b)   Greig & Somers is a partnership and thereby bound like companies by the requirement to lodge a form of proxy by the time and date stipulated in the notice convening the meeting.

The Chairman would be entitled to reject the proxy for voting purposes.

(c)   In the case of *Re Cardona (1997)* the Court held that the term 'proxy' meant simply the authority given, whether general or specific, and it would be absurd if a principal's authority could not be altered in the light of changing circumstances

In the case of *Re A Debtor No. 2001 (1995) and 2022 (1995)* (which related to an Individual Voluntary Arrangement) the Court held that a faxed proxy was valid if it bore upon it some distinctive or personal marking which had been placed there by or with the authority of the creditor. Chapter 8 of the Insolvency Rules 1986 applies to all Creditors' meetings governed by the Insolvency Act 1986 and Insolvency Rules 1986.

A creditor should mitigate its loss and in this instance the open market rental is at least three times the value of the rental reserved by the lease. Over the 18 years, the landlord will be able to profit from the demise of the company by £360,000.   .

The premises are in a good state of repair, thereby facilitating the immediate re-letting to the incoming tenant without dilapidation expenditure.

The Chairman should be advised to admit the landlord for voting purposes for the arrears of rent of £12,000 only.

(d)   Following the principle established under Rule 4.87 Insolvency Rules 1986, and if not already provided, the Chairman should be advised to call for the Bill of Exchange or a copy of it, certified by the Creditor or his authorised representative to be a true copy.

Under Rule 4.67(5) Insolvency Rules 1986, the liability of persons prior to Joseph Jester Ltd are to be treated as security held by Fairbrother Woodsmith Ltd provided that person has not become bankrupt or gone into Liquidation. Because a UK clearing bank is previously liable, then Fairbrother Woodsmith Ltd holds security for the full £15,450.

Because the value of the security is deducted from the Proof of Debt for voting purposes, the Chairman should be advised to reject the vote of Fairbrother Woodsmith Ltd.

(e)   In accordance with s184(3) the Enforcement Officer will be obliged to hold the net proceeds of sale for a period of 14 days because the judgement exceeds £500.

Under s184(4) the Enforcement Officer will presumably have been notified of the shareholders' meeting to pass a Special Resolution for Winding-up and the fact that such a resolution was passed prior to the Creditors' meeting held under s98 of the Insolvency Act 1986.

The Execution is invalid against the Liquidator (unless the Liquidator's rights are subsequently set aside by the Court) and hence Chester Jobb Ltd should not be treated as a secured creditor.

The Chairman should be advised to allow Chester Jobb Ltd to vote for the full amount of its claim in the sum of £26,750.

(f)   The debt due to the shareholder is not one due in his capacity as a Member. The claim (whereby Membership was a qualification for acquiring it) is not based upon the statutory contract between members and the company and hence membership is not the formulation of the cause of action. Accordingly, the claim should not be excluded as a debt under s74(2)(f).

The Chairman should, where in doubt due to the company disputing the claim, mark the proof as objected to, but allow the shareholder to vote for the full amount of its claim of £16,000 subject to such a vote being subsequently declared invalid if the objection to the proof is sustained.

(g)   A person who receives a Letter of Comfort is not a creditor of the author of that letter (*Re Atlantic Computers plc 1995*).

No contractual obligation exists where the statement was 'an expression of present intention by way of comfort only'.

The Chairman should be advised to reject the Proof and proxy for voting purposes.

(h)   Samuel Squires Ltd holds security over the property of a third party (ie Joseph Jester (Holdings Ltd) rather than the property of Joseph Jester Ltd to secure its debts (*Tager v Westpac Banking Corporation*).

Samuel Squires Ltd is not obliged to treat the legal charge as security for the purposes of voting in respect of Joseph Jester Ltd and the Chairman should be advised to admit the claim to vote for £58,950.

(i)   It is accepted that duly appointed officers of the Crown are entitled to vote on behalf of their relevant Crown department without lodging a form of proxy.

A Proof of Debt may be in any form (r4.73(6) of the Insolvency Rules 1986).

Preferential status is irrelevant in terms of voting entitlement and the Chairman should allow the local VAT officer to vote for £33,270.

Remuneration

> > > > > > > > > > > > > > > > >

Contents

Introduction

Examination context

Topic List

Introduction

Learning objectives

▶ Identify the statutory provisions relating to the calculation and approval of office holder's fees ☐

▶ Identify what information is to be provided to those responsible for the approval of fees ☐

▶ Understand the statutory provisions relating to the disclosure and drawing of disbursements ☐

▶ Understand what the Schedule 6 scale is and how it is applied in practice ☐

Working context

In all aspects of insolvency, at whatever grade you work at, you will be required to maintain a record of your working hours and details of expenses incurred. An insolvency practitioner is entitled to receive remuneration for his services when acting in any insolvency role. It is important therefore to know the rules for governing the calculation of remuneration (outlined in SIP 9) and who is charged with approving requests for remuneration.

Stop and think

Why are creditors responsible for agreeing office holder's remuneration? Why does the payment of certain expenses require approval? What information should be disclosed to creditors when an office holder takes remuneration?

Examination context

Office holder's remuneration is a very practical topic which could be tested in any of the three JIEB papers. It is important to understand the basis of calculation of remuneration and who determines and approves the office holders' remuneration.

Exam requirements

Past exam questions to look at include:

2006   Question 4(b)(iii)
2004   Question 3
1997   Question 2(d)
1997   Question 5(b)

1 Remuneration

Section overview

Office holders are entitled to be remunerated for work which they undertake, however the source of funds to pay the remuneration is the assets of the company which would otherwise be available for the benefit of creditors. It is important therefore that those with a direct financial interest in the level of office holders' fees should feel confident that the rules relating to the charging of remuneration have been properly complied with and that sufficient information about the basis of fees should be made available so that informed judgements can be made about remuneration levels.

The statutory provisions relating to the remuneration of office holders are set out in The Insolvency Rules 1986:

R4.127(1)   CVLs and Compulsories
R4.148A(1)   MVLs

1.1 SIP 9

SIP 9 sets out provisions regarding the remuneration of all office holders, liquidators, administrators, administrative receivers, trustees in bankruptcy and supervisors of individual and company arrangements.

SIP 9 ensures that office holders are familiar with the statutory provisions regarding remuneration and covers, amongst others:

▶ On what basis remuneration is to be calculated.
▶ What criteria should be used to judge the reasonableness of fees.
▶ Who should authorise the drawing of fees.
▶ What an office holder can do if he is dissatisfied with the level of fees.

The SIP also includes a series of pro-forma guidance notes which can be made available to creditors and which summarise their rights under insolvency legislation.

1.2 Basis of liquidator's remuneration

The liquidator's remuneration may be calculated on two bases, either (r4.127):

▶ A % of the value of assets which are realised or distributed or both, or
▶ By reference to the time properly given by the office holder and his staff in attending to matters arising in the insolvency.

The office holder cannot use a combination of the two bases.

In a CVL and compulsory liquidation it is for the liquidation committee to decide which basis is to apply (if there is no committee, a general meeting of creditors).

In a MVL, a general meeting of the members will determine the liquidator's remuneration.

If no determination is made the relevant statutory scale will apply. In liquidations which commence on or after 1 April 2004 the scale will be that set out in Schedule 6 to the Insolvency Rules. Essentially this is the same as 'the OR scale'. In pre 1 April 2004 cases the OR scale will continue to apply and this is set out below.

	Realisations	Distributions
First £5,000	20%	10%
Next £5,000	15%	7½%
Next £90,000	10%	5%
Balance remaining	5%	2½%

plus.

Sch 6

plus – r 4.127A(2)

The IP should always attempt to obtain the agreement of the relevant body (committee, general meeting etc) before claiming Schedule 6 scale remuneration, and should not claim Schedule 6 remuneration on an interim basis before obtaining agreement.

In determining the mode (and if appropriate the relevant %) the committee or general meeting should take the following factors into account:

▶ Complexity or otherwise of the case.

▶ Any responsibility of an exceptional kind or degree which falls on the office holder.

▶ The effectiveness with which the office holder appears to be carrying out, or has carried out, his duties.

▶ The value and nature of the property which the office holder has to deal with.

Liquidators selling secured assets can deduct remuneration on the same basis as the OR (or as agreed with the charge holder) would out of proceeds before paying the balance to the secured creditor.

Joint liquidators should decide between themselves an apportionment of remuneration failing which the court or the committee/general meeting can decide.

If the liquidator is a solicitor whose own firm does legal work on behalf of the company, the profit costs must be authorised by the committee, general meeting or court.

1.3 Dissatisfaction with decision on fees

If the liquidator is dissatisfied with the level of fees he can request an increase by resolution of the creditors.

If the creditors are not forthcoming appeal lies to the court with notification to the committee (or if none, to such creditors as the court directs).

If a creditor is dissatisfied, any creditor can apply to the court on the grounds that the remuneration is excessive, but must be backed by 25% by value of the creditors. The applicant counts towards the 25%.

The court now has a choice:

▶ To set venue, or

▶ To dismiss the application. It can only do this if it has first allowed the applicant to make representations *ex parte* on seven days' notice.

A disincentive to such applications is that costs are to be paid by the applicant unless the court orders otherwise.

The liquidator gets 14 days' notice and a copy of any evidence which the applicant intends to use in support of the application.

2 Provision of information

Section overview

▶ SIP 9 sets out best practice with regards to the provision of information to those responsible for the approval of fees.

▶ The office holder must ensure that those charged with approving his fees have access to sufficient information about the basis of fees to be able to make an informed judgement as to the reasonableness of the proposed fees when:

    – Seeking approval to the terms of remuneration
    – Seeking approval to fees to be taken.

▶ The guidance given in SIP 9 relates to all insolvency appointments not just liquidations.

2.1 Seeking agreement to the terms of remuneration

When agreement is sought as to the terms on which the office holder is to be remunerated, he should provide the meeting with details of the charge out rates of all grades of staff which are likely to be involved in the case.

Before any resolution is passed to fix the remuneration, the office holder should send to the creditors the appropriate SIP 9 Appendix C explanatory note or provide the equivalent information in some other suitable format .

S98 notices should state that resolutions regarding remuneration and costs may be taken at the meeting. Directors convening s98 meetings should be advised of this requirement. If this advice is given orally and not accepted by the directors, it should be confirmed in writing.

2.2 Content of SIP 9 Appendix C guidance note

The SIP 9 Appendix C guidance note contains the following information:

▸ Explanation that costs are payable out of assets, therefore creditors have a direct interest in cost/ remuneration levels. Consequently, legislation provides a mechanism for creditors to fix fees

▸ Brief description of the nature of the insolvency appointment

▸ Brief description of the constitution and function of the committee (not VA's).

▸ Explanation of:

▸ Basis of fees

▸ Criteria to be applied

▸ Who is responsible for deciding on the basis and amount of remuneration

▸ Information which should be provided by the office holder

▸ Rights of creditors if dissatisfied

▸ Rights of office holder if dissatisfied.

2.3 Seeking agreement to fees during the course of winding-up

When agreement to fees is sought the office holder should provide an up to date receipts and payments account.

Where fees are based on a time cost basis, the office holder should disclose details of time spent and charge out values and such additional information as may reasonably be required having regard to the size and complexity of the case. The additional information should form a sufficient explanation of what the office holder has achieved and how it was achieved to enable the value of the exercise to be assessed (while recognising that the performance of certain statutory duties might be seen to add no value for creditors).

The nature and extent of the supporting information which should be provided will depend on:

▸ The nature of the approval being sought.
▸ The stage during the administration of the case at which it is being sought.
▸ The size and complexity of the case.

The information would include an analysis of time spent on the case by activity and grade of staff. Appendix D of SIP 9 sets out a suggested format for producing the information required. This suggested format classifies work functions as follows:

▸ Administration and planning
▸ Investigations
▸ Realisation of assets
▸ Trading
▸ Creditors
▸ Case specific matters.

The table classifies the hours spent on those functions by grade of staff as follows:

- Partner
- Manager
- Other senior professional
- Assistants and support staff.

The degree of analysis should be proportionate to the size and complexity of the case.

2.4 Sub contracted work

Where fees are based on a percentage basis, the office holder must provide details of any work which has or is to be sub contracted out which would normally be carried out by the office holder.

2.5 Provision of information after fee approval

Where a resolution fixing the basis of fees has been passed before the office holder has substantially completed his functions he should:

- Notify the creditors of the details of the resolution in his or her next report or circular, and

- In subsequent reports specify the amount of remuneration drawn in accordance with the resolution.

- (As earlier) information on time costing and additional information should also be provided where relevant.

Generally sufficient information should be provided to allow the creditors to decide whether or not to challenge the amount of remuneration as excessive.

Where an office holder is appointed on or after 1 April 2005, under Regulation 36A they are required to provide certain information about the time spent on a case, free of charge, upon request. The persons who are entitled to ask for this information are:

- Any creditor in the case.
- Where the case relates to a company, any director or contributory, of that company.
- Where the case relates to an individual, that individual.

The information to be provided is:

- The total number of hours spent on the case by the office holder or staff assigned to the case.
- For each grade of staff, the average hourly rate at which they are charged out at.
- The number of hours spent by each grade of staff in the relevant period.

The information must be provided within 28 days of receipt of the request by the office holder.

2.6 Payments received from secured creditors

Where the office holder realises an asset on behalf of a secured creditor and receives remuneration out of the proceeds, he should disclose the amount of that remuneration to the committee, to any meeting of creditors convened for the purposes of determining his fees and in his report to creditors.

2.7 Official receiver (OR)

Where the OR is the office holder in a compulsory winding-up or bankruptcy and the order was made after 1 April 2004, the OR scale will no longer apply and he will be entitled to a flat rate administration as follows:

Bankruptcy	£1,715
Liquidation	£2,160

In addition the OR is entitled to revised hourly rates for work on the case.

3 Expenses and disbursements

Section overview

SIP 9 sets out best practice with regard to the disclosure and drawing of expenses and disbursements.

▶ All disbursements should be disclosed.
▶ Category 1 disbursements do not require approval.
▶ Category 2 disbursements require approval.

3.1 Disclosure

Office holders should disclose and explain how charges are made up and the basis upon which they have been calculated. They should be disclosed to those responsible for approving remuneration, that is, the creditors' committee or the general body of creditors.

3.2 Category 1 disbursements

Approval is not required for the drawing of Category 1 disbursements.

These comprise specific expenditure relating to the administration of the insolvency case and which are paid to an independent third party.

They generally comprise external supplies of incidental services specifically identifiable to the case. Examples include: identifiable telephone calls; postage; case advertising; invoiced travel; properly reimbursed expenses of personnel in connection with case and services specific to the case which cannot be provided internally such as printing, room hire and document storage.

3.3 Category 2 disbursements

Category 2 disbursements should be approved. They represent costs which, while being in the nature of expenses or disbursements include elements of shared or allocated costs.

The office holder can make a separate charge for such expenses providing they are incidental in nature, directly incurred on the case and the method of identification and calculation is reasonable (ie in line with cost of external provision).

The basis of the charge must be disclosed.

Examples given include room hire, routine/specialist copying/printing, allocated communication costs provided by the practitioner or his firm, any disbursements where payment is to be made to an associate and any disbursements where the liquidator is being paid on the statutory scale.

3.4 Priority of liquidation costs – Leyland Daf

Section overview

It had been believed that liquidation expenses were payable out of the proceeds of a floating charge in priority to the floating charge holder *(Re Barleycorn Enterprises Ltd)*, however the House of Lords gave judgement on 4 March 2004 in the appeal against the Court of Appeals decision in *Re Leyland Daf Ltd* and overturned the two decisions of the court on this issue.

3.5 Re Barleycorn Enterprises Limited 1970

The court held that the costs of a winding up were payable out of property comprised in a floating charge (which had crystallised when the company was ordered to be wound up) in priority to the claims of the holder of the charge.

3.6   Leyland Daf Ltd

The ruling in Leyland Daf in 2004 altered the way in which liquidators of companies could attempt to recover the payment of liquidation expenses and pay the liquidation preferential creditors where the company had granted floating charges over assets.

If a company is in administrative receivership and liquidation its former assets are comprised in two separate funds. Those which are subject to the floating charge (the debenture holder's funds) and those which are not subject to the floating charge (the company's funds) which are held in trust for the unsecured creditors.

Expenses of the administrative receivership are borne by the debenture holder's funds and the expenses of the liquidation are borne by the company's funds. The debenture holder has no interest in the winding up and the unsecured creditors have no interest in the administrative receivership, so neither should bear each others costs.

It follows therefore, that where the company has granted a floating charge, the costs and expenses of liquidation rank after sums payable to both the preferential creditors and to holders of a floating charge and would not be payable ahead of the floating charge security.

If the liquidator realises an asset forming part of the debenture holder's fund, the debenture holder should pay the costs of realisation (*re Regent's Canal Ironworks Company 1875*) but the debenture holder should have no liability for the general costs of the winding up.

The House of Lords decision in *Leyland Daf* has been much criticised.

▸   The decision creates an anomaly in that administrators may pay their general costs and remuneration out of floating charge realisations (see para 99(3) of Schedule B1) whereas liquidators may not. This is odd because:

   –   Both administrations and liquidations are collective insolvency procedures.

   –   It is possible to convert from administration to liquidation and *vice versa*.

   –   The statutory provisions which apply to administrator's remuneration were modelled on the pre-*Leyland Daf* rules which, it was believed at the time, applied to liquidators ie. Parliament intended the rules applying to liquidation and administration to be the same.

   –   The decision potentially distorts the judgement as to whether a company is more suitable for administration than liquidation. Clearly in the light of the ethical guide an IP should make the judgement based on what is in the best interests of the creditors as a whole NOT on what insolvency procedure best facilitates the payment of his or her remuneration.

3.7   S1282 Companies Act 2006

The Companies Act 2006 introduced a new s176ZA into the Insolvency Act 1986 with the effect of reversing the decision in Leyland Daf so that a liquidator's general costs will be payable as of right out of floating charge assets in defined circumstances.

The Insolvency (Amendment) Rules 2008 came into force on 6 April 2008 and apply to:

▸   Compulsory liquidations where the winding up order was made on or after the commencement date.

▸   Voluntary liquidations where the resolution to wind up was passed on or after the commencement date.

The Rules introduce an amended r4.218.

The expenses of the liquidation are payable out of:

(a)   The assets held by the liquidator in the course of carrying out his functions in the liquidation.

(b)   The proceeds of any legal proceedings which he has power to bring or defend, whether in his own name or in the name of the company, and

(c)   Subject as provided below, properly comprised in or subject to a floating charge created by the company.

The general priority of the expenses are as shown in r4.218(1) with the following amendments:

(Ai)   are properly chargeable or incurred by the Official Receiver or liquidator in preserving, realising or getting in any of the assets of the company or otherwise relating to the preparation and conduct of any legal proceedings which he has power to bring or defend whether in his own name or the name of the company.

(s)   litigation expenses and property comprised in or subject to a floating charge.

Definitions

Litigation expenses: those expenses or costs of a liquidation which are properly chargeable or incurred relating to the preparation and conduct of any legal proceedings which a liquidator has power to bring whether in his own name or the name of the company.

Where the assets of a company available for the payment of general creditors are insufficient to meet them, litigation expenses shall not have the priority provided by s176 ZA over any claims to property comprised in or subject to a floating charge created by the company and shall not be paid out of any such property save and to the extent provided by rules 4.128B to 4.128E.

Where the assets will be insufficient to meet the payment of general creditors, the liquidator must seek prior approval or authorisation of such amount for litigation expenses as the liquidator thinks fit. Approval must be sought from relevant creditors or the court.

Relevant creditors: creditors whose claim is to property comprised in or subject to a floating charge out of which the liquidator is seeking to pay litigation expenses.

Definitions

A **shadow director:** (s214(7)) A person in accordance with whose instructions the directors are accustomed to act (s251).

A professional will not qualify as a shadow director by virtue only of providing advice.

M C Bacon – although a bank can be liable as shadow director it will not become liable merely by the making of demands to a customer as a condition of its further support. The degree of influence which the bank would need to exert over the company would have to go beyond that which is normal in a banker-customer relationship.

De facto **directors:** Includes a person who acts as a director but has no formal appointment as one – so this includes a person who gives instructions, takes executive decisions, gets involved in company strategy, etc. There is a big overlap here with a shadow director (as defined in s251).

A *de jure* **director:** A company officer who is, by law, a director, being appointed by the company to that position, appearing on the Register of Directors.

A 'non-executive' director attends board meetings but is not a full time employee of the company and does not generally participate in the day-to-day management of the company.

Interactive question: Somerset Fruits Ltd

Somerset Fruits Limited was placed into creditors' voluntary liquidation and at the s98 meeting of creditors Mr Mathews, a major creditor of the company, agreed to sit on the creditors' committee. The liquidator has recently written to Mr Mathews advising him that he would like to draw £10,000 on account of his fees and would like to defer formal agreement of his fees until all assets have been realised. Mr Mathews has contacted your office for some clarification as to the powers and duties of the committee in relation to the liquidator's fees.

Requirement

Write a letter to Mr Mathews advising him of the following matters:

(a)   The basis on which the liquidator's remuneration may be calculated.

(b)   What information the creditor's committee should expect to receive from the liquidator when seeking approval for his fees.

(c)   Whether the committee are required to authorise the liquidator's expenses in the same way.

See **Answer** at the end of the chapter.

Summary and self-test

Summary

Summary of rules re: office holders' remuneration

Procedure	Basis	Criteria	Authorised	IP dissatisfied
CVLs and compulsory liquidations	▸ % value of assets distributed or realised or both or ▸ time costing (r4.127(2))	▸ complexity ▸ responsibility of exceptional kind/degree ▸ effectiveness ▸ value and nature of assets (r4.127(4))	▸ liquidation committee (r4.127(3)) ▸ ... failing which a meeting of creditors (r4.127(5)) ▸ ... failing which the schedule 6 IR 1986 scale (post-1 April 2004 cases)	With determination of: ▸ committee – may apply to creditors (r4.129) ▸ committee or creditors or with Sch 6 scale may apply to court (r4.130) giving 14 days' notice to committee (or if none then to creditors)
MVLs	As for CVLs and compulsories (r4.148A(2))	As for CVLs and compulsories (r4.148A(3))	▸ the company in general meeting (r4.148A(3)) ▸ ... failing which the Schedule 6 IR 1986 scale (r4.148B) etc for post-1 April 2004 cases	With determination of company in GM or with Sch 6 scale – may apply to court giving 14 days' notice to contributories (r4.148A(6) and (7))

Self-test

Answer the following questions.

1   On what basis is a liquidator's remuneration calculated?

2   What factors should the creditors take into account when determining the basis of a liquidator's remuneration?

3   If a liquidator is dissatisfied with the level of his remuneration what can he do?

4   What is a Category 1 and Category 2 expense?

5   Give three examples of Category 1 expenses.

6   Give three examples of Category 2 expenses.

7   Assets have been realised in the liquidation of G Smith and Sons Limited in the sum of £48,500. Dividends totalling £32,000 have been made to date. Calculate the liquidator's remuneration based on the scale laid down in Schedule 6 Insolvency Rules 1986.

Now, go back to the Learning Objectives in the Introduction. If you are satisfied that you have achieved these objectives, please tick them off.

Answers to self-test

1   A liquidator's remuneration shall be fixed by either:

   ▶   A % of the value of assets which are realised or distributed or both, or

   ▶   By reference to the time properly given by the office holder and his staff in attending to matters arising in the insolvency.

2   Complexity or otherwise of the case.

   Any responsibility of an exceptional kind or degree which falls on the office holder.

   The effectiveness with which the office holder appears to be carrying out, or has carried out, his duties.

   The value and nature of the property which the office holder has to deal with.

3   He can request an increase by resolution of the creditors, or he can appeal to the court.

4   A Category 1 expense comprises specific expenditure which relates to the administration of the liquidation and which are paid to an independent third party. They do not require approval.

   A Category 2 expense requires approval. They represent costs which, whilst being in the nature of expenses or disbursements, include elements of shared or allocated costs.

5   Category 1 expenses:

   ▶   Identified telephone calls
   ▶   Postage
   ▶   Case advertising
   ▶   External provision of printing, room hire and document storage

   The above must all specifically relate to the case involved.

6   Category 2 expenses:

   ▶   Room hire
   ▶   Specialist copying/ printing
   ▶   Internal document storage, copying
   ▶   Allocated telephone costs

7   Realisation fee:

£	£
5,000 x 20%	1,000
5,000 x 15%	750
38,500 x 10%	3,850
48,500	5,600

   Distribution fee:

£	£
5,000 x 10%	500
5,000 x 7.5%	375
22,000 x 5%	1,100
32,000	1,975

   Total fee 5,600 + 1,975 = £7,575

Answer to interactive question

Interactive question: Somerset Fruits Ltd

Letter format

(a)   There are two basis on which the liquidator could calculate his fees:

(i)   A % of the value of assets which are realised or distributed or both, or

(ii)   By reference to the time properly given by the office holder and his staff in attending to matters arising in the insolvency.

The office holder cannot use a combination of the two bases.

If not fixed as above the liquidator's remuneration shall be in accordance with the Schedule 6 scale (formerly the OR's scale).

In a CVL it is for the liquidation committee to decide which basis is to apply (if there is no committee, a general meeting of creditors).

The committee should take the following matters into account when assessing the level of the liquidator's fees:

▶   The complexity or otherwise of the case.

▶   Any respects in which in connection with the winding up, there falls on the insolvency practitioner (as liquidator), any responsibility of an exceptional kind or degree.

▶   The effectiveness with which the insolvency practitioner appears to be carrying out, or to have carried out, his duties as liquidator.

▶   The value and nature of the assets with which the liquidator has had to deal.

Where the liquidator sells assets for a secured creditor, he is entitled to take for himself, out of the proceeds of sale, a sum by way of remuneration equivalent to that which is chargeable in corresponding circumstances by Schedule 6 scale.

(b)   The committee should expect to receive the following information:

▶   SIP 9 guidance 'A creditors' guide to Liquidator's fees'.

▶   An up to date receipts and payments account.

▶   Where fees are based on a time cost basis, the office holder should disclose details of time spent and charge out values and such additional information as may reasonably be required having regard to the size and complexity of the case. The additional information should form a sufficient explanation of what the office holder has achieved and how it was achieved to enable the value of the exercise to be assessed (while recognising that the performance of certain statutory duties might be seen to add no value for creditors).

The nature and extent of the supporting information which should be provided will depend on:

▶   The nature of the approval being sought.
▶   The stage during the administration of the case at which it is being sought.
▶   The size and complexity of the case.

The information would include an analysis of time spent on the case by activity and grade of staff. Appendix D of SIP 9 sets out a suggested format for producing the information required. This suggested format classifies work functions as follows:

▶   Administration and planning
▶   Investigations
▶   Realisation of assets

> ▸ Trading
> ▸ Creditors
> ▸ Case specific matters

The table classifies the hours spent on those functions by grade of staff as follows:

> ▸ Partner
> ▸ Manager
> ▸ Other senior professional
> ▸ Assistants and support staff

The degree of analysis should be proportionate to the size and complexity of the case.

(c)   All disbursements should be disclosed.

> ▸ Category 1 disbursements do not require approval
> ▸ Category 2 disbursements require approval.

The liquidator should disclose and explain how charges are made up and the basis upon which they have been calculated. They should be disclosed to those responsible for approving remuneration, that is, the creditors' committee or the general body of creditors.

Practical issues

> > > > > > > > > > > > > > > >

Contents

Introduction

Learning objectives

▶   Content of an IP case record

▶   Statutory requirements re bonding

▶   Rules regarding reporting to creditors and others

▶   Statutory rules re receipts and payments accounts

▶   Decision to continue trading

▶   Dealing with Retention of title (ROT) claims

▶   Dealing with claims by employees

▶   Matters to consider when selling assets to directors

▶   Liquidator's duties following administrative receivership

Working context

This is a very practical chapter and many of the topics covered will be relevant to you in a working environment. You may be asked to assist in the handling of employee claims or claims received by ROT creditors or preparing reports to creditors.

Stop and think

In what circumstances would a liquidator continue to trade a company? How often should a liquidator report to creditors? What is a receipts and payments account? What monies may be claimed by an employee of an insolvent company? What is an ROT clause?

Examination context

The JIEB exam is very practical, you need to show not only that you understand the law but that you can apply it in practice. The topics covered in this chapter are all relevant and should be learnt.

Exam requirements

Past exam questions to look at include:

2007	Question 3(d), (c), (f)
2006	Question 2(a)
2006	Question 1(d)
2003	Question 5
2003	Question 4(a)
2003	Question 3(b)
2001	Question 1
2000	Question 3(a), (b)
1999	Question 3(a)
1998	Question 3
1997	Question 2(c)
1995	Question 5
1992	Paper II, Question 3(b)
1992	Paper I, Question 4

1 IP Case Records

Section overview

The Insolvency Practitioners Regulations 2005 require the office holder to maintain records in respect of each case in which he acts. The records must be preserved by the office holder until whichever is the later of:

▶ The sixth anniversary of the date of the grant to the IP of his release or discharge in that case.

▶ The sixth anniversary of the date on which any security or caution maintained in that case expires or ceases to have effect.

The minimum records to be maintained by the office holder are set out in Schedule 3 of the Regs:

▶ The name of the practitioner
▶ The insolvency practitioner number
▶ The principal address of the practitioner
▶ The authorising body
▶ The name of the company in liquidation
▶ The progress of the liquidation
▶ Bonding arrangements in the case
▶ Matters relating to remuneration
▶ Meetings (other than any final meetings)
▶ Disqualification of directors
▶ Vacation of office
▶ Details of any distribution
▶ Details of the filing of statutory returns and accounts
▶ Time recording.

The records must be maintained in such a way as to be capable of being produced separately from any other record.

The records must be maintained for a period of six years from the date of the liquidator obtaining his release.

The records must be available for inspection by the authorising body.

The insolvency practitioner must notify the insolvency body of the place where the records are maintained.

2 Books and records

Section overview

▶ On appointment the liquidator should take into his control all of the company's books and records.

▶ Destruction of books and records may take place one year after dissolution of the company following closure (Reg 16 (2) IP Regs 1994).

Non essential papers may be destroyed during the course of the liquidation but only with the written consent of the liquidation committee, creditors or shareholders.

The office holder's estate files must be kept separate from the client files. The IP's own records must be maintained for six years.

Skeleton files (including key documentation relating to the liquidation) must be retained for 10 years following the closure of a case.

3 Bonding

Section overview

Schedule 2 Part 2 Insolvency Practitioners Regulations 2005 requires office holders to have in force a bond in a form approved by the Secretary of State which:

▶ Contains provision whereby a surety or cautioner undertakes to be jointly and severally liable for losses in relation to the insolvent caused by:

— The fraud or dishonesty of the IP whether acting alone or in collusion with one or more persons.

— The fraud or dishonesty of any person committed with the connivance of the IP.

▶ Otherwise conforms to the requirements of this Part.

The liquidator must hold:

▶ A general penalty sum of £250,000.

▶ A specific penalty sum equal to at least the value of the insolvent's assets as estimated by the IP at the date of his appointment but ignoring the value of any assets which are:

— Charged to a third party to the extent of any amount which would be payable to that third party

— Held on trust by the insolvent to the extent that any beneficial interest in those assets does not belong to the insolvent.

Up to a maximum specific penalty sum of £5,000,000.

Interactive question 1: Rolling Bones Ltd

You have just been appointed liquidator of Rolling Bones Ltd at a s98 meeting of creditors.

The Statement of Affairs shows the following details:

	£
Fixed charge assets	526,000
Fixed charge holder	495,000
Floating charge assets	362,000
Floating charge holder	215,000
Preferential creditors	48,000
Unsecured creditors	297,000

For what amounts should you bond?

See **Answer** at the end of this chapter.

4 Reports to creditors and shareholders

Section overview

In a CVL the liquidator must summon a general meeting of the company and a meeting of the creditors at the end of the first year from the commencement of the winding up and of each succeeding year, or at the first convenient date within three months from the end of the year. The Secretary of State may allow a longer period. (s105)

The liquidator must lay before the meetings an account of his acts and dealings and of the conduct of the winding up during the preceding year.

In a MVL, the liquidator is only required to report to the members.

5 Receipts and payments accounts

Section overview

A receipts and payments account is prepared by office holders to:

▶ Provide information to creditors and other interested parties.

▶ Fulfil statutory requirements under IA re submission of annual returns.

5.1 Format

Reports to members, creditors, committees and other interested parties should include in the body of the report, or by way of an annexe, details of the office holder's receipts and payments.

The receipts and payments account is a summary of all receipts and payments made by the office holder during the relevant period.

The procedure for preparing a receipts and payments account is the same for whatever purpose the account is being prepared.

The layout will be determined to some extent by the requirements on individual cases. SIP 7 provides guidance to office holders when preparing receipts and payments accounts.

5.2 Additional considerations

The following points re presentation should be regarded as best practice:

▶ As far as possible receipts and payments should be classified under the headings used in the statement of affairs so as to facilitate comparison.

▶ The *Estimated to Realise* figures on the statement of affairs should be shown so that the comparisons with the actual realisations made to date may be made.

▶ Trading results should be shown separately from realisations of assets and costs of realisation.

▶ Any payments to pre-insolvency creditors should be stated separately by category indicating:

   – Amounts paid under duress
   – Reservation of title creditors
   – Payments to preferential creditors
   – Any other pre-insolvency items.

▶ Asset realisations should be shown gross.

▶ Cost of realising assets should be shown under payments.

▶ If assets are sold direct by a mortgagee so that the proceeds do not come into account, this fact should be stated in a note.

▶ Where assets subject to prior charges are sold and the prior charges are paid off by the solicitors out of sale proceeds, the net amount should be brought into account. Alternatively, the gross amount may be shown as a receipt and the disbursements as a deduction from receipts.

▶ If a separate bank account is opened for fixed charge realisations, these amounts should be included in the receipts and payments account without stating that a separate bank account is operated.

▶ Any sums received or paid out under the Employment Protection Act (EPA) should not be recorded as part of the receipts and payments account except where loans are made to employees under the loan scheme.

▶ The office holders' fees re EPA matters do not form part of the remuneration from the estate and should not be disclosed.

▶ Other amounts received and banked which are not part of the estate and are subsequently paid to the true owner should be shown in the account.

▶ Office holders' fees should be clearly stated and any additional management fee or fees for other services should be separately described.

▶ VAT – it is acceptable to show amounts net of VAT with the total net VAT being shown separately or show all amounts inclusive of VAT. (In a compulsory liquidation – Form 1 requires the amount of VAT included in each item to be shown separately.)

5.3 Summary of statutory returns

Statutory requirements for the filing of returns are laid down in the IA and rules, a summary of which is provided below.

	Form	Submit to	Timescale re submission	On closure
Creditors' voluntary liquidation S192 and R4.223	4.68	▶ Registrar of companies	Within 30 days of the end of the first year; thereafter at six monthly instalments	Final account with return of final meeting
Administrative receivership R3.32	3.6	▶ Registrar of companies ▶ The company appointee ▶ Creditors' committee	Within two months after the end of 12 months from the date of appointment; and every subsequent 12 month period	Within two months of ceasing to act
Receivers (other than administrative receivers) S38	3.6	▶ Registrar of companies	Within one month of the expiration of 12 months from the date of appointment; and every subsequent six month period	Within one month of ceasing to act
Administrator R2.47	2.24B	▶ Court ▶ Registrar of companies ▶ Creditors' committee	Within one month of the expiration of six months from the date of appointment; and every subsequent six month period	Within one month of ceasing to act

	Form	Submit to	Timescale re submission	On closure
Company Voluntary Arrangement R1.26	1.3	▶ Court ▶ Registrar of companies ▶ Bound creditors ▶ Company's auditors	Within two months after the end of 12 months from the date of appointment; and every subsequent 12 month period	Within 28 days of completion of the arrangement
Individual Voluntary Arrangement R5.31		▶ Court ▶ The debtor ▶ Bound creditors	Within two months after the end of 12 months from the date of appointment; and every subsequent 12 month period	Within 28 days of completion of the arrangement

Worked example: Receipts and payments account

If you are asked to prepare a receipts and payments account in the exam the question is likely to consist of a list of information regarding the realisation of company assets to date, assets still to be realised, expenses incurred and outstanding and details of creditors' claims.

Question

You were appointed liquidator of DOT Ltd following a s98 meeting of creditors twelve months ago. The following information is available:

1   The company's freehold property was sold for a sum of £285,000. The property was subject to a fixed charge held by Satby Bank plc in the sum of £115,000. Agents and solicitors fees paid in relation to the sale totalled £21,500. The property was shown in the Statement of Affairs in the sum of £240,000.

2   The company's other assets (machinery, fixtures and stock with a Statement of Affairs value of £55,000) were sold at public auction. The liquidator received the sum of £49,000 after the auctioneer deducted the sum of £5,750 in relation to his costs.

3   Book debts with an estimated to realise value of £93,000 have to date been realised in the sum of £72,000. Legal costs of £6,500 have been incurred in realising debtors to date.

4   Liquidator's remuneration has been drawn in the sum of £12,500 on a time cost basis.

5   Expenses totalling £2,500 have also been drawn relating to case advertising, copying etc.

6   Insurance costs of £1,800 have been paid.

7   A dividend has been paid to preferential creditors totalling £55,000. No dividend has yet been paid to the unsecured creditors.

Requirement

Prepare a Receipts and Payments account for DOT Ltd for the period from your appointment to date.

Solution

DOT Ltd in Liquidation – Receipts and Payments account for the period X.X.00 to X.X.01

	Per S of A £	Realised to date £
Receipts		
Freehold property	240,000	285,000
Machinery, fixtures, stock	55,000	54,750
Book debts	93,000	72,000
		411,750
Payments		
Satby Bank plc		115,000
Agents and solicitors' fees		21,500
Auctioneer's costs		5,750
Insurance		1,800
Legal fees re debt collection		6,500
Liquidator's remuneration		12,500
Liquidator's expenses		2,500
Payments to creditors		
Preferential creditors 100p in £		55,000
Balance in hand		191,200
		411,750

Interactive question 2: Aztec Clothing Ltd

You were appointed liquidator of Aztec Clothing Ltd following a creditors' voluntary winding up resolution passed on 10 November 2009.

A summary of the directors' Statement of Affairs is as follows:

	Book value £	Estimated to realise £
ASSETS		
Freehold property	275,000	298,000
Secured claim		(180,000)
		118,000
Book debts	110,000	65,000
Plant and equipment	60,000	35,000
Stock and raw materials	56,000	22,000
		240,000
LIABILITIES		
Preferential creditors		(48,000)
Unsecured creditors		(284,000)
		(92,000)
Share capital		(100,000)
Estimated total deficiency		(192,000)

The following transactions have occurred during the course of the liquidation:

▶ A motor vehicle was sold for £6,500. You subsequently established however that this vehicle was leased and repaid the funds to the leasing company less the costs of sale of £500.

▶ Raw materials were sold for £14,000 from which proceeds you discharged a ROT claim of £3,000 and the fees of your agents of £1,400.

▶ The freehold property was sold for £275,000 by agents who were paid a 2.5% selling fee. The secured creditor's claim of £180,000 was settled in full from the proceeds.

▶ Book debt realisations to date total £46,000. You have incurred debt collection fees of £4,000 in realising these debts.

▶ Finished stock was sold for £10,000 by the Court Enforcement officer who levied execution some time ago. After discharging the judgement creditor's debt of £8,000 and the Court Enforcement officer's fee and costs of sale of £900, you received the surplus.

▶ The plant and equipment was sold at public auction realising a sum of £28,000. Auctioneer's costs of £1,500 were incurred and paid after the sale.

▶ Interest of £5,000 has been received and £1,800 corporation tax paid.

▶ BERR fees amount to £620.

▶ Solicitor's fees incurred in the sale of the property and other various matters have been paid totalling £6,250.

▶ In accordance with r4.127(6) your remuneration has been approved on the basis of the scale laid down in Schedule 6 of the Insolvency Rules 1986. This has been settled on realisations and distributions to date.

The scale is as follows:

	Realisation %	Distribution %
£1 – £5,000	20	10
£5,001 – £10,000	15	7.5
£10,001 – £100,000	10	5
£100,000 +	5	2.5

In addition you were paid £4,000 direct by the secured creditor for dealing with the sale of the property.

▶ Your firm's paid disbursements total £650 and other sundry expenses settled during the liquidation total £711.

▶ You have agreed and paid all preferential claims in full.

▶ The balance in hand is held on deposit.

Requirement

Prepare a receipts and payments account for the period of the liquidation to date.

(**Note:** Ignore VAT)

See **Answer** at the end of this chapter.

6 Banking

Section overview

▶ In a compulsory liquidation the liquidator is required to pay all funds directly into the Insolvency Service Account (IS Account) at the Bank of England without deduction (Ins Regs 1994). If £5,000 or more is received, the funds must be paid into the IS Account immediately, but if less, within 14 days.

▶ The Secretary Of State can authorise a liquidator to hold a local bank account if it creates an administrative advantage, for example, if the liquidator is continuing to trade.

It is no longer necessary for a liquidator in a CVL to pay all funds into the IS Account with the Bank of England (within 14 days of six months from appointment), however he may pay monies into IS Account if he wishes.

In a winding up by the Court Secretary of State fees are paid on all monies paid into the IS Account. The fee is calculated as 17% of chargeable receipts over £2,000 to a maximum of £80,000 (reduced from £100,000 from 6/04/08). Chargeable receipts are sums paid into the ISA/c after deduction of sums paid to secured creditors and sums spent in carrying on the business of the company in liquidation.

7 Continuing to trade

Section overview

The liquidator has the power to trade the company, but he may only do so if it is for the beneficial winding up of the company. In a compulsory liquidation sanction of the liquidation committee or creditors is required. Sanction is not required in a CVL but it is usual for the liquidator to seek the support of the creditors. In a CVL, sanction of the court would be required in order for the liquidator to trade during the period before the holding of the s98 meeting of creditors.

7.1 Why would the liquidator continue to trade?

It may sometimes be necessary for the liquidator to continue to trade in order to:

- Complete a sale as a going concern
- Complete a profitable contract
- Increase debtor realisations.

7.2 Factors to consider when deciding whether to continue trading

In order to make the decision to continue to trade the liquidator should:

- Prepare cash flow forecasts

- Identify sources of working capital

- Identify employee requirements and make surplus staff redundant (employee contracts are only automatically terminated in a compulsory liquidation)

- Ensure employees will continue to support the company (duress payments re wage arrears may need to be paid to ensure co-operation of the work force)

- Identify customers and ensure they will support continued trading

- Ensure suppliers will continue to deal with the company

- Identify stock subject to ROT claims

- Consider health and safety issues

- Consider environmental issues

- Trading premises, if leased, will landlord allow continued use by liquidator?

- Give undertakings to utility companies.

8 Hiving down

Section overview

A hive down arises where an identified business and assets are transferred to a wholly owned subsidiary of the company in liquidation, established by the liquidator for such purposes, so that a potential purchaser may ultimately acquire the share capital of the solvent wholly owned subsidiary from the liquidator.

8.1 Advantages of hiving down

▶ Trading can be conducted through a company which is not insolvent and is not required to state 'In liquidation' on its letters, invoices etc.

▶ The hive down procedure creates a package of assets free from historic liabilities which may prove to be a more attractive proposition to a potential purchaser.

▶ A company in liquidation may experience difficulty in completing and disposing of work in progress due to customer reaction to that fact.

▶ It is likely to be easier to obtain funding through a solvent hived down company.

8.2 Disadvantages of hiving down

▶ Certain contracts may not be assignable to a wholly owned subsidiary for contractual reasons.

▶ Increases costs.

▶ Employee contracts are likely to vest with the hive down company. TUPR liabilities may make hiving down a less attractive proposition.

9 Retention of Title (ROT)

Section overview

Trade suppliers to companies often include in their standard conditions of sale a clause stating that title to goods supplied will remain with the supplier until all monies owing have been paid.

9.1 ROT clauses

A ROT supplier may, following the appointment of the liquidator, seek to recover their goods from the company in liquidation. If the liquidator wrongfully prevents the supplier from recovering the goods he may be liable to pay damages to the supplier. However, if the liquidator allows the supplier to remove the goods and the ROT claim later turns out to be invalid, the liquidator will have dissipated assets which should have been available for the creditors.

There are two types of ROT clause:

▶ **Simple clause**: provides that goods supplied under a specific invoice remain the property of the vendor until all goods on the invoice have been paid for.

▶ **All monies clause**: this holds that all goods supplied by the vendor remains their property until all sums due to the vendor, on whatever account, are paid.

If the clause is simple the supplier will be required to identify the remaining goods held by the company to an unpaid invoice.

With an all monies clause, the goods do not have to be identified to a particular invoice. All items will remain the property of the supplier until all monies owed are paid. However, when the purchaser has, at some date, cleared all sums due to the vendor, title to all goods supplied prior to that date will pass to the purchaser. It is important therefore for the liquidator to check whether the balance on the supplier's account has ever been reduced to zero.

The liquidator must ensure that the ROT clause has been accepted and incorporated into the contract. This should be done prior to the supply taking place ie on a separate agreement or order form. If the clause is on the back of an invoice this is a post contractual document and therefore it is not part of the contract. It is possible, where there has been a lengthy course of dealings that the ROT clause may be accepted as part of the contract because over the course of dealings the purchaser must have become aware of the terms.

ROT clauses which seek to assert title to the proceeds of sale are effectively charges which can only be valid if registered at Companies House.

When dealing with ROT claims the liquidator should:

▸   Request copies of all documentation relating to the claim, invoices, delivery notes, ROT clause etc.

▸   Obtain legal advice re validity of the claim.

▸   Invite the creditor to attend a stock take and identify goods subject to their ROT claim (simple clause – identify goods to specific invoice). Identification of goods can be difficult when the supplier supplies a product which is indistinguishable from that supplied by other parties or has no identifying marks. If the goods have been incorporated into other goods (ie. during the manufacturing process) and the claimed items cannot be removed from the manufactured product, the ROT claim will fail.

▸   Place goods identified to one side.

If the ROT claim is valid the creditor should be allowed to recover the goods. The liquidator should ensure that any proof of debt submitted by the creditor is amended accordingly.

10   Employee claims

Section overview

Employees will have claims in the liquidation for:
▸   Arrears of pay
▸   Holiday pay
▸   Pay in lieu of notice
▸   Redundancy.

The Employment Rights Act 1996 (ERA 1996) provides employees of an insolvent company with the right to make claims against the National Insurance Fund through the Redundancy Payments Scheme.

10.1   Arrears of pay

Up to four months' arrears may be claimed preferentially subject to a maximum claim per employee of £800. The balance of any claim will rank as unsecured.

Included as employees' remuneration will be statutory sick pay and contractual bonuses and overtime.

In respect of the ERA 1996 claim, employees may claim up to eight weeks' wage arrears. The weeks need not be the latest weeks of employment, nor need they be consecutive. They should be the eight weeks that are financially most beneficial to the employee.

10.2   Holiday pay

All holiday pay owed to an employee may be claimed preferentially without limit.

10.3 Pay in lieu of notice

This claim will be made where the employee has been dismissed without being given proper notice or pay in lieu of notice.

'Proper notice' is the statutory minimum notice period provided for by ERA 1996 (unless the contract of employment provides for a longer period in which case that period applies).

Statutory minimum notice periods are as follows:

Period of continuous employment	Minimum Notice
Less than one month	–
One month – two years	One week
Two years – less than three years	Two weeks
Three years – less than four years	Three weeks

....and so on up to a maximum of 12 weeks

Technical Release 5 (replaced SIP 5) applies where an employee of an insolvent employer has been dismissed without proper notice and as a result has a claim against a company.

The claim is essentially a claim for wrongful dismissal ie a breach of contract claim.

The individual will claim for remuneration lost and fringe benefits, for instance a company car, medical insurance and rent free accommodation.

In assessing the benefit of the company car an IP should have regard to the Tables published by the AA as the most accurate measure.

An employee may also claim for the lost employer's contribution to an occupational pension scheme during the notice period. In some circumstances a simple computation of payments may not do and an actuarial calculation may be necessary.

The employee will have a duty to mitigate his claim. The following table provides a summary of matters to be taken into account:

Matters in mitigation	Matters to ignore
Social security payments – Non-discretionary benefits eg Jobseeker's Allowance, Supplementary Benefit, Invalidity Pay, Maternity Allowance, and Sickness Pay	**Social security payments** – Discretionary
	Pension – All pension payments should be ignored – occupational, state and personal
Personal Tax – Up to £30,000 a deduction equivalent to the full amount of tax that would have been payable if the amount in question had been paid as salary	**Unemployment Benefit** – Paid by a Trade Union under a Welfare Scheme should be ignored as should any other similar benefits
Over £30,000 – the calculation is more complex. Three stages:	**Redundancy pay** – Redundancy is not founded on breach of contract and is therefore irrelevant
▶ Estimate the amount of tax that would have been deducted	**National Insurance Contributions** – The rationale is that the individual won't get the benefit of the equivalent NIC benefits, so it's not fair to penalise the employee deducting a notional amount representing NIC
▶ Less an amount for mitigation	
▶ Then take into account the individual's liability to tax on the damages	**Protective award** – This is not certain, but the best answer is probably that it is ignored. The reason being that the ECJ held in *EC Commission v UK 1994* that though a protective award represents remuneration, if it is deducted there would be no incentive on an employer to conform to the relevant labour relations legislation
Unfair Dismissal	
The basic award should be ignored (this is equivalent to the amount payable on redundancy)	
Only the proportion of the remaining damages that represents loss of earnings should be deducted	

Matters in mitigation	Matters to ignore
Remuneration received – which would not have been received but for the termination	However, there may be a problem of double proof if an employee claims for both
Notional earnings Usually only take these off if there's a long notice period or an unreasonable failure to take advantage of an opportunity of employment Up to three months the question of mitigation does not need to be pursued 'very far'	If in doubt, the RPS at the BERR can be approached for guidance

10.4   Redundancy pay

A claim for a statutory redundancy payment may be made where the employee:

▶   Is employed under a contract of *service* (as opposed to being a sub-contractor employed under a contract for *services* see SIP 4)

▶   Has been continuously employed for a period of two years

▶   Has been dismissed (or a fixed term contract has come to an end without renewal) and

▶   Redundancy is the reason for the dismissal.

Redundancy means the dismissal is attributable wholly or mainly to:

▶   Employer ceasing or intending to cease carrying on business or
▶   The requirements for employees to carry out work of a particular kind have ceased or diminished.

The amount of a statutory redundancy payment depends on the length of service and age of the employee and is as follows

Age of employee	No of weeks' pay
18–21 years old	½ week per year of employment
22–40 years old	1 week per year of employment
41–65 years old	1 ½ weeks per year of employment

Subject to a maximum of 20 years continuous employment.

A contract of employment may provide for termination payments exceeding these minimum statutory amounts. This is the 'contractual redundancy' referred to earlier.

10.5   The loan scheme

The ERA 1996 provides employees of an insolvent employer with the right to make claims against the National Insurance Fund through the Department of Employment (see summary). These claims include claims for arrears of pay.

The office holder may consider it expedient to pay arrears at an early stage to maintain employee co-operation.

Under the loan scheme.

▶   The office holder makes funds available for the company to pay the arrears of wages. These payments are deemed to be a 'loan' to the employees repayable out of any subsequent ERA 1996 claims that they may have.

▶   Employees fill in the ERA 1996 claim forms provided by the office holder and return them to the office holder who will submit them to the BERR on the employees' behalf in the event that they are made redundant.

▶ Employees also sign a written agreement in respect of the loan, a copy of which will be submitted to the BERR with the claim form.

▶ In the agreement the employee:

– Acknowledges receipt of the loan.

– Appoints the office holder as his or her agent to receive all monies payable to the employee under ERA 1996 in respect of the claim for arrears and

– Authorises the office holder to deduct the monies in respect of the loan from any monies received by him or her from the BERR.

In the event of a claim being submitted by the office holder, the BERR will remit monies in respect of the claim to the office holder.

If there is any balance of monies due to the employee the office holder is required by the BERR to forward such sums to the employee 'as quickly as is reasonably practicable' and normally within 14 days of receipt of the payment.

By recovering funds from the BERR, the office holder minimises the impact on floating charge realisations of paying the arrears.

However the BERR is subrogated to the position of the employees and is to the same extent therefore preferential.

The BERR's subrogated claim must be paid in full before an employees residual preferential claim (if any) can be paid. This may be important where there are insufficient funds to pay preferential creditors in full (s189(4) ERA 1996).

According to SIP 11 – monies received should be deposited in a separate bank account, segregating these funds from other case monies, and should be held to the account of the Secretary of State.

10.6 Claims by employees – a summary

Claim	Preferential	Unsecured	Against BERR
Arrears of wages/ salary	Restricted to four months pre-relevant date Maximum of £800 per employee	Any excess over the preferential limits	Restricted to the eight weeks accrued pre-'appropriate' date Maximum of £350 per week per employee
Holiday Pay	All accrued holiday pay is preferential	Not applicable	Restricted to six weeks accrued in the 12 months pre-appropriate date Maximum of £350 per week per employee
Pay in Lieu of Notice	Not preferential	Valid claim for greater of contractual or statutory period Employee has duty to mitigate claim	Statutory (but not contractual) notice Maximum of £350 per week per employee
Redundancy	Not preferential	Valid claim for greater of contractual or statutory redundancy	Statutory (but not contractual redundancy Maximum of £350 per week per employee

Claim	Preferential	Unsecured	Against BERR
Occupational Pension Scheme	Restricted to employer contributions in the 12 months prior to relevant date and employee contributions in the four months prior to relevant date	Any excess over the preferential limits	Employer contributions – lowest of ▸ 12 months contributions ▸ 10% of 12 months pay ▸ Amount certified to meet liability to pay employees pension 12 months employee contributions

Note: The 'appropriate date' in respect of the ERA 1996 claims for arrears of wages and holiday pay is the date of the order in Bankruptcy, Compulsory Liquidation and administration, the date an arrangement is approved in a CVA, the date of appointment of a Receiver and the date of the passing of the resolution in a CVL. However, none of these claims can be brought unless the employees are made redundant.

10.7 Claims by directors (Technical Release 6)

Many rights in employment law apply only to:

▸ Employees (ie those employed under a *contract of service*) and not to

▸ Sub-contractors (ie those employed under a *contract for services* – often referred to as 'self-employed').

Examples would be the right to statutory redundancy payment or compensation for unfair dismissal, as well as the right to a minimum statutory notice period etc.

It is not always obvious, particularly with directors, whether an individual is an employee or only a sub-contractor. Technical Release 6 deals with the treatment of directors' claims as 'employees' in insolvencies.

S230 ERA 1996 defines an 'employee' as 'an individual who has entered into or works under a contract of employment.' A contract of employment is defined as 'a contract of service ... whether express or implied, and ... oral or in writing'.

Factors to be taken into account in deciding whether to accept a director's claim as employee:

▸ In *SSTI v Bottrill 1999* the Court of Appeal advised that the first question that should be considered is has there been a genuine contract between the company and the director? For instance was the contract signed at a time when insolvency loomed?

▸ Assuming that the contract is not a sham, there are a number of factors to decide whether it actually gave rise to an employer/employee relationship.

▸ These are set out in the Bottrill case and other cases such as *Eaton v Robert Eaton Ltd 1988*, *McQuisten v SSE 1996*, *Buchanan v SSE* and *Ivey v SSE 1997*.

Remuneration

Firstly, did the director ever forgo salary as this implies that the individual was self employed. Employee factors will be the deduction of PAYE and Class 1 National Insurance Contributions. These do not mean that the director is conclusively an employee however (and *vice versa*, if PAYE was not deducted and self employed NIC contributions were paid this does not mean conclusively that the individual is self-employed).

Investment in the company/guarantor

Two other self-employed factors are the fact that a director is a controlling shareholder or guarantor of the company's debt.

Is the director an integral part of the company or another business?

The IP should consider whether the director had other employment. In addition the IP should consider whether the director was really in business on his/her own account?

The IP should also consider whether there is a 'mutuality of obligation' between the director and the company.

The degree of control exercised by the company over the employee.

Did the director work under control of the board of directors in respect of the management of his work? Even if a director is a controlling shareholder, this could still apply, for instance there could be directors other than the shareholder director or the Articles of Association could prevent the directors voting in matters in which they are interested (eg their dismissal).

Did the director take holidays and was the director entitled to holiday pay and sick pay?

If a director does not take holiday, and therefore seems to be in business on his or her own account, this may be a self employed factor. However, entitlement to holiday pay and sick pay do point towards employee status.

The director's title

For instance, 'Managing Director' gives an impression of a full-time employee.

No single factor is conclusive

Bottrill provides that no single factor is conclusive however and that all the factors must be weighed up to decide whether a director is an employee.

A director has the right to apply to the Employment Tribunal if he or she disagrees with a decision made by the RPS or an IP.

Sole Director employees:

▸ *Salomon v Salomon 1897* – A company is a separate legal entity from its owners (shareholders) and Directors.

▸ In *Lee v Lees Air Farming 1961* it was held that a Director may enter into a valid contract with a company of which he is a Director. This was so even if he was the sole Director and shareholder of the company. Contracts, obviously, include contracts of employment.

▸ In practical terms contracting with a company in these circumstances involves:

   – Assenting to the contract in ones capacity as the employee
   – Assenting on behalf of the company in ones capacity as director and agent of the company.

▸ In *Buchanan v Secretary of State for Employment and Ivey v Secretary of State for Employment 1997* the Employment Appeals Tribunal held that a controlling shareholder could not be an employee for the purposes of the ERA 1996 as it would be inconsistent with the purpose of the act to protect persons who were able to prevent their own dismissal as they had a controlling interest in the shares of a company.

▸ However, in *Secretary of State for Trade and Industry v Bottrill 1999*, it was held that a controlling shareholder of a company could also be an employee of that company.

▸ No single factor is conclusive, however, and each case should be decided on its own facts.

11 Pensions

Section overview

A company in liquidation will often have a pension scheme which the liquidator may have to deal with.

In relation to an occupational pension scheme the liquidator has a number of duties:

- ▶ Within 14 days of the liquidation (or the liquidator becoming aware of the pension scheme) he must send notification of the liquidation to:

  - – The Pension Protection Fund (PPF)
  - – The Pensions Regulator (TPR)
  - – The Scheme trustees

  (s120, s121, s126, s127, s129 Pensions Act 2004 and Regs 2, 3, 4, 5 of the PPF (Entry Rules) Regs 2005).

  If there are more than one pension fund, a separate notice is required for each.

- ▶ If the PPF decides that the scheme should enter assessment, the liquidator must inform the PPF whether or not he considers that the scheme can be rescued (s122, s123 and 148 Pensions Act 2004 and Regs 6, 9, 11 of the PPF (Entry Rules) Regulations 2005).

- ▶ If the liquidator considers that the scheme can be rescued, he must issue a withdrawal notice to the PPF and the scheme will continue or be wound up outside the PPF.

- ▶ If the liquidator is uncertain whether or not the scheme can be rescued he will issue an 'uncertain' notice to the PPF.

- ▶ If the liquidator considers that the scheme cannot be rescued, he must issue a scheme failure notice to the PPF. The scheme will continue throughout the PPF assessment period.

12 Utilities

Section overview

Where the liquidator requires a continued supply of gas, water, electricity by a utility company, the utility company may not make it a condition of the giving of the supply that any outstanding charges in respect of supplies made to the company before the commencement of the liquidation are paid. The supplier may however, require the liquidator to undertake personal responsibility for payment of any new supply (s233).

13 Sale of assets to directors

Section overview

- ▶ The duty of the liquidator to maximise realisations of the company's assets does not preclude a sale of the company's assets to the directors. However, the creditors of the company may be concerned that the directors are acquiring assets at an undervalue.

- ▶ SIP 13 (Acquisition of assets of insolvent companies) sets out guidelines for office holders to follow (not just liquidators) when disposing of assets to directors.

The directors should be advised of their obligations.

The overriding duty of the directors is to act in the best interests of the company, its creditors and members. Failure to do so exposes directors to risk of:

▶ Claims for breach of duty or
▶ Misfeasance.

They should refrain from entering into transactions which may be set aside as transactions at undervalue or preferences.

They must obtain prior approval in general meeting where directors (or connected parties) enter into substantial property transactions with the company (s190 CA 2006). This is where the transaction exceeds in value the lower of:

▶ £100,000 or
▶ 10% of the companies net asset value (subject to a minimum of £5,000).

If approval is not obtained the company can avoid the contract.

The directors should be made aware of their obligations under Phoenix company rules (s216).

In order to avoid any claims when selling the assets the liquidator should:

▶ Advertise or circularise sales particulars to potentially interested parties.
▶ Obtain agents' advice re mode of sale.
▶ Obtain professional valuations of the assets.
▶ Ensure transactions are at arm's length, on the basis of a professional valuation.

Any connected party transactions should be fully disclosed (SIP 8).

Where the directors indicate to the liquidator prior to the s98 meeting that they intend to make an offer for some/all of the business, the liquidator should advise the directors that:

▶ He will advise any committee of the director's offer who will have an opportunity to comment (although strictly sanction not required).

▶ In both CVLs and compulsories there is a statutory duty to notify the committee of disposals of property to connected parties.

The details which should be disclosed are:

▶ The date of the transaction.

▶ Details of the assets involved and the nature of the transaction.

▶ The consideration for the transaction and when it was paid.

▶ The name of the counterparty.

▶ The nature of the counterparty's connected party relationship with the vendor.

▶ If the transaction took place before the appointment of the member as office holder, the name of any advisor to the vendor.

▶ Whether the purchaser and (if the transaction took place before the appointment of the member as office holder) the vendor were independently advised.

▶ Where the transaction took place before the commencement of liquidation, the scope of the office holder's investigation and the conclusion reached.

▶ Where the disclosure is to a liquidation committee and the committee has not been consulted prior to contract, the reason why such consultation did not take place.

▶ Where, in a liquidation, the disclosure is to creditors, whether the liquidation committee (if there is one) has been consulted and the outcome of such consultation.

14 Liquidation following administrative receivership

Section overview

There may be occasions when a company in administrative receivership enters into liquidation. The administrative receiver will retain custody and control of the charged assets and the power to realise and sell company property subject to the charge. He may continue to carry on the company's business and retains his general powers of management. The administrative receiver has a duty to co-operate with the liquidator (s235(3)(e)).

The liquidation of a company will have a number of consequences for an administrative receiver appointed in respect of that company. He has a statutory duty to provide the liquidator with the following:

▶   A copy of the s48 report.
▶   A copy of the Statement of Affairs (s48(3)).

The liquidator may, under s41, require the administrative receiver to:

▶   Render proper accounts of receipts and payments
▶   Pay over any amounts properly payable.

All post appointment company documentation should be forwarded to the liquidator (SIP 9).

The liquidator has the power to apply to court for the removal of the administrative receiver (s45(1)) or for the public examination of the administrative receiver.

S245 will be triggered by the liquidation so that a floating charge created within 12 months of the onset of insolvency, at a time when the company is insolvent, will be invalid except to the extent that fresh consideration is provided.

The liquidator must ensure that:

▶   The appointment of the administrative receiver is valid.
▶   That the charge under which he is appointed is valid.

Self-test

Answer the following questions.

1 For how long must an office holder retain the Case records required under IP Regs 2005?

2 When can a liquidator destroy the books and records of the company in liquidation?

3 How often must a liquidator in a CVL summon meetings of the company's creditors?

4 What information must be given at such a meeting?

5 (a) A liquidator in a compulsory liquidation realises an asset in the sum of £7,200. What should he do with the proceeds received?

   (b) Assuming this is the first realisation made by the liquidator, what Secretary of State fees will be payable?

6 What is the difference between a 'simple' and an 'all monies' retention of title clause?

7 What sums may be claimed preferentially by an employee?

8 What mitigating factors would be taken into account when assessing an employee's claim for pay in lieu of notice?

Now, go back to the Learning Objectives in the Introduction. If you are satisfied that you have achieved these objectives, please tick them off.

Answers to self-test

1   For a period of six years from the date of his release.

2   After one year after dissolution of the company following closure (Reg 16(2) IP Regs 1994).

3   At the end of the first year from the commencement of the winding up and of each succeeding year.

4   An account of the liquidator's acts and dealings and of the conduct of the winding up during the preceding year, a receipts and payments account.

5   (a)   Since the amount is greater than £5,000 he must pay the money into the ISA/c immediately.

    (b) $(7,200 - 2,000) \times 17\% = £884$.

6   Simple clause – provides that goods supplied under a specific invoice remains the property of the vendor until all goods on the invoice have been paid for.

    All monies clause – this holds that all goods supplied by the vendor remains their property until all sums due to the vendor, on whatever account, are paid.

7   All holiday pay without limit.

    Up to four months' wage arrears, subject to a maximum preferential claim of £800.

8   Non-discretionary social security benefits – jobseekers' allowance, maternity allowance, sickness pay etc.

    Personal tax which would have been paid if that amount had been paid as salary.

    Remuneration received during the period.

    A proportion of an unfair dismissal award which represents damages for loss of earnings.

    Notional earnings that could have been earned during the period (if employee fails to pursue alternative, reasonable employment).

Answers to interactive questions

Interactive question 1: Rolling Bones Ltd

The amount of the bond is the amount which would be available for the unsecured creditors of the company (unsecured includes preferential creditors in this regard).

	£
Assets subject to fixed charge	526,000
Less fixed charge holder	(495,000)
Assets subject to floating charge holder	362,000
Less floating charge holder	(215,000)

Bond for £178,000.

Interactive question 2: Aztec Clothing Ltd

AZTEC CLOTHING LTD IN LIQUIDATION
SUMMARY OF LIQUIDATION RECEIPTS AND PAYMENTS
FOR THE PERIOD FROM 10 NOVEMBER 2008 TO DATE

	Per S of A £	Realised £
RECEIPTS		
Freehold property	298,000	275,000
Book debts	65,000	46,000
Plant and equipment	35,000	28,000
Raw materials	22,000	14,000
Finished goods		1,100
OTHER RECEIPTS		
Gross interest		5,000
Motor vehicles		NIL
		369,100
PAYMENTS		
Agent's fees (freehold property)		6,875
Debt collection fees		4,000
Auctioneer's costs		1,500
Agent's fees (raw materials)		1,400
Corporation tax		1,800
BERR fees		620
Solicitor's fees (freehold property)		6,250
Liquidator's remuneration		26,980
Liquidator's disbursements		650
Sundry expenses		711
		48,411
PAYMENTS TO CREDITORS		
Secured claim – in full		180,000
Retention of title claim – in full		3,000
Preferential creditors – in full		48,000
		330,197
BALANCE IN HAND		
On deposit		38,903
		369,100

Notes:

(1) The finished stock was sold for £10,000 by the Court Enforcement Officer following a pre liquidation execution. The judgement creditor's claim for £8,000 and the Court Enforcement Officer's costs of £900 were settled. The balance shown of £1,100 is the surplus received.

(2) The balance shown for liquidator's remuneration has been drawn on the basis of the statutory scale. In addition, the secured creditor also paid the liquidator a fee of £4,000 direct in relation to the sale of the freehold property which is not included in the above figures.

WORKINGS

(1) *Liquidator's remuneration on Schedule 6 scale*

	£
Realisations	369,100
Distributions	48,000

Realisations

£	£
5,000 x 20%	1,000
5,000 x 15%	750
90,000 x 10%	9,000
269,100 x 5%	13,455
369,100	24,205

Distributions

£	£
5,000 x 10%	500
5,000 x 7.5%	375
38,000 x 5%	1,900
48,000	2,775

Total remuneration = £26,980

(2) *Leased motor vehicle*

A motor vehicle was sold for £6,500. It subsequently transpired however that this had been leased and the proceeds, net of costs of £500, were returned to the lessor.

(**Note:** Could show receipts and payments on the face of the receipts and payments account.)

Liquidations

228

BPP
LEARNING MEDIA

13

Vacation of office

> > > > > > > > > > > > > > > > >

Contents

Introduction

Examination context

Topic List

Summary and self-test

Answers to self-test

Answer to interactive question

Introduction

Learning objectives

▶ Identify the circumstances in which a liquidator vacates office ☐

▶ Understand the liquidator's duties upon vacating office ☐

▶ Learn the statutory procedures to be followed when calling final meetings ☐

▶ Identify practical steps to be taken when closing cases ☐

Working context

As part of your role you may be asked to review cases ready for closure. It is important therefore to know the relevant statutory provisions when finalising a liquidation.

Stop and think

Why is it important for cases to be closed properly? What information should be given to creditors by a liquidator when he vacates office?

Examination context

Vacation of office and closure are not topics which have been regularly tested in the liquidations paper of the JIEB exam, however they are on the exam syllabus and the closure checklist is also relevant to other insolvency appointments. The topics covered in this chapter are therefore relevant to the exam and should be learnt.

Exam requirements

Past exam questions to look at include:

2007	Question 2(a)(ii)
2007	Question 3(g)
2000	Question 5(d)
1992	Paper II, Question 3(a)
1990	Paper I, Question 3

1 Vacating office

1.1 Removal

▶ In a compulsory liquidation, s172 provides that a liquidator may be removed by:

    – An order of the court.

    – By a meeting of creditors called specifically for that purpose in accordance with the Rules (r4.113).

▶ In a voluntary winding-up, a liquidator may be removed from office by (s172(2)):

    – An order of the court.

    – In a CVL by a meeting of the company's creditors summoned specifically for that purpose in accordance with the Rules.

    – In a MVL, by a general meeting of the company summoned for that purpose.

▶ If the liquidator was originally appointed by the court, the meeting for removal can only be summoned if:

    – The court directs.

    – The liquidator sees fit.

    – Creditors representing more than 50% of the total value requisition the meeting. In a MVL, this % relates to those creditors entitled to vote at the meeting.

If the liquidator was appointed by the Secretary of State then he may be removed by a direction of the Secretary of State.

▶ In a voluntary liquidation, the court may, on just cause, remove a liquidator and appoint another (s108).

In *Re Keypak Homecare Ltd 1987* it was held in relation to the words 'on just cause' that:

▶ Onus is on the applicant to show why the liquidator should be removed.

▶ No personal misconduct or unfitness need be shown on the part of the liquidator.

▶ The court need to be satisfied only that it was for the general advantage of those interested in the assets of the company that the liquidator be removed.

▶ It might be appropriate to remove a liquidator even though nothing could be said against him either personally or in his conduct of the particular liquidation.

The procedure for dismissal is:

▶ Application is made to the court for removal or for an order that the liquidator be directed to call a General Meeting for the purpose of removing him (r4.143).

▶ The court may dismiss the application if no sufficient cause is shown. The court can only do this if the applicant has had the opportunity to be heard ex-parte, on at least seven days' notice.

▶ If the court grants the application it fixes a venue. It may require the applicant to make a deposit or give security for the costs to be incurred by the liquidator on the application.

▶ The applicant must give 14 days' notice of the venue to the liquidator and a copy of the application and any evidence which he intends to adduce in support of it.

▶ The costs of the application are not payable out of assets unless the court orders to the contrary.

Where the court removes the liquidator it will give two copies of the order of removal to him. He keeps one and sends the other to the Registrar of Companies along with his notice of ceasing to act.

The court may include such further provisions as the court thinks fit.

The liquidator has to apply to the Secretary of State for his release.

1.2 Resignation

R4.108 provides that the grounds upon which a liquidator may resign from office are:

▶ Ill health.

▶ Intend ceasing to be an insolvency practitioner.

▶ A conflict of interest or change in personal circumstances which make it impossible or impracticable to continue.

▶ Where joint liquidators are appointed and it is no longer expedient to continue with that number of joint liquidators.

In a CVL, a meeting of creditors must be called for the purpose of receiving the liquidator's resignation. The notice of the meeting must indicate that this is the purpose of it and draw attention to the rules on release, r4.121 and r4.122.

The liquidator will have his release from the date on which he gives notice of his resignation to the Registrar of Companies.

In a MVL, the liquidator must call a meeting of the company for the purposes of receiving his resignation (r4.142). The notice of the meeting must state that this is the, or a, purpose of the meeting. As soon as reasonably practicable, following the meeting, the liquidator gives notice on Form 4.33 to the Registrar of Companies, and has his release from that date (r4.144).

In a compulsory liquidation, a meeting of creditors must be summoned to receive the liquidator's resignation. The OR (if not chairman of the meeting) must be notified of any resolution passed to accept the liquidator's resignation.

1.3 By operation of the law

A liquidator will also cease to be in office in the following situations:

▶ Death (r4.132 and r4.133)
▶ Ceasing to be an IP (r4.134 and r4.135)
▶ Following the final meeting of creditors (s171(6) and s172(8))
▶ In a CVL, on the making of a winding-up order (r4.136).

2 Duties on vacating office

Section overview

The liquidator has a number of statutory duties to comply with upon vacating office.

2.1 Statutory duties

Must deliver up forthwith to any successor:

▶ The assets, after deducting any properly incurred expenses and distributions made.
▶ The records of the liquidation including any correspondence and proofs.
▶ The company's books, papers and other records.

In a compulsory liquidation, the liquidator must give notice of his intention to vacate office to the Official Receiver together with the notice of any meeting of creditors to be held.

This notice must be given at least 21 days before any creditors' meeting is held.

If the liquidator vacates office after a final meeting in a compulsory winding-up, all records not already disposed of must be delivered up to the Official Receiver.

3 Final meetings and release

Section overview

The liquidator must summon final meetings of creditors (in both voluntary and compulsory liquidation) in order to receive his account of the winding-up and for the purpose of receiving his resignation.

3.1 The position in Compulsory liquidation

When a company is being wound up by the court and for practical purposes the liquidation appears complete, the liquidator must summon a final meeting of creditors to:

▶ Receive the liquidator's report of the winding-up
▶ Determine whether the liquidator should have his release.

Creditors must be given at least 28 days' notice of the meeting. This notice should be sent to all creditors who have proved for their debts. In addition, notice of the meeting must be advertised in the Gazette at least one month before the meeting.

The liquidator's report to be laid before the meeting should include:

▶ An account of the liquidator's administration of the winding-up.

▶ A summary of receipts and payments.

▶ A statement that he has reconciled his account with that held by the Secretary of State.

▶ A statement of the amount paid to unsecured creditors by virtue of the prescribed part of the company's net property (s176A).

Once the meeting has been held the liquidator must give notice to that effect to the court together with a copy of the report laid before the meeting and whether he has been granted his release. A copy should also be sent to the Official Receiver.

If there is no quorum at the meeting the liquidator must report this fact to the court together with the fact that the meeting was summoned in accordance with the rules. The meeting will then be deemed to have been held and the creditors not to have resolved against the liquidator having his release.

Provided that the creditors have not resolved otherwise, the liquidator will be deemed to get his release on the date the notice of the final meeting is filed at court.

If the creditors resolved that the liquidator should not have his release then it must be obtained from the Secretary of State. The date of release will be the date specified in the certificate issued by the Secretary of State.

3.2 The position in Creditors' voluntary liquidation

As soon as the company's affairs are all wound up the liquidator is required to call a general meeting of the company and a meeting of creditors for the purpose of laying before it an account of the winding-up.

The meeting must be advertised in the Gazette at least one month before being held. 28 days' notice must be given to all creditors who have proved their debts.

Within a week after the meeting has been held the liquidator must send a copy of the account to the Registrar of Companies, together with a return of the holding of the meeting. Failure to file these documents will render the liquidator liable to a fine.

If a quorum is not present at the meeting the liquidator makes the return stating that the meeting was convened but that no quorum was present. In these circumstances it is deemed that the requirements have been complied with and the creditors are deemed not to have resolved against the liquidator having his release.

If the liquidator fails to call the meeting as required he will be liable to a fine.

At the final meeting, the creditors may question the liquidator with respect to any matter contained in the account and may resolve against the liquidator having his release.

If the creditors resolve against his release, the liquidator may apply to the Secretary of State (r4.126). The date of release will be the date specified in the certificate issued by the Secretary of State.

3.3 The position in Members' voluntary liquidation

The rules regarding the final meeting in an MVL are the same as in a CVL.

The liquidator is deemed to be released from office from the date of giving notice to the Registrar of Companies of his ceasing to act.

Interactive question: Preston Stationery Ltd

Your principal, Adam Jones, was appointed liquidator of Preston Stationery Ltd at a s98 meeting of creditors. All assets have now been realised and Adam is keen to close the case.

Requirement

Write a memo to Adam outlining the procedure for calling final meetings to close the case and obtain his release.

See **Answer** at the end of this chapter.

4 Closure checklist

Section overview

There are a number of practical steps to be taken by the liquidator when closing a case.

4.1 Checklist

The following points should be included in a closure checklist. Note that this list is not exhaustive, add any additional matters that you can think of to the end of this list.

1   Review files.

2   Ensure all creditor claims have been admitted or rejected.

3   Ensure all assets have been realised.

4   Ensure all expenses of the winding-up have been settled.

5   Ensure liquidator's remuneration approved and drawn.

6   Obtain written confirmation from agents and solicitors that their remuneration has been settled.

7   Withdraw any undertakings given.

8   Ensure all employee claims dealt with.

9   Ensure D returns submitted and all necessary proceedings against officers and others have been disposed of.

10   Obtain HM Revenue and Customs' clearance that all tax and VAT matters have been completed.

11   Check final dividend has been paid:

  ▶   Calculate final dividend
  ▶   Send notice of intention to declare dividend
  ▶   Pay dividend.

12   Ensure all uncashed dividend cheques are returned to ISA.

13   Close all bank accounts.

14   Notify insurers of ceasing to act and cancel bordereaux.

15   Complete IP records.

16   Call final meetings of members and creditors.

17   Prepare final account of winding-up.

18   Send return of final meetings to Registrar of Companies.

19   Do not dispose of company's books and records until at least one year after dissolution.

20   Retain financial and administrative records for at least six years.

Summary and self-test

Summary

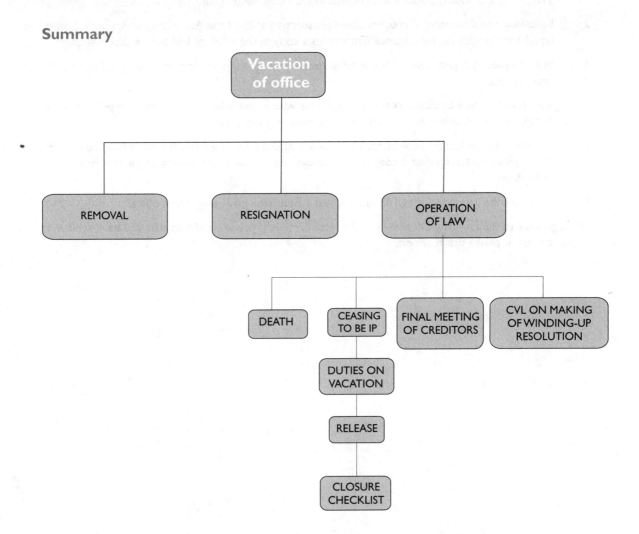

Self-test

Answer the following questions.

1   When may a company's books and records in a CVL be destroyed?

2   Following a final meeting of creditors held pursuant to s106 of the Act, within which period must the liquidator file with the Registrar of Companies a copy of the account laid before that meeting?

3   In a compulsory liquidation, what period of notice must the liquidator give to the creditors of the final meeting?

4   If a vacancy occurs by death, resignation or otherwise in the office of a liquidator appointed by the company in a members' voluntary liquidation, how may the vacancy be filled?

5   In a members' voluntary liquidation, within which of the following periods must a liquidator send to the Registrar of Companies a copy of his account and return of the holding of the final meeting and of its date?

6   What are the grounds per r4.108 upon which a liquidator may resign from office?

Now, go back to the Learning Objectives in the Introduction. If you are satisfied that you have achieved these objectives, please tick them off.

Answers to self-test

1   One year after the company has been dissolved.

2   Within one week.

3   28 days.

4   By the company in general meeting, subject to any arrangements with creditors.

5   Within one week.

6   (a)   Ill health.

          (b)   Intend ceasing to act as an IP.

          (c)   A conflict of interest or change in personal circumstances which make it impossible or impractical to continue.

          (d)   Where joint liquidators are appointed and it is no longer expedient to continue with that number of joint liquidators.

Answer to interactive question

Interactive question: Preston Stationery Ltd

Memo format

▶ Liquidator must convene a general meeting of the company and a meeting of the creditors.

▶ 28 days' notice must be given to all creditors who have proved their debts.

▶ The meeting must be advertised in the London Gazette at least one month before being held.

▶ At the meeting:

– Lay before it an account of the winding-up showing how it has been conducted and the company's property disposed of.

– The creditors may question the liquidator with respect to any matter contained in the account.

– Creditors may resolve against the liquidator having his release.

▶ Within a week after the meeting, the liquidator must send a copy of the account to the Registrar of Companies, together with a return of the holding of the meeting.

▶ If a quorum is not present at the meeting the liquidator makes a return stating that the meeting was convened but that no quorum was present. It is deemed that the requirements have been complied with and the creditors are deemed to have not resolved against the liquidator's release.

▶ If the creditors resolve against his release, the liquidator may apply to the Secretary of State. The date of release will be the date specified in the certificate issued by the Secretary of State.

▶ If creditors have not resolved against his release, the liquidator will have his release from when he gives notice of the final meeting to the Registrar of Companies.

Index

> > > > > > > > > > > > > > > >

A

Actions or proceedings (litigation) against the company, 156
Advising member, 64
All monies clause, 214
Antecedent transactions, 136
Arrears of pay, 215
Associate, 145
Avoidance of floating charges, 137

B

Banking, 212
Bonding, 207
Book value, 72
Books and records, 206
Brumark case (Agnew v Commissioner of Inland Revenue), 73

C

Category 1 disbursements, 194
Category 2 disbursements, 194
Centre of main interests, 14
Centrebind procedure, 40
Closure checklist, 236
Code of Ethics, 6
Collective insolvency proceedings, 15
Commencement, 38, **158**
Commercial Rent Arrears Recovery (CRAR), 160
Compulsory liquidation, 94
Confidentiality, 6
Connected person, 145
Continuing to trade, 213
Course of dealings, 215
Creditors' voluntary liquidation (CVL), 38, 64

D

D1 report, 122
D2 return, 122
De facto directors, 196
De jure director, 196
Debts payable in a foreign currency, 174
Declaration of dividend, 179
Declaration of Solvency, 51
Deficiency account, 76
Directors returns, 122
Discounts (R4.89), 174
Dismissal, 232
Disqualification of directors, 120
Disqualification order, 122
Disqualification undertakings, 124

Dissolution, 41
Distress, 159
Distribution, 50
Distribution in specie, 54
Double Proof, 175

E

EC Regulation, 14, 15
Employee claims, 215
Enterprise Act 2002, 4
Establishment, 16, 19
Estimated realisable value, 72
Execution, 157
Extortionate credit transaction, 137
Extraordinary resolution, 50

F

Final meetings, 234
First meeting of creditors, 104
Fixed charge, 71
Floating charge, 72
Foreign tax, 176
Fraudulent trading, 138
Fundamental principles, 6
Future debts, 177

G

General penalty sum, 207
Grounds for winding-up petition, 94

H

High value dealer, 13
Hiving down, 214
Holiday pay, 215

I

Inability to pay debts, 94
Incorporated, 215
Insolvency Act 2000, 4
Integrity, 6
Interest, 176
Insolvency Act 1986, 4, 27
Insolvency Services Account, 212
Investigations, 118
IP Case Records, 206
ISA/c, 212